Acting Male

Acting Male

□□□

MASCULINITIES IN THE FILMS OF JAMES STEWART, JACK NICHOLSON, AND CLINT EASTWOOD

Dennis Bingham

□□□

Rutgers University Press
New Brunswick, New Jersey

Bingham, Dennis, 1954–
      Acting male : masculinities in the films of James Stewart, Jack
Nicholson, and Clint Eastwood / Dennis Bingham.
            p.   cm.
      Includes bibliographical references and index.
      ISBN 0-8135-2073-8 (cloth) — ISBN 0-8135-2074-6 (pbk.)
      1. Men in motion pictures.   2. Sex role in motion pictures.
3. Machismo in motion pictures.   4. Stewart, James, 1908–
5. Nicholson, Jack.   6. Eastwood, Clint, 1930–   .   I. Title.
PN1995.9.M46B56   1994
791.43′652041—dc20   93-37678
                                                                                                        CIP

British Cataloging-in-Publication information available

For Christine

Contents

□□□

□□□

Acknowledgments

□□□

In its eight-year development from concept to publication, this book has undergone as many reversals, close calls, and last-minute rescues as may be found in any of the movies mentioned herein. The project went through several distinct stages, and those who were with me along the way were more responsible than many of them know for the book's movement from step to step.

Morris Beja and Judith Mayne were there at the beginning, and what I owe each of them is beyond measure. I hope I've been able to apply a little of what I learned from these two exemplary people—and scholars.

The book started its way toward publication in 1990–91, the year I spent at Wayne State University. Lesley Brill, Robert Burgoyne, and Cynthia Erb showed tremendous enthusiasm and encouragement for my work and its progress. The students in my fall 1990 course at Wayne State—on masculinity and the films of James Stewart, Jack Nicholson, and Clint Eastwood—opened up new possibilities, many of which found their way into the manuscript. I remember with special fondness the contributions made by Alit Amit, James Loter, Kelly Otter-Cooper, and Lynn Pellerito; I wish them good fortune.

At Indiana University–Purdue University at Indianapolis (IUPUI), I have enjoyed the support of Dean John Barlow and Associate Dean Barbara Jackson of the School of Liberal Arts, and Chair Richard Turner of the English Department. The IUPUI Summer Research Fellowship I received in 1992 greatly eased my writing (which finally ended a year later). I also received a School of Liberal Arts Manuscript Preparation Grant.

William Touponce, my colleague and mentor, has helped me in preparing this manuscript and in other ways, not least of which was introducing me to the wonderful world of laser discs. My colleagues, in particular Kristine Karnick, Frank Dobson, Ken Davis, and Susan Shepherd, have helped me keep things in perspective, as well as exchanged ideas about the fields we love. Marianne Wokeck arranged my January 1993 Work-in-Progress Seminar on James Stewart, which helped me refine my ideas for that section.

I have probably learned as much from a number of my IUPUI students as I hope they have from me. They have often asked questions or made comments that sent me scurrying to add to or change the manuscript. They include Edie Scherrer, Jane Winters, Dwayne Wolfe, Lee Warren, Beth Kelley, and Jennifer Bingham (no relation).

Leslie Mitchner of Rutgers University Press is an editor without peer, as unstinting in praise as in criticism; whatever this book is is due greatly to her contributions. Managing editor Marilyn Campbell and copy editor Susan Llewellyn are helpful, conscientious professionals. The outside reviewers, Virginia Wright Wexman and Peter Lehman, were the appreciative and astute readers I knew they would be. Thanks also to Joanna Hitchcock and Valerie Jablow.

All photographs are courtesy of the Museum of Modern Art/Film Stills Archive. Archivist Terry Geesken assisted in the selection of stills.

A version of first part of the Clint Eastwood section was published as "Men with No Names: Clint Eastwood's 'The Stranger' Persona, Identification, and the Impenetrable Gaze" in *Journal of Film and Video* 42.4 (Winter 1990). I thank two anonymous reviewers for their comments and then-editor Michael Selig for editing and publishing the article. "Masculinity, Star Reception, and the Desire to Perform: Clint Eastwood in *White Hunter, Black Heart*," a longer version of the book's discussion, appeared in *Post-Script* 12.2 (Winter 1993). Carole Zucker, guest editor of an issue on film acting, solicited that piece, and I am grateful to her.

Finally, Christine Bratkowski, my wife, lives daily with my projects and me and contributes in countless ways, big and small, to the development and well-being of both.

Acting Male

Introduction:
I'm Not Really a Man,
But I Play One in Movies

□□□

On March 27, 1973, Marlon Brando—protesting Hollywood's depiction of Native Americans—upset the self-congratulations of the Academy Awards by sending an actress, dressed in Apache garb and calling herself Sasheen Littlefeather, to decline his Best Actor award. She was later followed to the stage by a lean, insolent actor who jokingly refused to present the Best Picture award "on behalf of all the cowboys who have gotten shot in John Ford Westerns" (Wiley & Bova 478). While Brando's absentee activism may have left viewers unsure how to react, Clint Eastwood's comment was less equivocal. Andrew Sarris called the '73 Oscars "a night fully worthy of the growling nastiness of the Nixon years" ("Oscar Wiles" 71). Eastwood was very much identified with that "nastiness," due to the rightist backlash of *Dirty Harry* (1971). His remark, like his films, cavalierly reinstated the white male as the center of things, and movies as "just entertainment" of no ideological import. Eastwood's wisecrack reinforced the reactionary reputation of his films. Awaiting release was *High Plains Drifter*, his second film as director and the eighth from Malpaso, Eastwood's production company. In the film's first ten minutes the world's most popular film star rapes a woman and shoots three men between the eyes. This disreputable money machine and the staid "excellence" promoted by the Academy Awards embarrassed each other. He did not attend another Oscar show for twenty years.

On March 29, 1993, Clint Eastwood, still "the most powerful actor in the industry," according to that week's *Time* (Witteman 56), returned to the Oscars, a first-time nominee. The film that brought him this mark of official respect was made from a mid-1970s-vintage script about a reformed Old West murderer, a vigilante sheriff whose authority is mixed up with sadism, and a cocky gunslinger who can't see ten feet away. Not quite a movie for vindicating cowboys. The only Native American in the film is a woman married—in a bit of revisionist history—to the African American sidekick of the Eastwood protagonist. The plot is set in motion by a group of women who strike back against male violence and injustice. Like many reviewers, Eastwood himself noted that *Unforgiven* "demythologizes idolizing people for violent behavior" ("Accolade" 2).

Academy Awards often go to performers in "lower" genres, like action films and comedies, when they make a film that cuts against their persona, when they show their "seriousness." By renouncing the violent representations that made him rich and famous, Eastwood attracted the Academy's attention and perhaps transformed his long-fixed persona. The Oscars are also known to honor late-career stars for sheer longevity. Eastwood in 1993 was sixty-three, the same age as John Wayne when that weathered star (whose successor as male icon Eastwood was often assumed to be) won a "sentimental" Best Actor award in 1970. Nevertheless, a time traveler from Oscar week '73 would have been thunderstruck. Eastwood's two awards were for directing and producing, exceeding the resemblance to John Wayne while joining the company of John Ford. While Ford spent his late films revising myths he had helped to propagate, Eastwood had been more brutal with the myths of masculinity he had not only spread but embodied.

Previous studies of stars and gender have assumed that star personas are produced by fantasies that enforce the dominant "reality." Some may change "or at any rate—'deepen'" (Dyer *Stars* 110); others may stay essentially the same. Gender identity, which is complexly and intrinsically tied to star images, may similarly appear to be in flux. Steven Cohan and Ina Rae Hark write: "The suspicion lingers that the more things change in outward appearance, the more they have thus far stayed the same in their fundamental political structure, with the game fixed so as always to produce a white heterosexual male winner, who routinely overcomes the other—the Indians, the aliens, the feminine" (8). Accordingly Paul Smith downplays *Unforgiven*, asserting that "Eastwood has changed, but he hasn't necessarily evolved" (quoted in Chethik 3J). It can be argued, on the other hand, that because Eastwood's revisionist films (of which *Unforgiven* is the culmination) move the threat to stability from "the other" to the white male himself, they *do* constitute an evolution into a less "masculinist" male identity.

Moreover, given the contradictions in the construction of a star persona and of masculinity itself, both of which appear natural and coherent, probably no male star persona—or the masculinity it embodies—is ever as monolithic as Eastwood's appeared to be in 1973. He had already starred in one atypical film that was thoroughly contradictory in its gender politics, *The Beguiled* (Don Siegel, 1971). In addition his earlier, unplanned appearance on Oscar night '73, when the show's producer pulled him out of the audience at the last minute to fill in for host Charlton Heston, who had had a flat on the freeway, showed an affable, flustered Eastwood never glimpsed in his films of the period (Weinraub 214). As he stumbled over the lame Moses jokes (written out for Heston) on the cue cards, he ad-libbed, "Man, this isn't my bag," hip argot that in the early 1970s might have come from Jack Nicholson or the peace symbol-sporting villain in *Dirty Harry*, but never from Harry himself.

Furthermore, one must ask whether a general evolution of gender is ever possible in commercial cinema. Concurrent with honoree Eastwood's born-again nonviolence was a raft of press stories scorning the Oscar show's theme—"the Year of the Woman"—borrowed from 1992 electoral politics. The Academy's tone-deaf ballyhoo came at a time when more films than ever were directed at young males (with 91 percent of Hollywood films in 1992 featuring male protagonists) (Corliss 59) and the Best Actress category could barely come up with five candidates—exactly as in the "From Reverence to Rape" 1970s.

As if to prove that Eastwood's "conversion," which had been in progress for about a dozen years, changed little about film masculinity, from the cover of the March 29 *Newsweek* glared another male action star, Michael Douglas. Emblazoned over his photo was the headline WHITE MALE PARANOIA, the stock-in-trade of the 1970s Eastwood. The article, a facetious cataloging of imagined hurts to white men caused by the modest progress of a resurgent feminism and multiculturalism in the early 1990s, took as its starting point *Falling Down*, a Douglas vehicle in which a somewhat-deranged "average guy" storms out of his car amid an L.A. traffic jam and goes on a rampage. The film was received as a freshened-up backlash item "which evokes the self-pitying 'silent majority' rhetoric of the Nixon era: that appalling sentimentality about one's own beleaguered and underappreciated virtue" (Rafferty 99). "The more things change" indeed.

It has become virtually a commonplace in feminist film criticism to see overbearing action-film icons like Eastwood as responses to "male hysteria," because "popular versions of what it is to be a 'real man' have become so outlandish as to prompt the idea that all is not as it should be for the male sex" (Metcalf and Humphries quoted in Smith "Action" 88). Richard Dyer finds in Eastwood an "outlandishness" just short of parody, "as if the values of masculine physicality are harder to maintain straightfacedly and unproblematically in an age of microchips and a large-scale growth (in the USA) of women in traditionally male occupations" (*Heavenly Bodies* 12). With the succession of action stars—from the earthy Wayne and streamlined Eastwood to the musclebound

Stallone, humanoid (but determinedly turning humane) Schwarzenegger, and sternly androgynous Steven Seagal—the heroes have grown less human, more mechanical, and, it has been argued, more objectified. However, the violence, invincibility, and body count are turned up as well. Masculinism may be harder to take seriously, but it's also portrayed as harder to challenge. So the question is Does Dirty Harry, originally a product of and for the "silent majority," appear to reform because he has seen the error of his ways or because younger, sleeker reinforcements have arrived to relieve him?

Eastwood's own debatable evolution shows, if nothing else, that masculine domination represents not nature but artifice and effort, that it is a burden for men repeatedly to convince themselves and their peers of their indispensability. Arguably, then, the patterns of subversion and recuperation cited in film studies have recurred throughout film history, demonstrating the fragility of patriarchal gender constructions, offset by a resilience rooted in power. Hence Susan Jeffords, discussing "kinder, gentler" Hollywood male characters in the early 1990s, writes that "the transformations undergone by white male characters do nothing to address the consequences of the privileges associated with white U.S. masculinities" ("The Big Switch" 205).

With the "gentling" of white masculinity an apparent strategy for holding on to power during shifting times, this book is concerned with male star personas that, however intermittently, have indeed addressed the consequences of white male privilege before a mass audience, deliberately, passionately, as if unable to keep from doing so. The undermining of masculinism and the revelation of "femininities" that conventional masculinities work to contain have seemed to occur more often in movies since the fall of the studio era, which began in the late 1940s, but they can be seen in films of earlier eras as well. Such subversions take place in cycles—and in different corners of an increasingly fragmented movie industry in different eras.

Take the actor who handed Eastwood his Academy Award for producing *Unforgiven*. Given the Oscar pageant's penchant for displaying stars as their "real selves" while still confusing them with their movie roles, Jack Nicholson's entrance as final presenter mingled the banal and the bizarre. He was introduced, mock portentously, by host Billy Crystal as simply " . . . Jack." Striding onstage to the strains of a Sousa march (because he happened to have played a marine in *A Few Good Men*, his most recent hit), this man who had ridden to stardom twenty-four years earlier as a putative hero of the counterculture broke the ludicrous military airs by abruptly flashing a Joker wave. Though Robert Redford once complained that a star is regarded as "a cartoon character," Nicholson in public often retreats to just that level. His delivery of the nominees' names that night had an ironic subtext, as if to parody the role of the big-star Oscar presenter while performing it flawlessly. It was a brilliant postmodern moment, a pastiche of blank allusions and performance codes signifying little besides fame. Following Nicholson, Eastwood looked like a coherent, sincere individual, thanking his mother and honoring Steve Ross, the CEO of Time Warner, who died in January 1993. All this allowed "Jack" to slink back into the gaudy secrecy of his star persona.

The time traveler from 1973 would have been startled to see the two of them together, perhaps for the first time—the gracefully aging, athletic Eastwood and the pudgy imp Nicholson. For years they had been re-garded as cultural opposites, Nicholson the modern, "now" actor and Eastwood the lowbrow action star (Haskell "Gould vs. Redford" 46, Cole 125). Molly Haskell in 1974 took care to separate "culturally pres-tigious stars" like Nicholson from "action heroes like John Wayne, Steve McQueen, Clint Eastwood, Charles Bronson, and Burt Reynolds, who have formed an unbroken line parallel to them" ("Gould vs. Redford" 46). Robert B. Ray included Nicholson in a group representing a "new kind of star" produced by the 1960s "self-consciousness about the re-ceived American myths" (260); Ray also assigned Eastwood to the op-posing camp—that of a "traditional star" (261).

Nicholson's self-consciousness had become a large part of his star mythology, touching his film roles with an air of absurdist theater. When the absurdism was directed at others around him, as in *Five Easy Pieces* (1970), he played the self-destructive but helpless victim of a rebellious-ness brought on by a culture that restrains him, a 1950s "rebel male" with whom the times have finally caught up. As an actor with a decade's experience in low-budget exploitation films before stardom, Nicholson was able to become much more an industry "player" than Brando, Dean, and Clift, the original "rebel males," victims of Hollywood whose latter-day romanticization seems a confirmation of feminists' worst suspicions of "sensitive" men. Unlike the rebel males, whose rebellion was often against such bogeys as femininity and "momism" (Nicholson's biggest hit of the 1970s, *One Flew Over the Cuckoo's Nest*, was also in this vein), he excelled in roles that posed the male as not so much a player of the game as a player of parts, with the codes of masculinity reduced to a series of roles, sensitivity just another in the repertoire. As Nicholson could not present an Oscar straight, in his best roles (such as *The Last Detail*, *Chinatown*, *The Shining*, *Prizzi's Honor*) he could not play mas-culinism straight. He made a masquerade of masculine conformity, re-vealing a character's confident male identity as an unconscious oedipal identification with monstrous paternity.

In 1974 Haskell saw Nicholson as a potential transitional figure, the star "best equipped to bridge the old and new, the funky and traditional, to invest modern absurdism with a new whiff of heroism" ("Gould vs. Redford" 57). Eventually the Reagan-Bush years and the generic film-making that accompanied them forced Nicholson to choose between his career as a star actor (stardom and acting being hard to separate for all three of the men in this book) and the counterculture modernism that was his professed project as an actor (Wolf 36, Schatz *Old Hollywood* 217–241). Thus an actor who did much through his art to display the monstrous identification that is male identity became known to a later generation for playing funny monsters. The acting that had been seen as risky exploration at the edge evolved into over-the-top craziness that was permitted as a temporary diversion in otherwise very conservative films. Nonetheless, Nicholson remains a vivid example of a male star who often displayed the consequences of male privilege and the void that it obscures.

While journalists started to notice Eastwood's steady output of cinematic eccentricities, they began to write off Nicholson as just a Hollywood deal maker. A surprised *Esquire* reporter sent to interview Eastwood before the release of *Bird* (1988), his Charlie Parker biopic, admitted that he had assumed that Eastwood "was a fascist" (Giddins 133). Two years later the same magazine ran a cover story debunking Nicholson's counterculture mythos, on the premise that after an actor reaped a reported sixty million for his share in *Batman* trinkets, it was unseemly for him to go on invoking Beckett and Godard (Walker 56–59). In films such as *The Witches of Eastwick* and *Batman*, moreover, Nicholson's misogyny appeared not so ironic, while such Eastwood films as *Sudden Impact* and *Tightrope* partly atoned for the patriarchal fantasies of rape given play in *High Plains Drifter*. The coup de grace came in a 1990 *Esquire* piece on Nicholson by a writer named Michael Ventura, who exclaimed: "Nicholson a rebel? Give me a break. You want a rebel in the Hollywood system? Clint Eastwood is ten times the rebel Nicholson is. Nicholson *is* the Hollywood system" (Erickson 172).

Hence Oscar night '93 seemed to be a summary of Hollywood stardom of the previous quarter century. Here was Eastwood on a level with those against whom he was formerly judged—not just Nicholson, but also Al Pacino, Dustin Hoffman, and Gene Hackman, the latter having agreed to appear in *Unforgiven* only after "Clint convinced me this was not a Clint Eastwood film" (Biskind 60). These stars—in addition to Barbra Streisand, who handed Eastwood his Best Director prize, and others who were absent, such as Robert Redford, Robert DeNiro, Warren Beatty, and Woody Allen—had represented the "new kind of star." A massive generational turnover, the likes of which had not been seen since the coming of sound, took place in only a few years—roughly 1967–71. It gave these "New Hollywood" actors opportunities for lasting power as producers, directors, or actors as *auteurs*.

They displaced a generational cohort that, in the youth wave and the collapse of the mass-audience blockbuster, lost the bankability many of them had owned for two decades or more. Among these were Bob Hope, Bing Crosby, Frank Sinatra, Doris Day, Audrey Hepburn, Rock Hudson, Burt Lancaster, Kirk Douglas, John Wayne, Charlton Heston, Henry Fonda, Gregory Peck, Elizabeth Taylor, Jerry Lewis, Dean Martin, William Holden, Jack Lemmon, Marlon Brando, and James Stewart. Of this group some—such as Lemmon, Lancaster, and, for a while, Brando—took chances as actors and survived, though without their former box-office clout. Many (Hope, Crosby, Sinatra, Stewart, Taylor, Day, Lewis) eventually retired from moviemaking. All, except Brando and Lancaster (a favorite of prestigious European directors and an early innovator of star-owned production companies like Eastwood's Malpaso), were establishment figures. Although many have since gained a retrospective luster, in the early 1970s they were discards, aging remnants of a studio system whose outmoded genres and icons were unwelcome in a polarized society in which everything seemed to have changed overnight. In the wake of near bankruptcies at the end of the 1960s, the studios—what was left of them—out of some degree of desperation turned to new faces.

Much was written, in the early 1970s and since, about the difference between the old style of star and the new. Barry King sees the studio system star as a fixed image that predominates over characters the star plays. Since the studio era, according to King, stars have been actors who subsume their personas to the roles they play (169–170). Robert B. Ray elaborates: "While the Classic stars had depended on the cumulative power of typecasting and genre conventions, these new performers specialized in playing against the expectations created either by a film's nominal genre or by their own previous roles" (260). These axioms hold up over the careers of many studio-era stars, including those of some, such as James Cagney and Bette Davis, who resisted the studio's relentless typecasting, and others, like Humphrey Bogart, who did seek to display their versatility once they became free-lancers (Sklar 251). They also explain why Nicholson, like most "new stars," insists that he does not have a persona. Even the "revised" Eastwood, when asked by a CNN reporter in 1992 whether he considered his persona when deciding to play a role, claimed, "I don't think about that at all."

The first star actors whose personas actually formed through highly

publicized struggles against fixed star images were the Actors Studio–
trained "rebels" of the fifties: Montgomery Clift, Marlon Brando, and
James Dean. Ray cites Brando as the model for the post-1967 "new
stars." His "desire to avoid typecasting had frequently led him to adopt
a mannered, campy style as a defense against conventional material"
(260). In describing what made the rebel actors so fresh when they first
appeared, Graham McCann calls them

> fascinating neurotics, exuding a primeval sexuality.
> Whereas the old Hollywood stars, such as Clark Gable and
> John Wayne, regarded acting as a rather lucrative "trick,"
> an enjoyable recreation, the new young rebel males were
> . . . far more serious in their approach. . . . Clift, Brando,
> and Dean were in search more of "authenticity" than of
> stardom. This caused them to clash with directors and pro-
> ducers . . . publicists . . . and the guardians of morality. (6)

The distinctions between "old" and "new" stars are accurate to some
extent, but they evoke some unfortunate dualisms. Although Clift,
Brando, and Dean did go to Hollywood to practice their craft, they were
hardly the first to take their jobs seriously. McCann singles out Wayne
and Gable, two classic stars without formal acting training. But other
studio-era male stars (Tracy, March, Muni, Fonda, Stewart) had dramatic academy and stage backgrounds. While later "new stars," most
famously Dustin Hoffman, have continued the Method actors' reputation
for difficulty and exactitude on the set, others—as director Tony Richardson said of Nicholson—"are what thirties and forties stars were like.
He can come on the set and deliver, without any fuss" (Wolf 38).

Nor were the "new" stars the first to rupture the unitary heterosexuality
of conventional gender identities. Given the difficulty a performer has
staying inside the lines of the star persona, feminist critics were quick to
point to such classic female stars as Marlene Dietrich, who embodied an
intriguingly aggressive androgyny, and Doris Day, whose projection of
independent strength was generally misconstrued and whose performances were more complex in terms of gender politics than her popular
persona would have one believe (Clarke and Simmonds 1–20). The personality coherence connoted by the mere mention of "John Wayne" or
"Jane Fonda" is, as Dyer maintains, the greatest of stardom's structuring
illusions.

A star's gender revision invariably involves rupturing the smooth surface of the coherent "masculinity" or "femininity" of which every star
persona is an individual version. With male stars especially, what breaks

through is a kind of polymorphous presocial bisexuality that itself can have tremendous appeal—although generally not to male spectators (at least not consciously)—as Miriam Hansen and Gaylyn Studlar have pointed out in studying Rudolph Valentino's appeal for women in the 1920s. Freud explained that bisexuality refers not just to sexual preference (although that is included), but to an infant's original possession of what are understood later in life as the traits of both genders, traits repressed by the postoedipal construction of gender identities (*Three Essays* 141). Revising the masculine persona means deconstructing "masculinity" and revealing man's identification with his repressed femininity.

In contrast to the coherent and controlling male subject drawn lastingly by Laura Mulvey in "Visual Pleasure and Narrative Cinema," a revisionist gaze at the "screened" male (to use Cohan and Hark's all-purpose pun) reveals him as an object, his masculinity as an act, and his identification with the phallus as an illusion. Unitary masculinity disperses into multiple masculinities and learns to live with ambivalence and contradictions rather than divide up the world into either-or dualisms. The male confronts the patriarchy in himself. Thus a revisionist Eastwood film, *Unforgiven*, attacks the notion of the Western man's gun as a reflection of the phallus. *The Shining*, with Nicholson, displays the white male's egoistic attraction to patriarchal images as an ironic expression of a desire to be the other sex.

In one of the most interesting studies of bisexuality in the presumably unproblematic masculinity of classic male stars, Andrew Britton found that Cary Grant's 1930s screwball comedies celebrate the passage of the Grant character from patriarchal masculinity into a polymorphous presocial sexuality. In films such as *Bringing Up Baby* and *The Awful Truth*, "the sophisticated couple is the couple whose sexuality is no longer organised by the phallus" ("Comedy and Male Desire" 7). For Britton the narrative action of these films is the hero's "unlearning" of patriarchal conditioning and his acceptance of his "feminine" traits.

Nevertheless critics have noted a tendency of the new stars to worry less than earlier actors about projecting a consistently "masculine" screen image. McCann writes that "anything in [the classic stars'] personalities which undermined the straightforwardly virile image . . . was repressed or 'corrected' by the studios" (8). Clift, Brando, and Dean, on the other hand, "were not afraid of roles which made them look weak, or foolish, or slow-witted, or sexually insecure. They sought out roles that led to suffering, both emotional and physical, and were frequently violent and always disturbing" (6).

In his important studies of stardom Richard Dyer asserts that the relationship between the classic movie star and the audience turns in part on a notion of what the star is like as a "real person." This established personality then forms a continuous line with the characters he/she plays on screen. Thus the bisexual orientations of Brando, Clift, Dean, and also Grant, what Joan Mellen, writing about Brando, saw as a new kind of screen male "capable of expressing feelings"—that is, "femininity"— (199) might be in fact considered an extension of the "real person," as McCann argues. However, such an explanation hardly accounts for the stolidly heterosexual demeanor Rock Hudson managed to maintain throughout his film career. Nor does it explain the persistent traces of femininity in the performance style of one presumptively classic male star whose off-screen image was the epitome of "straight," average virtue. This actor started out in the studio system, hit his career peak in the fifties, and, according to James Naremore, projected an "important quality that made him different from any other male star of his period. He was the most emotional leading man to emerge from the studio system— perhaps the only one who could regularly cry on the screen without losing the sympathy of his audience. There was . . . a troubled, cranky, slightly repressed feeling in his behavior" (254).

The actor, of course, is James Stewart. As dominant in the film industry in his day as Eastwood and Nicholson have been in theirs, Stewart in retrospect has had two coequal personas: the earnest idealist, the nostalgic figure of the homespun boy next door; and the risk-taking actor who probably performed in more films for more canonical *auteurs* (Frank Capra, Ernst Lubitsch, Alfred Hitchcock, John Ford, Anthony Mann, Otto Preminger) than any other American star. Not incidentally, he is the star who most clearly marks the transition between the studio period—when he was a contract player for MGM (he reached star status, significantly, on loan-out to other studios)—and the era of free-lance actors, independent production, and powerful talent agents that made possible the "new kind of star" of the late 1960s.

Stewart was not the first star free agent (Grant was a free-lancer from 1937 on, followed by Gary Cooper in 1940). However, his mythic sweetness and idealism were combined with eccentric physical equipment and a capacity as an actor to enact emotion, anxiety, and pain. All this made him the only star of the transitional 1950s with a foot firmly planted in each era's kind of stardom—the studio star system, by which the audience identified with the sense of a star as real person; and the more iconoclastic poststudio independent mode. Most important, Stewart was no less uninhibited in front of the camera than were the 1950s rebels. Like them, he was not afraid to appear weak, neurotic, or even psychotic. In his films for Hitchcock and his Westerns for Mann he explored the boundaries of male coherence and decency without fearing for his image. Like the 1930s Cary Grant he indulged—in *Harvey*—a fantasy of desire free from the phallus. Like Brando and Nicholson he showed the psychic trouble and oppression proliferated by phallic masculinity.

His ability to "play"—even symbolize—honesty and "American ideals" made him an icon into whose mold later male stars tried to pour themselves. Kevin Costner in particular has emulated the "beloved" Stewart. *Field of Dreams* (1989) draws explicitly on the charm of *It's a Wonderful Life* (1946) and *Harvey* (1950). Early in that film, Roy Kinsella (Costner) comes into the kitchen to tell his wife about the voices he's heard in his cornfield. He stands next to a TV that is showing the scene in *Harvey* in which Elwood Dowd describes the first time he saw the six-foot-three-inch rabbit leaning on a lamppost. *JFK* (1991) borrows for its rhetorical project the remembered aura of *Mr. Smith Goes to Washington* (1939), transforming the quirky Jim Garrison of New Orleans into the archetype of the earnest, determined little man defending American ideals against massive corruption and conspiracies. Oliver Stone's film even transports its hero to Mr. Smith's mecca, the Lincoln Memorial. *Dances with Wolves* (1990) may be seen as a veritable remake of *Broken Arrow* (1950). On the other hand, Eastwood's demythologizing *Unforgiven* draws on the five "adult Westerns" Stewart made with Anthony Mann in the early 1950s. Eastwood's sexually neurotic detective in *Tightrope* (1984), moreover, is an apparent descendant of Stewart's Scottie Ferguson, the lost obsessive of *Vertigo* (1958). (This Costner/Eastwood opposition does not take into account *A Perfect World* [1993], which costars Costner and Eastwood, under the latter's direction.) Thus, if Stewart's career sets examples for the creation of myths, it supplies models for problematizing them as well.

As Hollywood movies take down a brick from one part of the wall of dominant ideology, they put back another elsewhere. Film studies may never answer the question of what matters more—the apparent subversion of the dominant ideology or its restoration. This question applies especially to Stewart. The new-style jaggedness and unpredictability of his performance style after World War II (in which he served) are regulated by his "real life" as a war hero and family man, a pervasive off-screen image included in his films (especially his 1950s biopics) often enough to keep the discrepancy between on- and off-screen from becoming obvious.

Steven Cohan points out in his study of the exhibitionism of William Holden in *Picnic* (1955) that a male star persona that is taken as a guarantor of masculine normality can help neutralize whatever the film may be doing to subvert those very norms (64). In a less dichotomous way than with Stewart, the axiomatic personas of Eastwood and Nicholson, like those of all really popular stars, hover in the mind of a spectator who watches these actors play characters. Eastwood's critique of violence or masculinism is nonetheless performed by "Clint Eastwood," thus mitigating for many audiences even his sharpest indictment. "Jack Nicholson" promises the pleasurable breaking of rules and flouting of conventions, even when, as is increasingly the case in his 1980s films, the conventions are in no danger.

Andrew Britton discusses the interplay of subversion and affirmation in star vehicles. On the one hand, what Britton sees as the subversiveness of a film such as *Beyond the Forest* (King Vidor, 1949) "is possible because it is 'just' a Bette Davis film and we all know the kind of thing that Bette Davis gets up to: the structural assimilation of the subversive product is given in advance." On the other hand:

> Every Hollywood movie of whatever genre must at least allow for a conservative reading. No film can explicitly authorize the transgression, or assert the bankruptcy, of the ideological absolutes without adopting, as protective camouflage, the ostensible affirmation of them which many Hollywood films offer *without* irony. Indeed, the very condition of the ironic happy ending is a happy ending which is *not* ironic. ("Stars and Genre" 201)

It was the ability of Stewart, Eastwood, and Nicholson to walk the tightrope between normality and difference, between consistency and change, that made them such extremely successful, durable stars. The success maintained by each actor's balance of a coherent persona and the capacity to reinvent himself through changing times and the actor's own aging makes these stars different from the trios that have constituted several recent books on stardom. As if to prove the Fitzgerald axiom that there are no second acts in American lives, *Rebel Males*, Graham McCann's cross between psychobiography and 1970s "images of men" criticism, chronicles exciting young actors whose failure to fulfill the promise of their early performances shows the romantic futility of their "rebellion." Richard Dyer's *Heavenly Bodies* examines stars as complex cultural sign systems, whose reading is influenced by the public's knowledge of and identification with the "real person." Dyer chooses performers—Marilyn Monroe, Paul Robeson, Judy Garland—"whose sense that they had been used, turned into something they didn't control"

(6)—allows him to analyze them as codes of gender and race in a system manipulated by others. Robert Sklar's historiographic *City Boys* examines "Golden Age" actors (James Cagney, Humphrey Bogart, John Garfield) who were limited by ethnic stereotyping and political oppression (Garfield), or by age and typecasting (Bogart and especially Cagney), to the one-dimensional personas they chafed against.

Star performances and the performance of gender roles have been discussed by a number of writers as "masquerade," after Joan Riviere's 1929 concept by which a professional woman feels compelled to overcompensate for taking a "male position" in the culture by putting on mannerisms and flirtations that mime "femininity." As Judith Butler puts it: "Femininity is taken on by a woman who 'wishes for masculinity,' but fears the retributive consequences of taking on the public appearance of masculinity. Masculinity is taken on by the male homosexual who, presumably, seeks to hide—not from others, but from himself—an ostensible femininity" (51). Masquerade is a specific way of dealing with gender roles as performed rather than as manifesting "nature." Butler finds masculinity and femininity as made up of "acts, gestures, enactments." "The essence or identity that they . . . purport to express are *fabrications* manufactured and sustained through corporeal signs and other discursive means" (136, emphasis in original). The effect of these "fabrications" is the "construction of coherence [which] conceals the gender discontinuities that run rampant within" our understanding of gender identity and sexual orientations (135).

While traditionally "femininity has been analyzed as a masquerade in implied contrast to the 'naturalness' of masculinity" (Cohan 69), masquerade has been applied to movie masculinity to point out the performative aspects of the "real man." To Cohan, William Holden's performance as Hal in *Picnic* involves a complex masquerade: An insecure man builds muscles and poses as a husky man; the husky young man is a pose for a man in his late thirties who won't "act his age"; Hal's past as a sports hero is a excuse for his display of his body for female and homoerotic gazes; and "Holden's secure star image as 'a solid citizen on-screen and off' . . . help[s] overcome the role's disturbing implication that masculinity is constituted in a performance of virility" (63). In effect the "disturbing implication" moves the filmmakers to masquerade the role from William Inge's play as "William Holden"—itself a fabrication. Moreover, Chris Holmlund, analyzing two 1989 Sylvester Stallone vehicles, *Lock Up* and *Tango and Cash*, in terms of the "queer" masquerade of "the butch clone" (the muscular macho man), finds that "the doubling and hyping of masculinity in these films only highlights how much masculinity, like femininity, is a multiple masquerade" ("Masculinity as Multiple Masquerade . . . " 224).

The three actors in this book exemplify the male masquerade in myriad ways. Nicholson and Stewart (in his Westerns especially) often foreground a man playing the role of "Man," while projecting the pose as separate from the insecure male behind it (in Stewart's case) and as virtually constituting the male identity (in Nicholson's). Like Holden's persona in *Picnic*, but over a longer period covering a great many films, Stewart's persona allowed him to play "disturbing" roles under the shelter of the all-American "Jimmy Stewart" persona.

I am uncomfortable, however, analyzing Eastwood's "formula" movies as evidence of the "hysteria" that motivates masquerade. These films elaborately deny the performing aspect, and there is little in them to confront a male spectator with that hysteria. Eastwood's revisionist films, on the other hand, elaborately articulate the persona "Clint Eastwood" as a "performance of virility." (The formula films are "inarticulate," as befits the ultrasilent persona.) Indeed, Eastwood's career renovations culminate in *White Hunter, Black Heart* (1990). By playing John Huston, a figure much unlike himself, Eastwood finally shucks off the minimalist acting style that effaces "feminine" performance and dons the ostentatious trappings of masquerade, pointing out the mask of the "Hemingway male" by emphasizing a mask of his own. When a male star's film *confronts* its spectator with the mask *as* mask, therefore, the contradictions take on valuable subversive—even educative—potential. This is my answer to the objections already being voiced about "performance criticism." Lee Edelman asks: "Might it not be useful to inquire just what, if anything, is getting subverted . . . or to ask how the miming of heterosexual privilege by a heterosexual male differs from the persistently oppressive enactment of that privilege in the culture at large?" (quoted in Tasker 230–231).

This seems a very valid point, which brings to mind the early 1990s Jack Nicholson, self-consciously miming—and perpetuating—privilege in a style emptied of criticism. A "masquerade" that is not made apparent to the film's implied spectator expresses less any genuine affront to dominant certitudes than it does the wishful thinking of the critic who analyzes it, much like 1980s leftists who were sure that "any day now" the American public would "see through" Ronald Reagan. Near the end of her against-the-grain reading of Stallone, Holmlund concedes: "It is not coincidental . . . that Stallone's fans are so often conservatives: his mask of healthy, happy, heterosexual, white masculinity is eminently reassuring to the right" (225). However, they see not the mask but what it represents. Conservatives and leftists have been enamored of aspects of

Stewart and Eastwood for very different reasons, perhaps proof of a divergence between the cultural meaning of their personas and the contradictions of many of their films, between the wearing and lowering of the mask (and the difficulty of determining which is which).

The performative aspects of masculinity bring it close to acting and the star persona. In his groundbreaking elucidation of film acting, James Naremore pointedly connects the role playing of actors, with their control of body, voice, facial expression, and persona, to the roles played by people in everyday life, based on ideological identifications. In his careful analysis of performance style, mostly in characteristic films of legendary stars like Grant, Chaplin, Brando, and Katharine Hepburn, Naremore details how acting technique organizes human behaviors into a coherence of personality and individuality. Using Erving Goffman's theories of the "presentation of self in everyday life," alongside the philosophies of Stanislavsky and Brecht, Naremore demonstrates "the way acting makes persons of us all" (285). The actor on the screen mirrors our self-images as "unified, transcendent subjects of experience who express an innate personality through daily activity, ultimately becoming star players in our personal scenarios" (5).

Naremore builds on the earlier work of Richard Dyer on stars. Both writers provided a methodology and vocabulary for dealing with the previously neglected topics of stardom and acting and their contributions to the way a spectator watches a movie. Dyer emphasizes the importance of the individual in Western society and the appeal of the star as a magnified "individual" who represents a unique, continuous personality that is nonetheless produced by, and reproduces, cultural standards of race, class, and gender. A male star is always "James Stewart," "William Holden," "Kevin Costner"—"solid citizens on-screen and off." Of great importance to Dyer is the sense of the star as "real person," unifying changes in him- or herself over time and a variety of film roles, thus bearing "witness to the continuousness" of the star's own self.

"There is a rhetoric of sincerity or authenticity," writes Dyer, "two qualities greatly prized in stars because they guarantee, respectively, that the star really means what he or she says, and that the star really is what she or he appears to be" (*Heavenly Bodies* 11). John Ellis, on the other hand, sees a definite gap between "star image" and film performance.

> There is always a temptation to think of a "star image" as some kind of fixed repertory of fixed meanings (Joan Crawford = tough, independent, ruthless, threateningly sexy, etc.). [However,] star images are paradoxical; they are composed of elements which do not cohere, of

> contradictory tendencies. . . . The star image is an *inco-*
> *herent* image. It shows the star both as an ordinary person
> and an extraordinary person. . . . The cinematic image
> (and the film performance) rests on the photo effect, the
> paradox that the photograph presents an absence that is
> present . . . the star image is not completed by the film
> performance, because they both rest on the same paradox.
> (92–93, emphasis in original)

While they may appear to disagree, Dyer and Ellis are really making the same point: Stardom works to maintain a coherent sense of the star, one the film performance appears to confirm but cannot because it is based on illusions that contradict the sense of "truth." The apparent authenticity—and consistency of image—which helps boost certain performers to star status to begin with, becomes fraught with contradictions as the star ages or accepts a variety of roles.

For example, Stewart's personality was so credible and well established by the early 1950s that his choice of roles couldn't affect it; indeed, his career threatened to stagnate if his performances did *not* sometimes veer from his accepted image. Nicholson's "real personality" hinges on almost a parody of personality; his public image teases the very idea of knowing what Dyer calls "the star's private self": An *Entertainment Weekly* cover (8 January 1993) wittily proclaimed "You don't know Jack." However, Nicholson's coyness maintains an element that has been a key to movie stardom from its earliest development, what Richard deCordova calls "the distinction between surface and depth, and the construction of knowledge about the players as a secret" (*Picture Personalities* 139–140).

John Ford, in a candid remark about Stewart, seemed to maintain that his acting, persona, and projected "real personality" were deliberately mingled: "Wayne, Cooper, and Gable are what you call natural actors. They are the same off the screen as they are playing a part. Stewart isn't like that. He isn't a thing like he is on the screen. Stewart did a whale of a job manufacturing a character the public went for. He studied acting" (Gallagher 378). Ford repeated the perceptions of many that while "Wayne, Cooper, Gable" are "natural actors," which amounts to calling them "natural men," there is an artifice to Stewart ("he studied acting") that separates him from "natural" manliness and makes "masculinity," when he tries to project it, something of a bad fit, a put-on like the "character the public went for."

The persona of an action star is clear in one sense and obscure in another, since it is based mainly on the films. The indomitability of

"John Wayne" is blurred when the mighty "Duke" is conflated with the real man's two bankruptcies and his long affliction with cancer. The "real" Schwarzenegger is another bundle of contradictions that are seldom conjured with: a notorious hedonist in his *Pumping Iron* days who more recently taught kids to exercise as President Bush's star-spangled physical fitness chief, a homosexual fantasy figure and the avatar of heterosexual "health," and a Kennedy in-law who hobnobs with Republican politicians. The action star is received as a monolithic icon whose "real self," however incoherent, is mostly beside the point.

The unitary extreme of the action star persona mirrors that of macho masculinity; to problematize one, as Clint Eastwood's career shows, is necessarily to problematize the other. Eastwood's revisionism since the early 1980s has involved an attempt to assert the "real person." His TV interviews present a laid-back, soft-spoken guy, almost dull with "ordinariness." Adam Knee, in an article on *Play Misty for Me*, points out the tension, little recognized (or believed) between, as a 1974 biography described, "an actor whose trademark is violence" and a man who "abhors violence in real life, especially cruelty to animals" (Knee 90). In 1993 Eastwood said, perhaps a bit disingenuously given the fortune he's made from representations of violence:

> You get trapped by an image, but I've overcome it to some degree. . . . You make an impact in a certain kind of role and everyone thinks you're that person. . . . It's nice in a way—you've set out to do what you want to do. But I don't carry a .44 Magnum around. And if I were to play in a remake of *Dr. Kildare*, the audience might say "Wait a minute. He's doing a few operations now, he's tending to pediatrics, he's helping a couple of old people. But eventually he better start shooting." . . . I've fought my way out of the genre. (Weinraub 214)

Therefore, the coherence that constitutes the personality in a capitalist society often collides with the coherence that defines a commodity in the same commercial culture. We are objects masquerading as subjects; gender and stardom convey the illusion of a similar transformation. Film studies has until very recently defined the star, the spectator, and particularly the male specimens of each, in psychoanalytic terms of subjectivity and the "ego ideal." As in the Mirror Stage of Jacques Lacan, the person "misrecognizes" an object of the other as one's self. This illusion of identity, as Jean-Louis Baudry and Christian Metz theorized, is related to the illusion of a "transcendental" movement through space and time. The star image is fundamentally a commodity and hence an object, but one with the characteristics and mobility of a subject—an "individual" with what Dyer calls an "irreducible core."

In light of recent film criticism on the male body as an object, a 1974 quotation by Robert Redford now looks particularly interesting. "I hate being stared at by anybody," he said. "That whole feeling of becoming an object rather than a person bothers me. I don't mind being an object on the screen, because that's what a role is, something you've created. Off screen, I'm not some kind of *thing*. I'm a human being" (quoted in Bingham " . . . Crawling into the Spotlight" 20). Actually, a star is a combination of both subject and object, but Redford's understandable discomfort at being objectified is a privilege granted as a rule to men, but not to women. Despite recent critical efforts to highlight the "invisible" outlines and pleasure in looking at the male body as object on screen, Laura Mulvey's often-quoted line, "Man is reluctant to gaze at his exhibitionist like," still seems accurate, based on illusion and displacement though this reluctance may be. The gaze at the male star often (though by no means always) deemphasizes the body and focuses on the face, upper body, and voice, as sites of individuality as well as avatars of "sincerity" and "coherence." The filmed object of the male body masquerades as a subject, with the passive spectator positioned as an "active" participant.

The tension between the male persona and the man who acts, between the commodity and the masculine subject, has not been much explored in film studies. In attempting to do so, I analyze how film changes an object into the subject of fictions and the spectator's gaze. Each section takes a somewhat different approach. With Stewart, I am interested in the dialectic between his off-screen persona as the paragon of virtue next door and his highly emotional screen personality. With Nicholson, the emphasis is more on acting that puts the masquerade into the foreground— on masculinity as a set of roles one "performs." The section on Eastwood starts with the construction in his early films of the star as a projection of spectatorial ego and works through the evident instability over time of this highly masculinist fantasy.

This book is not a comprehensive study, such as Paul Smith's 1993 *Clint Eastwood: A Cultural Production*, of a star's entire career from a number of cultural standpoints. Rather it seeks primarily to find the meaning of the star's persona in the films themselves, from a spectator's point of view, following my inclination to look for answers to research questions mainly in the evidence on the screen. Although I appreciate the importance of such extratextual approaches as historiography and cultural studies and find them useful, I believe that the most important relationship remains the one between the "magic" images on a screen and the person who watches.

I approach the texts as cinematic narratives built around the appearance of a popular actor, who trails behind him a long-accumulating stream of expectations and connotations. Thus I look at how an actor's performance creates meaning in the context of the film's narrative and cinematic strategies. I've chosen films that have been important in a star's career, paying special attention to the star's turns—roles that either stretch him beyond his fixed persona or may not be permitted to—by audiences and the industry.

Accordingly genres are crucial in understanding how star personas are developed and maintained (Eastwood's evolution through Westerns and police films, for example). As Andrew Britton and Richard deCordova have discussed, genres also ring ideological changes in interaction with stars whose personas and performance styles in some way run counter to generic expectations (for example, the changes the tough Western archetype and the emotional Stewart demeanor brought to each other in the 1950s, or Nicholson's subversive effect on horror conventions in *The Shining*).

Fundamentally, Hollywood movies show the process by which gender is represented—and masculinism maintained and threatened—in our culture. The sense of gender identity as a coherent unit is strong. Virtually all the previous books on stars, acting, and film masculinities have begun with an assumed monolith or conventional wisdom through which the writer must pierce. This was true of simplistic early studies of the harshness and invincibility of film masculinity, such as Joan Mellen's *Big Bad Wolves* (1977), which merely recycled patriarchy's dualistic definitions of "masculine" and "feminine." It was also true of the work of Mulvey, whose excluded female spectator and omnipotent male subject gave the dualisms the pedigrees of semiotics and psychoanalysis.

I try to play out the dialectics of the stable gender identity (and its counterpart, the movie star persona) and the multiplicities that belie it. The personas of Stewart, Nicholson, and Eastwood—three of the most popular and durable male stars in film history—show the discontinuities of fabricated roles and the problems of playing them. The categories assumed by film studies, reviewers, and the movie industry—"prestigious" and "action star," "new star" and "classic star"—obscure the common cultural tradition of maintaining male dominance as well as the fragmentation that makes unitary masculinity a difficult—even impossible—construction to maintain.

PART ONE
□□□

James Stewart:
Your Average Bisexual
□□□

2

"Hollywood Didn't Invent Him": Mythology and "Naturalness"

□□□

A close shot on a stone curb marker, engraved "Dowd," dollies up to settle on a full shot of a handsome Victorian house on a backlot Anytown, U.S.A. The front door opens and out steps tall, lanky James Stewart, age forty-two, as Elwood P. Dowd. On the soundtrack a lighthearted cross between a gavotte and fanfare announces the presence of the star. Dowd/Stewart slowly ambles toward the street and also toward the camera. His tweeds are worn, his hair wavy and long in back. His walk is loose, shambling, and relaxed; Elwood is clearly open to whatever comes his way. He looks around and sniffs the air. Opening the front gate and motioning to his invisible companion with a slight flourish— "After you"—he licks his lips as if in anticipation of the day, or of a drink. A postman rides into the shot on a bicycle and asks Dowd to sign for a special-delivery letter. Dowd/Stewart stands with pelvis out and shoulders back and answers the mailman's pleasantry about the weather in a tone that is faraway but firm: "Every day's a beautiful day." The postman does a triple take and hurries to his bike and out of the shot. Dowd looks to his "friend," smiles pleasantly, and mutters, "Nice man," while tearing up the letter and tossing it into the street with a motion and look at once methodical and careless.

Stewart's entrance in *Harvey*, an eagerly awaited and popular presold property when new, and one of his best-remembered roles now, displays luminously the essential Stewart persona—a small-town friendly neighbor, with a gentle face and voice and a slim body that is at once graceful and awkward. He has about him as well a kind of privacy that projects as "vision." The actor portrays that private vision with a sincerity and conviction that make it convincing, be the vision a six-foot rabbit, a concept of American ideals, or a murder across an apartment courtyard. This active sight projects the persona out toward its object in a way redolent of the goal-oriented "male" behavior of Mulveyan feminist theory. However, it also suggests something withheld, a "secret" that gives Stewart a charismatic, curious demeanor that, like his vision, can take a number of forms and adopt seemingly any behavior while staying true to the essential image. It makes him, in short, both a "personality" star and a chameleon, and chameleons know no fixed gender.

When James Stewart began his film career as a studio contract player in the 1930s, his failure to fit the masculinity of a "straight" leading man, his lithe physique, and emotional demeanor confronted the studio publicity department with the problem of selling as a "real man" a personality that was evidently bisexual. They succeeded in etching an appealing character into the public mind, but Stewart actually became a star in films that capitalized on his sexual ambivalence and the ambivalence of the diegetic world toward him. To study the contrasting facets of James Stewart's persona, which the star and actor made a career of balancing, is to explore an ambivalence at the heart of ideologically constructed masculinity, to find a distinction between stardom and acting (Stewart made a virtually separate career of each), and to seek—like the answer to an unanswerable riddle—dialectics of conservatism and rupture, subversion and recuperation, the familiar and the peculiar. Stewart encompasses the farthest extremes of American masculinity, from Reaganite militarist patriotism to Hitchcockian perversity. The issue involves the multiple meanings of Jimmy Stewart and what keeps competing meanings balanced and coherent.

I am concerned here with the films and publicity that defined Stewart's fifty-plus-year career as a star presence at three distinct historical points. The first two eras are demarcated by Stewart's World War II military service, which interrupted his career. First is his prewar stardom, in which he became defined as a shy, earnest boy next door, but one of unusual emotional intensity. The postwar years, which marked Stewart's most sustained success, often show a dramatic contrast between the offscreen image of an exemplary war hero and family man and film performances that appear free to veer wildly from it. The final portion explores the meaning of "Jimmy Stewart" as he was remembered in the late 1980s and early 1990s, when the still-living actor remained a popular, nostalgic presence in American culture. From this latter-day vantage point, I revisit the 1950s and two films, *Harvey* and *Anatomy of a Murder*, in order to show the selective, forgetful, and restorative process by which the historical and cultural legacy of a star, especially one as contradictory as Stewart, is constituted.

James Stewart is unique in that of the "Golden Age" film performers who became household names under the pre-1948 studio system, he is the only one whose greatest success came in the 1950s during the decline of the studios. The deal Lew Wasserman of MCA (then a talent agency) engineered for Stewart with Universal-International in 1950 was the first of its kind and paved the way for the system by which stars gained wealth and independence unheard of since Charles Chaplin's halcyon days in the twenties; Stewart took no salary in return for a large percentage of the profits on two films, *Winchester '73* and *Harvey*. From 1950 to 1957, Stewart made roughly a film a year for U-I while remaining free to work for other companies, sometimes developing his own projects, usually as part of director-star packages put together by MCA (Schatz *The Genius of the System* 470–472).

Thus we approach Stewart both as a star groomed by the studio system and as an actor who at his peak exercised relative control over his career. The straddling of eras helps account for the curious way in which Stewart's performances often seem parallel to but separate from his persona. The image of Jimmy Stewart as American hero—decent, hardworking, loyal, with an air of the rural, the unsophisticated (despite a degree from Princeton), and the inarticulate (with his famous stammer)—stayed constant throughout his career even when his film roles varied from it. David Thomson in 1979 referred to Stewart as "one of the most intriguing examples of a star increasingly cast against his own accepted character" (*Biographical Dictionary* 582). While Humphrey Bogart, in Robert Sklar's account, made films in the early fifties that display versatility beyond his accepted persona, these are not the Bogart films that are remembered now. Stewart, on the other hand, is well remembered in movies that deeply problematize the "gee-whiz," small-town persona MGM began promoting in the 1930s.

After Stewart was brought to Hollywood from Broadway in 1935 and signed by MGM to the standard seven-year contract, the studio was dismayed by his gangling, scrawny physique. Ted Allan, a publicity photographer, explained the confusion. "Was he a comedian, or a romantic leading man? We tried photographing him outside, leaning over fences, working with a shovel, with a tennis racket—but while that worked with Robert Taylor in helping to make him more athletic, it didn't work with Stewart" (Eyles 42). Realizing that they would never have a he-man or a sex symbol in Stewart, MGM began promoting him as "the upright average man . . . product of a small American town and God-fearing parents . . . endowed with a keen sense of humor" (Robbins 39). His simplicity was emphasized; one press release described Stewart's preference for a "beat-up windbreaker" over a "three-piece business suit" (Robbins 39). It was at about this time that the publicity and press articles began to refer to "Jimmy" Stewart, his name among family and friends, while film credits and ads billed him as "James." A formal distinction was thus set up between "Jimmy," the "upright average man" who is everybody's friend, and "James," the actor. The result was a commodity that combined perceptions of the artist, the film image, and the "real" person.

There was truth to the studio's publicity; James Maitland Stewart was raised in the small western Pennsylvania town of Indiana. He later described his hometown as "the way all of America should be like. Open and friendly" (Robbins 15). His parents were college educated; his father, who graduated from Princeton, owned and ran the local hardware store until the mid-1960s. The hardware store became part of Stewart's mythology; his 1940 Academy Award for Best Actor stood in the window of the mom-and-pop store for more than twenty years, signifying that in the United States even the most humble can gain fame and fortune without losing touch with their origins. Military patriotism is a given in this all-American persona. Reportedly Stewart's great-great grandfather was a soldier in the Revolutionary War; "since then, there has been a Stewart in every American war. It didn't matter if they were underweight or overage—somehow they managed to find ways to serve their country" (Robbins 16).

Therefore the image to which Stewart and his Anglo-Saxon Yankee background lent themselves fit comfortably with Louis B. Mayer's vision of MGM as a vessel for homogeneous American values. However, it does not appear that Stewart's "personality" needed to be shaped to fit the studio image; for once, the publicity was tailored to the personality. This "naturalness" ironically became part of his mythology, as summarized by a headline such as: JIMMY STEWART: HOLLYWOOD DIDN'T INVENT HIM (*Christian Science Monitor* 1980). His image does not have the appearance of a construction but is presented as the sum of such "natural" attributes as honesty, sincerity, modesty, idealism, naïveté, and shyness. The publicity props described by the studio photographer come off as the phony trappings of media manipulators next to the simple virtues of the small-town Stewart, a populist theme that rang through many of his films. He embodied the underestimated "common man" who gets in the last word on the sophisticated and the privileged.

However, Frank Capra, with whom Stewart made *You Can't Take It With You* (1938) and *Mr. Smith Goes to Washington* (1939) on loan-out at Columbia, recognized in Stewart a blend of the "common touch" and upper-class breeding. Capra wrote in his autobiography, "I had seen Jimmy Stewart play a sensitive, heart-grabbing role in MGM's *Navy Blue and Gold*. I sensed the character and rock-ribbed honesty of a Gary Cooper, plus the breeding and intelligence of an ivy-league idealist" (242).

The prewar, physical Stewart was easily caricatured. He said of his first film, *Murder Man* (1935), "I was all hands and feet. Didn't seem to know what to do with either" (Robbins 37). A 1940 Warner Brothers cartoon parody of Hollywood personalities shows Stewart, with long neck, shoestring arms and legs, drooping eyelids, and large lips, in the throes of a stammering fit as a saronged Dorothy Lamour puts the make on him. The cartoon Stewart exits stage left, putting a sign on the table: "Mr. Smith Goes to Washington." While such caricatures take off on the star's bashfulness and boyish ungainliness, the prewar Stewart film persona was honest, open, and gentle. His extreme height and slimness (he was six foot three and a half inches tall and 130 pounds on his arrival at MGM) were sometimes exploited for comic effect, as in his fright-stricken encounters with the senator's daughter in *Mr. Smith*, which leave the Stewart character unable to put on a hat or hold a telephone.

More often, however, the awkward physique was balanced by the fixity of Stewart's gaze and sincerity of his verbal delivery. The classical Hollywood style, with its stress on close-ups and medium shots, favored Stewart, deemphasizing his ungainliness. Comic use of Stewart's scarecrow frame called for long shots and objectified his body; the more the camera ignored his body, as, for example, in Lubitsch's romantic comedy-drama *The Shop Around the Corner* (1940), the more graceful he seemed. His honesty and intelligence were emphasized by a focus on the face, eyes, forward-bent shoulders, and an expressive voice that was both eccentric, in the manner of many early stars in the first two decades of sound film, and seemingly common.

The first stage of Stewart's star career ended with his induction into the U.S. Army in March 1941. By then the personality described by the MGM scout as "unaffected and decent" was so well established that it could be transported in films across lines of class, history, social milieu, and nationality. Stewart materialized as the heir to a Wall Street banking fortune (*You Can't Take It With You*), a law-abiding but unorthodox sheriff in the Old West (*Destry Rides Again*), a big-city newspaper reporter (*The Philadelphia Story*), and a jaded store clerk in Budapest (*The Shop Around the Corner*).

The Jeff Smith character, with his Boy Scout worldview and his emotional bond with an anachronistic frontier America, would be the basis of the Stewart persona, enhanced by what the audience knew about the "real" Stewart. Before *Mr. Smith*, however, Capra had cast him in *You Can't Take It With You* as an eastern, urban scion of wealth and power, one who credibly renounces his upper-class status because it sits on the "average" Stewart so "unnaturally." Thus the broad adaptability of Stewart's persona and his emotional range as an actor probably ensured that in time Stewart would grow too complex to be contained within the sort of fixed star image that John Ellis finds essentially "incoherent" (92–93).

The prewar Stewart, with his gentle manner and unathletic body, played characters who were closer to the home—to the realm of boys and their mothers—than to the world of "experience," the arena of aggressive, striving, driven men. All three of the Capra films, as Nick Browne has remarked, open with the Stewart character living with his mother (4). Stewart's characters falter when they try to act as men in the world. Conversely, the Stewart hero who stays too close to home collides with his own feeling that he should be doing something more, that there is nothing manly about being the boy next door in a world ruled by Mother. The very notion of "the boy next door" connotes middle-class conformity. "Boys next door" live at home in a domestic world partway between boyhood and manhood. They are close to the late-nineteenth-century feminine values of harmony, charity, and domestic order. A "boy next door" represents the antithesis of a rebel hero such as Huckleberry Finn because his world is the "sivilisation" Huck Finn rejects, needing no other reason than its perceived femininity and the restrictions it represents.

As Stewart was described as boyish, especially in the prewar publicity and press, later appraisals have found "femininity" in his acting style. In a 1987 PBS documentary on Stewart, actor Richard Dreyfuss referred to Destry, the Wild West deputy who refuses to use a gun, as "a very feminine hero." One recent account states that "from the first, Stewart's performances stood out: raw, edgy, full of nervous energy. While his rivals played with masculine understatement, Stewart mirrored the vital excesses of those most American of rising actresses—Crawford, Davis, Hepburn" (Monaco et al. 515).

"Boyishness" gives way to "femininity" because both "read" as something other than masculine. Oedipal narratives such as Capra's *Mr. Smith* and *It's a Wonderful Life* lead their naïve young protagonists from youthful dreams and irresponsibility to the eventual taking of a noble (dead) father's place, by means of martyrdom in *Mr. Smith* and a virtual death and rebirth in *Wonderful Life*. In both the characters are problematized by the films' own ambivalence. Charles Wolfe and Capra himself have written about the stormy reception that *Mr. Smith* received in federal government circles because of its depiction of a jaded and corrupt official Washington into which the patriotic Boy Scout innocently wanders. Indeed, the film's view of American government is thick with pessimism, and Smith's heroic filibuster is not enough to dispel it. *It's a Wonderful Life* can barely separate the responsibility and maturity—which it appears to celebrate in its protagonist's unrewarding life of drudgery—from feelings of disgust for George Bailey's small-town life. The film blames the hero's plight on the women who keep him there, homebound creatures without an ounce of the man's imagination or curiosity.

Both of these famous films have recently aroused critical debate because they unlock, at the heart of American male mythologies, contradictions greater than they themselves can resolve. The Stewart character at last arrives, scarred and battered, at the attainment of his manhood, but the films are unsure about whether he is better off there. Stewart as actor articulates the characters' visions, expectations, pain, disappointment, and final revelations with more clarity than the script and direction, reasserting the star's image as an honest, open person whose vision and receptiveness to experience break through the world's muddles and ambiguities. This openness makes Stewart different from many male stars of this period and beyond. In comparison to the man as "hermetic being, closed up in himself," Octavio Paz sees women in patriarchy as "inferior beings because in submitting, they open themselves up" (quoted in Schwenger 43). Peter Schwenger adds that "it is by talking that one opens up to another person and becomes vulnerable. It is by putting words to an emotion that it becomes feminized" (44–45). When Stewart doesn't speak, it's not because he won't but because he can't. Furthermore, in big speeches Stewart is often breathless, the words tumbling out. If his stammering and reticence mark him as "natural" and "ordinary," they also show him to be not in complete control of himself. His openness is double edged, making him a "nice guy" but leaving him vulnerable.

3
□□□

"Boy's Stuff" and
the Surrendering Gaze:
Mr. Smith Goes to Washington

□□□

As Stewart's verbal traits leave him with both "masculine" and "feminine" characteristics, his version of the male "look"—the foundation of feminist spectatorship theory—is also marked by ambivalence. The intensity and magnetism of Stewart's gaze would seem to make the star a male identification figure; his eyes clearly direct the gaze and project him toward its object. So many of the well-known images from Stewart films involve a fixed, intense gaze that the actor could be called a specialist in the eyeline match and the reaction shot.

A type of look not associated with masculinity, however, is the enraptured gaze. While the male's look, according to feminist theory, fixes objects for his possession, the gaze of rapture posits its owner as a receptor who gives him- or herself over to the object and becomes a vessel for the values it connotes. Stewart films teem with moments in which, rather than seeing something and thus finding and possessing it, he looks at, and loses himself to, the object of his gaze.

In *Mr. Smith Goes to Washington*, on his arrival in the nation's capital, the callow young leader of the Boy Rangers, who has been appointed to the U.S. Senate as the unwitting pawn of a corrupt political machine, takes a bus tour. In a sequence assembled by montage expert Slavko Vorkapitch, Jeff Smith/Stewart is seen at first in an establishing shot, sitting in the bus and looking all around him. In a close-up, Stewart's head turns 180 degrees; his eyes are wide and his mouth slightly agape. He purses his lips, miming the awe of an uninitiated rube seeing the big city for the first time.

The ensuing montage of historic sights and monuments in Washington is punctuated by Smith's excited gaze, and the rhythm of the editing is matched by an orchestral medley of patriotic tunes. The sequence mirrors the ambivalence of the film, placing a spectator in a position to follow the young patriot's awestruck journey while remaining somewhat detached from it. Charles Wolfe, in a contextual study of *Mr. Smith*, identifies the film's "central political question": "What *is* Washington, a repository of political ideals or the scene of their inevitable compromise?" (*Mr. Smith* 316). For most of its length, the film persuasively depicts the latter, with the idealistic hero observed through a scrim of cynicism.

At the climax of this montage, Smith finds himself at the Lincoln Memorial. First, in a long shot that dwarfs Smith among the columns of the memorial, the panning camera follows him until he is framed, gnat size, at the foot of the memorial, craning his neck to gaze at it. A point-of-view shot shows the lettering over the monument and moves down until the screen is filled by the alabaster Lincoln. What follows is the first of several reaction shots. A sidelong Smith/Stewart is shown from the waist up, his head cocked and eyes fixed. He turns to read the engraved Second Inaugural Address, which is shown in another point-of-view shot, a shaft of light seeming to underscore the "with malice toward none" passage. Then, in a close-up that repeats the second shot on the bus, Stewart turns his head, toward us this time, and looks up again at the monument; his eyes are slightly watery, his jaw slack, his lips parted and trembling. A side view of the monument, looking impermeable and eternal, is followed by a return to the medium shot of Smith, with Stewart's face in the same expression, transfixed by the monument and walking toward it as if utterly in its thrall.

Stewart's open, receptive look recalls the typical Marilyn Monroe pose as Richard Dyer analyzes it, in which the actress's lips are parted and slightly quivering. Dyer states that the open lips, while not necessarily crude symbols of the vagina, signify "'yielding sexuality'" and "'vulnerability'" (*Stars* 158). The prototypical Monroe waits to be given form by the male desire her look is designed to excite. While it would be simplistic to say that Stewart's gaze makes him "feminine," the open, trembling mouth and spellbound gaze spell receptivity and submission, divorced from male sexuality. The focus on the gaping mouth and staring eyes, and the lack of emphasis on Stewart's body, render him formless; he is shaped by what he looks at and gives himself to—monuments to American democratic ideals. Stewart does look, whereas the Monroe pose is there to be looked at. However, both code passivity, availability, and the surrender of individuality.

The montage is a cinematic patriotic pageant, but it is problematized because the patriotism is identified with Smith, the impressionable hick. The scene vividly exemplifies Louis Althusser's discussion of the "interpellation of the ideological subject," whereby an individual is "hailed" and turns around to acknowledge that the "hail" is addressed to him or her (Althusser gives as an example a shout like "Hey, you there!") (86–87). As Althusser adds, however, "Those who are in ideology believe themselves by definition outside ideology" (87). In classical Hollywood cinema, Americana is a given, not an expression of ideology. Hence the notion of recognition within dominant ideology of the subject's interpellation by that same ideology is oxymoronic. The need to negotiate this obvious contradiction accounts for the film's ambivalence; Smith/Stewart's "hailing" by "Lincoln" is much like subject construction in Hollywood cinema. In rendering such an "invisible" process visible, the film must distance its spectator from it. Thus Smith's gullibility and naïveté combine with Stewart's pantomime of the act of being "hailed" to make it admirable but also embarrassing, in the way that Saunders lectures Jeff about "fools with faith" in the second Lincoln Memorial sequence: To be a martyr is to embarrass oneself for a cause.

Stewart's is an adoring gaze, a look of eager surrender. Mary Ann Doane describes the end of *The Purple Rose of Cairo*, in which Mia Farrow is shown "in spectatorial ecstasy, enraptured by the image, her face glowing. . . . What the shot signifies, in part, is the peculiar susceptibility to the image . . . attributed to the woman in the culture." She adds that "there is a certain naïveté assigned to women in relation to systems of signification—a tendency to deny the processes of representation, to collapse the opposition between the sign (the image) and the real" (*The Desire to Desire* 1). In the first half of the film the inability to separate sign and reality makes Smith a figure of fun in the narrative; his interpellation by an ideology to which the sophisticates are "wised up" is neatly summarized in dialogue with the world-weary Saunders (Jean Arthur). "Gee whiz, why, Mr. Lincoln—there he is," he says breathlessly. "He's just lookin' right straight at you as you come up those steps." "Well, he's got nothing on me," she replies.

In its passive submission to the signifier, a loss of identity in looking as Stewart/Smith gives himself over to the ideological position signified by the Lincoln Memorial, the gaze at "Lincoln" does associate Stewart's Smith with the "feminine." There is a profound difference between the depiction of Smith/Stewart's looking and the classic positioning of the spectator's "look." The spectator in an Eastwood film fantasizes— "misrecognizes"—himself in the position of the masterly hero and is guaranteed "the confirmation of the subject's mastery over the signifier" (Doane *Desire* 15). This difference is the reason behind the detachment and ambivalence that mark many of *Mr. Smith*'s key scenes; the spectator looks at what Smith sees but also looks at Smith. The constant reminder of the submissive gaze keeps the spectator from total involvement in Smith's enthusiasms.

1. *Mr. Smith Goes to Washington.* The awkwardness of a boy cast into an adult world. With Beulah Bondi, Guy Kibbee, and Ruth Donnelly.

The fixity of Stewart/Smith's gaze in the presence of "Lincoln" contrasts with his weak, wavering glance in social situations, which find him unsure of what to look at. In Smith's entrance into the film, he is next to the governor at the political banquet in the new senator's honor. He is seated in a low chair, in the bottom left-hand corner of a shot busy with people and decoration. His eyes wander, and his head moves queasily. In the next shot the governor's hand dominates a medium shot of Smith, who flinches as the hand motions at him. When he does rise to speak, his soft, stumbling delivery indicates the sincerity of an amateur. The slow, faltering speech and erratic vocal tone, which Stewart exaggerates in *Mr. Smith*, are effective dramatically. Stewart's line readings contrast with the rapid-fire delivery of thirties comedy, slowing down the rhythm of a dialogue scene and making Smith the center of attention by focusing on the awkwardness and unpredictability of a boy in an alien, adult world.

Jeff is thrown to castrating, primal father figures, political bosses whose instruments of emasculation are, as Wolfe suggests, technological—mass-circulation newspapers, radio, the smooth political operation Boss Taylor runs, and the telephone into which he barks his orders (320).

Jeff's identification figures are dead men who signify courage in fighting for "lost causes"—his father, a small-time editor who was killed by a mining syndicate he sought to expose—and the "Fathers of Our Country," from whom Jeff draws his inspiration.

Smith identifies with death and with a way of life that can hardly be said to survive in a modern urban media world. He identifies with ideals that appear to have died but can still be revived, as the film would have it, by a martyr who reaches back through history and saves them for the twentieth century. Wolfe calls the dramatic filibuster "a spectacle of martyrdom" (*Mr. Smith* 318). With Smith's instinctive identification with lost causes and signifiers of dead men—even down to the style of hat that his father wore during his crusades and on the day he was killed—the narrative strains toward a giving over of self, martyrdom as the culmination of Stewart's surrendering gaze.

This accounts for the film's odd ending, in which the hero has passed out on the Senate floor and the chief villain is still at large, as the galleries cheer. The film fades out with the martyr/hero having sacrificed himself for the ideals he signifies, but the ending shows again an uncertainty about whether those values can actually survive in the world. The film betrays doubts about what constitutes constructed masculinity—the brutal, primal manhood associated with advanced technology or the credulous, moral subjectivity of the respectable citizen that the film associates with archaic frontier legends.

This star-making film displayed for the first time Stewart's talent for masochism, for playing characters whose pain spectators can feel and identify with. As we will see, the masochism of Stewart's roles in Anthony Mann's Westerns and Alfred Hitchcock's thrillers in the 1950s emerges from Stewart's complex postwar persona and is more in the vein of the Freudian masochist whose suffering results from self-willed punishment. However, the Italian-Catholic Capra puts his protagonist through a secularized Christian ritual of castration and suffering that does not break violently with Stewart's earnest prewar image, but does derive from the persona's "femininity."

Freud theorized three kinds of masochism: erotogenic, "the lust of pain"; feminine, which, to quote Kaja Silverman, "positions its [presumably male] sufferer as a woman" (*Male* 189); and moral, in which "an unconscious sense of guilt" gives way to a "need for punishment" ("Economic Problem in Masochism" 192–197). He focused on moral masochism, which he said begins when "the ego reacts with feelings of anxiety . . . to the perception that it has failed to perform the behests of its ideal, the super-ego" (197). Such guilt feelings result in a resexualization of the Oedipus complex, whereby transgressions against the father

lead to punishment and castration at his hands. Senator Smith, by fili-
bustering, both confronts and submits himself to the castrating primal
father, Boss Taylor. However, this is not the same as submitting to what
Freud called "the reproaches of the sadistic conscience." The conscience, or superego, is once again signified by Lincoln, Jeff's father,
and the "lost ideals" men must teach to boys.

Mr. Smith's "spectacle of martyrdom" follows primarily the "Christian masochism" described by Theodor Reik. In Reik's formulation, the
ego is more central to masochistic fantasy than is the superego, with "the
desire to be rewarded for good behavior" foremost in the masochist's
mind. The Christian masochist is an exhibitionist. In Reik's examples,
from the lives of saints and martyrs as well as the life of Christ, the
essentials are an external audience, a central display of the body, and a
"master tableau [such as] Christ nailed to the cross, head wreathed in
thorns and blood dripping from his impaled sides" (Silverman *Male*
197). Silverman explains that "what is being beaten here is not so much
the body as the 'flesh,' and beyond that sin itself, and the whole fallen
world." In Christian masochism lies "the desire to remake the world in
another image altogether, to forge a different cultural order" (Silverman
Male 197–198).

Smith talks for twenty-three and a half hours without stopping or sitting down, as dictated by Senate rules that allow him to keep the attention of the Senate but that make excruciating demands on his body. By
the twenty-fourth hour, Stewart/Smith's fragile, spindly physique seems
to buckle and break. He uses his desk to prop himself up; leaning forward, he could as easily fall facedown as punch out the words of his
"extemporaneous" speech. The actor swabbed his throat with a solution
prepared by a physician to induce laryngitis (Molyneaux 73); to the
hoarseness he adds a wheeze and occasional cough.

As Wolfe points out, Jeff is not aware, as the film's spectators and the
other characters are, of the mounting futility of his stand (*Mr. Smith*
318). Jeff is unconscious when Paine attempts suicide and dramatically
confesses all. As the film ends Jeff is a sacrificial lamb ignorant of his
"triumph born of defeat," in Wolfe's words, as all about him celebrate.
"What is perhaps most remarkable about Smith as a heroic figure,"
Wolfe writes, "is the limits placed on the range of his knowledge . . . ,
his lack of any sense of destiny (or premonition of personal doom), a
mystical motif that runs through the legends of Lincoln and [Martin Lu-
ther] King" (318).

The dynamic of the martyr legend, then, is almost completely opposite
that of the goal-oriented conflict narrative. The nobility of the martyr is
proved by his defeat, which is assured by a lack of knowledge that keeps

him innocent and guileless. His good works are almost inadvertent (but natural; he can't help but do the right thing), free of the calculation that would make him a more conventional, masterly male hero (like Destry in *Destry Rides Again*) rather than a martyr who sacrifices himself for the good of all. As with many of the saints, the good brought about by Smith's suffering is apparent only later.

Silverman finds fault with Reik's notion that the Christian masochist is motivated by victory and reward, arguing that "what is rendered visible" in Reik's own account "is the subject's 'suffering,' 'discomfort,' 'humiliation,' and 'disgrace'" (*Male* 198). Jeff's motives are as pure and selfless as those of the Christian martyrs. Just as Smith is unprepossessing and uncalculating throughout the film, so his triumph is shown to be unexpected; the point is his suffering, not victory over Taylor. This appears to suit Capra, who rejected a number of scripted happy endings showing Jeff, Saunders, Paine, and Ma Smith reunited back home, one of which was evidently filmed (Wolfe *Mr. Smith* 318). Capra seems too persuaded by the depiction of sold-out ideals to wipe it away definitively.

Finally Silverman points out the distance of the Christian masochism formula from conventional oedipal masculinity:

> Insofar as such an identification implies the complete and utter negation of all phallic values, Christian masochism has radically emasculating implications, and is in its purest forms intrinsically incompatible with the pretentions of masculinity. . . . Christianity also redefines the paternal legacy; it is after all through the assumption of his place within the divine family that Christ comes to be installed in a suffering and castrated position. (*Male* 198)

The film culminates in the emulation of the martyrdom of Jeff's father, who is invoked at the moment of Jeff's most profound humiliation, the arrival at the Senate of hundreds of hate telegrams trumped up (unbeknownst to Smith) by the Taylor machine. Were the film to follow through the paternal legacy as fully as the classic film normally does, it would have to end with Smith's death, rather than with the symbolic martyrdom of a fainting spell. The film dilutes the paternal legacy with its array of father figures. Besides the symbolic fathers (Jeff's real father, Lincoln) and the primal father (Taylor), there is the symbolic father reduced to actuality, Paine, "a man I've admired and worshipped all my life."

Moreover, the vice president (Harry Carey), pure iconography and little characterization, functions as a kind of living Lincoln Memorial. A

2. The surrendering gaze at the moment of rapture.

veteran B-Western actor, Carey was cast because he fit Capra's require-
ment of "a good American face" for a character who has considerable
screen time but few lines, and thus is important as a "presence" (Capra
263). The "good American face" means white, Anglo, with "ordinary"
features and tousled hair; the vice president could be a composite of all of
Jeff's Boy Rangers (or Jimmy Stewart) at fifty—a combination of the
codes of boyish idealism and fatherly authority. Thus the vice president's
kindly looks at Smith, especially near the moment of Jeff's "martyrdom," suture the young senator to original American values in ways that
recall the "celestial suture" in Silverman's reading of *It's a Wonderful
Life*.

The Christian masochism paradigm accounts for the film's peculiar
handling of its love story. The relationship between Saunders and Smith
is more maternal than romantic; this is a romance without so much as a
kiss. Jeff never professes love for Saunders. She proclaims her love for
him to her "buddy," Diz, the newspaperman (Thomas Mitchell), and has
a love note delivered to Jeff on the Senate floor from her perch in the
gallery. (It could be said that the "feminine" surrendering gaze is finally
displaced onto the face of the woman, where it "belongs.") But Saunders's submissive gaze at Smith at the end of the film seems less the
traditional woman-as-mirror affirmation of masculinity than an indica-

tion that Jeff is beginning to take his place as a living Lincoln, a symbol of lost values, with Saunders as a vessel for his greatness.

Moreover, as Jeff must emulate his martyr-father as his initiation to manhood, Saunders is compelled to rediscover her femininity, which has been buried, as the thirties film would have it, by her career as a trusted assistant to important men. Her femininity is signified by her first name, Clarissa, which she hides like a humiliating secret. It is a pattern of the film's cutting and shot placement to begin scenes with Saunders in a superior, gaze-controlling position and Smith in the inferior position of object of the gaze. In the "bill-writing" scene, for example, Saunders explains to Smith the logistics of getting a bill passed in Congress. During her long explanation the shot/reverse-shot pattern alternates a low-angle shot of Saunders, who is standing, and a head-on shot of Jeff, who is seated and listening like an eager schoolboy. However, once Jeff dictates the ideas for his bill, he stands and paces, commanding the stage and the look of the camera. He even holds a pipe in his hand, dispelling somewhat the character's "boyishness," while a loose forelock of hair signifies hard work.

If the martyr's suffering and emasculation collide with the requirements of the Hollywood romance, they also help explain why the Stewart persona came to be oddly asexual for a male star of this period who was not mainly a comedian. Countering the prevalent present-day impression of Stewart as some sort of lifelong virgin, Kathleen Murphy wrote of Stewart's passion and abandon: "Few actors have ever matched Stewart's ability to project flat-out enthusiasm for the fall into love. In his youth, he was never afraid to give himself away" (36).

"Giving himself away" can be read as exposure or surrender—or perhaps both at once. Masculinity that "gives itself away" gives up control and invites collapse and disablement. The scene in It's a Wonderful Life in which Stewart shows George succumbing to Mary's domesticating charms while fighting them presents a masculinist critique of Stewart's propensity to surrender, displaying misogynist contempt both for the force he gives himself up to and for the submissiveness in himself that allows him to do it.

Just as few actors fall in love as wholly as Stewart, few actors faint as gloriously as he does. In a bodily gesture he would repeat in later films (notably Vertigo) at Smith's moment of overwhelming defeat, Stewart's lips quiver, his head and shoulders waver, the hand limply reaches for the mouth, and his eyes roll to the tops of their sockets just before falling shut. Smith/Stewart's head and shoulders slump to the edge of the frame, and the body, which had been framed in the right half of the shot, now sinks out of frame entirely; a match-on-action completes the fall in full shot, as the towering body tumbles, bringing down a storm of paper with it.

The Stewart persona gives himself up to women in the same way that Jeff surrenders to "Lincoln" and the cause. Stewart's passion mingles with his masochism, requiring the "love interest" to share his pain; thus, when Smith collapses, Saunders/Arthur's scream is heard above all others in the crowded chamber. Moments earlier she says, "I can't stand it. I can't stand to see him hurt like this." This shared pain is necessary because the Stewart character's masochism and longing for "the fall" (both toward death and back into the womb) deprive the love story of the phallus around which, as Lacan maintains, a heterosexual relation centers (Heath "Difference" 54).

For proof of Stewart's lack of the solidity expected from a male icon, look at the comparison between Stewart and Gary Cooper made by Jean Arthur, who worked with both actors in Capra films:

> Jimmy Stewart's marvelous, but Cooper's better. You get to know Stewart too well, and with Gary there are always wonderful hidden depths that you haven't found yet. Stewart is almost too much when he acts; I get tired of his "uh, uh . . . "—his cute quality. With Cooper it just seems to *happen*. I can't remember Cooper saying much of anything. But it's very comfortable working with him. You feel like you're resting on the Rock of Gibraltar. (McBride 345)

These remarks are rich with assumptions about "masculinity" and "femininity" in acting. The emotional accessibility that Arthur finds in Stewart, his excess, and his obvious performance are contrasted with Cooper's laconic stoicism, his effacement of performance, and coherent solidity. With conventional masculine behavior as the standard in the culture, Cooper's acting is "comfortable" because of the virility that does not need to be stated; it is "implicitly known," in Steve Neale's phrase. The emotionalism patriarchy displaces onto femininity but reads as mysterious is "too much" for a male actor to display, for the same reason that masochism is associated with femininity in spite of—or perhaps, alas, because of—the fact that the great majority of Freud's masochistic patients were men (Silverman *Male* 189).

The question that becomes more pointed as Stewart's career progresses is how an actor who projected so much femininity remained so popular. It is true that Stewart's films, especially as he grew older, balanced his emotional propensities as an actor and his physical idiosyncrasies against his "real life," which became only more exemplary with time. It is also true that the films themselves negotiate what Silverman calls "the dominant fiction" with currents that work against it. Both of these balancing acts fit the familiar pattern in Hollywood cinema of sub-version made right by recuperation. It is small wonder, then, that Stewart goes forth from this film with an utterly ambivalent persona.

4

Gender Trouble at the OK Corral: *Destry Rides Again*

□□□

Given the contradictions that Stewart's image manages to contain, it is probably no surprise that he became such a durable and acclaimed star: The contradictions made him more complex than at first glance and made him interesting as a box-office commodity by mixing familiar and new elements. After *Mr. Smith* Stewart's next film after was a comic Western that dealt as openly as a Hollywood movie could with "femininity" in a masculine domain. *Destry Rides Again* (1939) was made at Universal and was perceived primarily as a successful comeback film for Marlene Dietrich. In many ways a typical showcase for the unfailingly nice, unwaveringly honest prewar Stewart, *Destry* features him as a deputy sheriff who doesn't believe in guns. One interviewee in the 1987 PBS documentary commented, "When I was a kid, if the hero didn't carry a gun, I just thought that was terrible. But with Stewart's Destry, you sense that he could be a man of action; that danger is always lurking." That the speaker was a pre-*Unforgiven* Clint Eastwood playing to his popular persona ought to make clear the standard of masculinity expected in the Western, as well as an appreciation of the feminine traits held in check by constructed masculinity.

In her feminist study of the Western, Jane Tompkins sees the popularity of Western novels at the beginning of the twentieth century as a male backlash against female domestic culture and the heroic Christian sacrifice and social reform celebrated in late-Victorian popular novels. Tompkins sees the Western as a direct answer to the feminine sentimental novel, an attempt to write femininity out of American culture. To Tompkins "The Western doesn't have anything to do with the West as such" but is "about men's fear of losing their mastery, and hence their identity, both of which the Western tirelessly reinvents" (45). Thus the axiomatic binary oppositions of the Western (book vs. gun, garden vs. wilderness, parlor vs. mesa, word vs. deed, culture vs nature, and so on) add up to the conquest of civilized Victorian "feminine" values by masculinism's rough simplicity. The Western novels of Zane Grey, Owen Wister, and many others, and the movie genre that grew out of them, amount to "American men . . . taking their manhood back from the Christian women who have been holding it in thrall. Mercy and religion, as preached by women and the clergy, have stood in manhood's way too long and men are finally rebelling" (33).

The project of the Western, according to Tompkins, is the suppression of women, and the creation of an imaginary world in which women are unnecessary encumbrances, in which female protests against male violence are made in order to be proved wrong, and in which language, negotiation, and introspection are ineffectual female contrivances dangerous to men's survival. While the Western sees woman as a creature of culture, man is an extension of nature. Moreover, while the heroine's capacity to face life is the central test of her character, the Western hero's manhood is determined by his ability to face death; thus prowess with guns and fists is the standard of the male's fitness for life (and death) in the West.

Therefore a Western that sets out to spoof, complicate psychologically, or revise the conventions of the genre necessarily confronts a narrative that safeguards masculinity from femininity. When Stewart, with his ambiguous gender image, made Westerns, the "feminine" aspects of his persona and performance style were means of questioning and revising generic conventions steeped in sexual politics. In his prewar era the only sort of Western Stewart would have been (and in fact was) cast in was a comedy, whose humor was derived from inversions of the genre's conventions.

In his structuralist categories for the Western genre, Will Wright classifies *Destry* as a "classical Western" (30), a plot he summarizes as "the story of the lone stranger who rides into a troubled town and cleans it up, winning the respect of the townsfolk and the love of the schoolmarm" (32). While *Destry* does ultimately respect this plot structure, the film finds comedy in it by inverting gender values. Tom Destry (Stewart) comes into town and fails to live up to the blazing reputation of his father, a tough sheriff killed in the line of duty. He is first shown toting a birdcage and parasol for a lady as she gets off the stagecoach, defusing a confrontation with the villain by announcing that he doesn't carry guns, and ordering milk at the saloon.

Masculinity, not femininity, is the problem. The frontier town of Bottleneck suffers from an excess of testosterone. The opening-credit sequence is a hyperbolic montage showing cowboys punching each other, shooting guns into the air, and generally blowing off excess sexual energy. Instead of weak-willed women threatening safety by relying on words and prayers in the face of death, trigger-happy men endanger the homes and families of the town—and themselves—by their violent impulsiveness. To work its comic inversions, the movie returns to the Western's origins as a reaction, in Tompkins's argument, to the Victorian female values of mercy, domesticity, and negotiation, in order to make comic the genre's values of confrontation and force as solutions to all problems.

Like *Mr. Smith*, *Destry* keeps Stewart off screen for the first fifteen minutes, while the corrupt world he will enter is set up. As in the earlier film, he is brought to center stage very gradually. As Destry rides into town on the stagecoach with Jack Tyndall (Jack Carson) and his sister, Janice (Irene Hervey), Carson, a brawny character actor who often played blustering bully types, is seen first, sticking his head out the window and threatening to blow the driver's head off for driving too fast on mountain ridges. The costumes of the two men contrast: Carson wears the open shirt and loose clothing of a cowman; Stewart is dressed in tweeds, looking more like the stock clergyman of Westerns than the lawman. When he and Stewart are shown together in a shot, Carson still occupies the foreground. Stewart/Destry responds to Tyndall/Carson's threat with the first of many anecdotes meant to show the foolishness of violence.

Destry delivers all his dialogue in this scene while carving a napkin ring, a practice he recommends because of the "genuine rage you can work off" doing it. When the forceful man remarks about Destry's "peculiar ideas," his sister adds that "they make sense." So right away the masculinism of Westerns, epitomized by the short-fused Tyndall, is set up as a foil to Stewart's "peculiar" deputy. Destry warns against male violence to the assent of his female listener; he whittles away at a napkin ring, a domestic ornament a woman would use; and he is visually in a "feminine" position, dominated in the shot by the more forceful man. Thus Stewart/Destry is immediately identified with the feminine, clashing comically with the expectations of Sheriff Wash (Charles Winninger), who has told the ornery townspeople that they're "gonna meet a man."

James Naremore wrote that in the late 1930s, "Stewart seemed prepared to inherit the mantle of Will Rogers," with "clod-kicking shyness and innocence concealing 'natural' intelligence and passionate idealism. Thus in *Destry Rides Again* . . . one almost expects him to do rope tricks" (254). The "feminine" might seem a ruse, simply the most obvious way the script could devise to make Destry underestimated and poise him to catch the crooked tinhorns and politicians off guard.

Stewart/Destry is cast in the familiar folk type of the "trickster," a figure who comes in numerous guises but who manages to flout convention and fleece his adversaries, after letting them believe that they have things well in hand and need not take him seriously.

Stewart's affect as Destry is quite different from that of Mr. Smith. In the scene in which he arrives in town, the Stewart character once again emerges from the background of a busy group shot. His back is to the camera as the shot begins. His posture is loose and loping; he is again physically passive, allowing himself literally to be pushed around by the older sheriff. This physical self-effacement, however, hides an unshakable belief in the rightness of his position. When the emphasis is on Stewart's full frame, the character seems a boorish rube. As soon as the camera focuses on his earnest gaze and evident sincerity, however, he becomes the idealistic hero, his voice rising to a higher register and taking on a misty quality in lines like, "You gotta give me a *chance* . . . we'll fool 'em, Wash."

Thus the "feminine" values served by Destry's nonviolence are balanced by the sense of vision, male self-confidence, and goal orientation that Stewart was always able to project. Unlike Smith, who is victimized by events, Destry/Stewart conveys the illusion of what Ian Green calls "active control of the narrative" (44). Destry's certainty that Bottleneck will "settle down into a pretty peaceful place one of these days" carries the spectator's interest with it. This comedy cares little about the rueful paradox of the "straight" Western, whereby the hero's success over lawlessness brings the West another step closer to its extinction (Tompkins 101–102). The film sees with relief the coming of civilization and the end of anarchy.

The rhyming opening and closing sequences make clear how the oedipal pattern has been bent and the paternal legacy changed. The wild nocturnal town of the opening scene, in which bottles are shot from atop a crudely fashioned "Welcome to Bottleneck" sign, is replaced at the end by a quiet, orderly community in which farmers and merchants go about their business and people invite their friends over for Sunday dinner, embodied in a quaint sampler sign shown in daylight at the town's entrance. A little boy, seen earlier toting a shotgun, now mimics Destry as they walk down the serene main street, both of them whittling napkin rings as a repression of the aggressive energy that used to be worked off by firing pistols. The town now resembles the safe haven idealized in the nineteenth-century domestic novels, with Destry an acceptable symbolic father for such a society.

The courageous, can-do cowboy who defies the crooked syndicate is here a hotheaded fool who endangers Destry's plan to stop the crooks by lawful means. The scene in which the conventional reach-and-draw between the new deputy and the slick villain (Brian Donlevy) is defused by Destry's lack of guns is followed directly by a compensatory wrestling match between two women. When Wash's death moves Destry to strap on his six-guns and lead the good men against the bad, the women save them from themselves by entering the fray with garden rakes and rolling pins, subverting, as it were, the gunfight at the OK corral. Destry/Stewart is, finally, a composite of male goal orientation and the female values of domesticity and peace. However, he does not simply represent a marginalization of women by combining masculine and feminine virtues in a single (male) character; when Destry no longer does the women's bidding, they do it themselves.

For all this the women characters do not stray far from genre conventions. While Destry is identified with the feminine and does seem to act in the interests of female values, women do not help him or ally with him, his ideas still stemming from the "horse sense" of the Western hero as well as the "natural" integrity of the Stewart persona. The women characters divide along the virgin/whore boundary that separates the schoolmarm from the dance-hall hostess. However, the "good woman" destined for the hero is kept on the sidelines. This is perhaps because the nonviolent male hero himself performs the traditional function of the peace-seeking schoolmarm; however, since he is a male hero, he has the authority to enforce words (the law) over forceful deeds.

The often-discussed androgyny of Marlene Dietrich's screen persona appears to operate here. She is almost indistinct from the world of the men, the only woman given equal weight in the all-male preserve of the saloon. The moral force of Stewart/Destry moves Frenchy/Dietrich to accept her "proper" femininity, much as Smith induces Saunders to unearth the femininity she has supposedly buried with her first name. While the "bad woman" must be sacrificed, taking a bullet aimed at Destry, once again the romance between Stewart and the "love interest" comes off without the sorts of love scenes considered requisite for Hollywood movies. In this Stewart film one cannot be sure if the romantic reticence is a result of the generic reluctance of the Western hero to commit to marriage or due once more to a film's inability to reconcile the gender-ambivalent Stewart persona with the demands of the Hollywood heterosexual romance.

Thus, even in so uncommon a vehicle as *Destry Rides Again*, we see how awkwardly Stewart fits with the conventional masculinity arbitrated by the Western, a fact of which his postwar Westerns with Anthony Mann will take full advantage. He projects an authority, however, which betrays its gender by its obvious "rightness." In *Mr. Smith* it is Stewart's vision that "unmans" him and aligns him with the feminine; in *Destry* his extraordinary vision compensates for his refusal to line up behind phallic fantasy, which endangers home, family, community, and law. What he envisions is in fact a more stable patriarchy ordered by force of law rather than raw power. The Stewart figure's mastery of a clear, "commonsense" vision that comes naturally to him completes the oedipal drama by positing him as the symbolic father of a new order rather than as the successfully assimilated son.

This desexualizes him as surely as the martyr pattern of *Mr. Smith* does. In the last scene Destry/Stewart appears to the ingenue, Janice, as the lawgiver. His proposal of marriage is made without so much as a touch; he tells her an anecdote, unheard by the audience, as the end titles roll and the music swells. In a two-shot the entranced young woman looks up at Stewart in the familiar gaze of the pupil standing at the foot of the father and teacher. Stewart's feminine aspects are again alchemized with the power of idealism and a homely vision of what is right.

However, this recuperation makes him once again an unbalanced figure for a romantic lead. It removes him from the realm of "normal" sexuality signified by the oedipal route to manhood. We will soon see what could be called a balanced imbalance in Stewart's persona. Its dichotomy of the visionary and the "feminine" is placed alongside the heroic "real-life" Stewart, who becomes more vividly known during and after World War II.

A connotation of the cultural coding of femininity in men that I have not addressed is the homoerotic. With the "feminine" stereotype of male homosexuality, coded as a figure Vito Russo in *The Celluloid Closet* calls "the sissy," a dominant group inoculates itself against the danger of "difference" by turning it into a joke (4–59). Indeed, Robin Wood defines homophobia as "the inability to accept one's own bisexuality" ("Cat and Dog" 41). Thus, to stigmatize gay men as "female males" is to be at once homophobic and misogynist; femininity is used to caricature homosexuality, making both trivial alongside the heterosexual male standard. Such conventions stretch the contrast between animated supporting performances and the understatement of the leading actor to its extreme, grotesquely exaggerating the already wide chasm between subject and other. Thus the star system, which sutures the alienating gap between subject (self) and image (other), cannot accept intimations of homosexuality in the persona of a male star.

This is not to say that there isn't the potential for homoeroticism in the persona of any male star, including James Stewart. This potential is managed and contained in some ways that we've already seen. Hints of homoeroticism in *Destry*, for example, are headed off, despite the initial appearance of Destry/Stewart as a "sissy." Destry may make his entrance into Bottleneck toting a canary cage and a parasol, but he does it for a young woman already coded as his "match." Hence what is "sissified" to the townspeople is just chivalry to us who know "our" Jimmy Stewart. In *Destry* the "sissy" is a foil for heterosexual male insecurities; the hoax of the trickster in the film is that the deputy's "sissiness" lulls the men into false security and masks Destry/Stewart's "rock-ribbed honesty." The "sissification" of Destry is a ruse, another of the comedy's inversions, which switches the hero's association with "inverts," Freud's term for homosexuals.

The question of homosexuality figures in the boy-next-door persona's close association with motherhood. The equation of homosexuality and femininity is reinforced by such dubious notions as Freud's "negative" Oedipus complex, in which a gay male subject reverses the Oedipus and castration complexes, fixing the father as an erotic object and identifying with his mother. Thus, the gag about Destry's drinking milk at the saloon is actually a complicated metaphor, suggesting either a "positive" identification with the father still in process, or a "negative" emulation of the mother. In a later Western, *Winchester '73* (1950), the patricidal brother of the Stewart character infuriates him by ordering milk for him at a saloon, a clear insult to his masculinity that emphasizes their blood feud. On the other hand, one of the mitigators of the early Stewart's "femininity" is the unformed quality that keeps him "boyish," an arrested twelve-year-old. A child, after all, would ask for milk.

There is much homoerotic tension in Stewart's later work, especially his Westerns of the 1950s. We'll see that there is latent homoerotic romance in two of Stewart's most warmly received films of the 1950s, *Anatomy of a Murder* and especially, *Harvey*. The trick is in the packaging.

Thus femininity and homosexuality are not the same in signification because of the persistent gap between actual homoeroticism and its homophobic representations. Freud's work on bisexuality, although laden with contradictions, provides a convincing account of original bisexuality. In his 1905 studies of "inverts," Freud found that

> A certain degree of anatomical hermaphroditism occurs normally. In every normal [*sic*] male or female, traces are found of the apparatus of the opposite sex . . . an originally bisexual physical disposition has in the course of evolution, become modified into a unisexual one, leaving behind only a few traces of the sex that has become atrophied. (*Three Essays* 141)

Beyond this ancestral physical bisexuality, Freud finds no unisexual orientation in the unconscious:

> By studying sexual situations . . . it has been found that all human beings are capable of making a homosexual object-choice and have made one in their unconscious . . . psychoanalysis considers that a choice of an object independently of its sex . . . is the original basis from which both the normal and inverted ones develop. (*Three Essays* 145)

(Freud, ever the barometer of sexism and homophobia, semantically contradicts his own findings, stating that homosexuality is normal in the unconscious, but then differentiating between normality and homosexuality.) In 1925 Freud concluded that men, "as a result of their bisexuality and cross-inheritance, combine in themselves both masculine and feminine characteristics, so that pure masculinity and femininity remain theoretical constructions of uncertain content" ("Some Psychological Consequences" 193).

The confusion of femininity and homoeroticism, then, stems in part from the often imprecise use of the word *bisexuality*. The notion of bisexuality in a star persona like Stewart's is assumed to refer to the reappearance of repressed aspects of the male, which are usually displaced as "feminine" traits. It rarely refers to heterosexual man's repressed homosexual "half," despite Freud's clear alignment of gender identification and sexual orientation.

Fundamentally, sexual orientation is one of the characteristics critics have in mind when they discuss repressed male bisexuality, which can include heterosexual ideals, such as man's admitting that he needs women or his ability to share in an equal partnership with a woman. In my emphasis on the multiple possibilities of masculinity, homoeroticism is seen as one repressed trait, but not one that necessarily equates with man's buried femininities.

5

Bombing Missions,
Station Wagons, and Bisexuality:
Stewart Postwar

□□□

Stewart's military service in World War II had a great effect on the way he was seen by the public. Stewart had only just arrived at stardom before joining the army and approached moviemaking very uncertainly after the war: "When you've been away for four and a half years, you know, maybe you forget how to act. Maybe the whole thing's gone" (*The 'It's a Wonderful Life' Book* 77). His MGM contract having lapsed during the war, Stewart took his agent's advice not to sign with another studio and was actually considering going back to Pennsylvania to run his father's hardware store (McBride 524). He is said to have worried that acting was not a "decent" enough profession for "someone who had experienced what he had in the war" (McBride 525–526). It is typical of the publicly known Stewart to worry about the "decency" of movie acting—a concern shared since the earliest days of movies by some of the "average people" with whom Stewart was identified—rather than fret, as many male actors have, that it is not a "manly enough" occupation.

Stewart was drafted nine months before Pearl Harbor, in March 1941, and was inducted despite the fact that either his low weight or his age (thirty-two) could have disqualified him. He took flight instruction, entered the Army Air Corps (later the Army Air Forces), did publicity for the army, and worked as a flight instructor before being sent overseas in late 1943. Stewart commanded the 703rd Bomber Squadron, based in England, and flew a total of some two thousand hours in bombing missions over Germany. By the end of the war he was a colonel and was awarded the Distinguished Flying Cross, the Air Medal, the croix de guerre, and seven battle stars (Robbins 57).

These facts were widely reported during the war and figured in the press coverage surrounding the release of *It's a Wonderful Life*, his first postwar film, in December 1946. His war record and status until his retirement in 1968 as an officer in the Air Force Reserve remained

3. Stewart in uniform, circa 1942.

powerful elements of Stewart's film persona. During the sixties, more-over, he was "virtually the voice of the United States Air Force," appear-ing in or narrating a series of propaganda documentaries (Molyneaux 28). However, parts of Stewart's military record, especially his war ex-periences, were minimized and suppressed by the actor himself. His agents were forbidden to sign him for films that would capitalize on his war experience. His film contracts included the clause: "In all advertising and publicity issued by the corporation, or under its control, the corporation will not mention or cause to be mentioned the part taken by the artist in World War II or as an officer of the U.S. Army" (Robbins 58).

Biographies of Stewart remark on his refusal ever to discuss his war experiences; "Those memories are private," states the 1987 PBS special. Moreover, as Kaja Silverman points out apropos Capra, who had been a colonel in the Army Signal Corps, *It's a Wonderful Life* seems an attempt to repress the memory of wartime experiences by stressing the importance of doing one's bit at home. Capra's effort to repress the war works for Stewart as well. The movie about a man compelled to appreciate his life in a dreary small town, while others have lives in the world—World War II included—makes a perfect vehicle for a star seeking to downplay his war record and reestablish himself as an actor.

Stewart's role in *Wonderful Life* paves the way for a continuing separateness between screen and real-life roles, between "James" and "Jimmy," between the actor, the real person, and the persona that was somehow a combination of the two. Stewart's military record was actually enhanced in the public mind by his modesty about it and the mystique created by the information blackout around it. As a subtext of his persona, the war service allowed Stewart to broaden his range. Producers reportedly had reservations at first about casting Stewart in Westerns because they feared that he "would seem too weak and irresolute to carry off the role of a tough western hero, but they were persuaded by the thought of his war record" (Eyles 99). His public vagueness about his military experiences gave the actor freedom to make films that might go against the audience's sense of the real Jimmy Stewart, without fearing for his image.

This distinction between the actor and the person—a separation many stars are unable to make precisely because of the way stars are promoted as personas continuous with their film roles—meant that when Stewart made a *Vertigo* or a *Naked Spur* he did not receive anguished letters from fans of the sort that Doris Day, for example, reported getting after the release of *Love Me or Leave Me*; these letters demanded to know how she could play such a sordid role and caused Day not to veer so far from her accepted image again (Clarke and Simmonds 50).

Nevertheless, casting Stewart as a voyeur, an obsessed bounty hunter, or a tricky lawyer makes those characters into magnetic identification figures. Otto Preminger said that Stewart's appearance in *Anatomy of a Murder* made the Production Code–busting producer-director's film "acceptable," despite unprecedentedly explicit sexual language (Robbins 96). This is because of the charm and magnetism of the screen ego-ideal. It is also because Stewart's exemplary real life sanctions the film's public airing of subjects that, in the Kinsey Report atmosphere of the 1950s, the public considered impolite to discuss but really wanted to hear. Stewart's presence makes safe and permissible a thrill of transgression in knowing in 1959 that behind the irrepressible screen character sits a paragon of official virtue—Brig. Gen. James Stewart of the U.S. Air Force Reserve, a rank to which he was promoted the very month of the film's release (the Army Air Forces having become a separate branch of the military—the Air Force—in 1947).

Stewart's marriage also was important to his persona. Single until he was forty-one, Stewart married Gloria Hatrick McLean in 1949. His long bachelorhood had matched the prewar persona of the boy-not-quite-turned-man. Lew Wasserman of MCA said, "By [age forty-one] a lot of big Hollywood stars are working on their third or fourth wife. . . . But [Stewart is] very old-fashioned about such an important step. Why, even in a movie, he didn't pop the question until the last reel" (Robbins 69). Stewart's choice of a bride, the ex-wife of a millionaire whose mother owned the Hope diamond, showed his tendency to gravitate toward the upper class despite his "average" image; he described her as "a thoroughbred" (Robbins 70).

His percentage deals on successful films made Stewart himself a millionaire by the early 1950s. A 1955 *Look* feature story proclaimed him "the highest-paid actor in film history" (95). Typical of such profiles, the article downplayed the star's wealth and portrayed the Stewarts as an ordinary couple. It stressed that their home, while a "comfortable" house in Beverly Hills, was "on a good but not gaudy street." It described Stewart's preference for old clothes (as had the MGM publicity nearly twenty years earlier) and included a photo of the star driving a station wagon—in the 1950s a signifier of the suburban American family—with kids in the backseat. ("A station wagon is the only thing to have when you've got a mess of kids like us," he is quoted as saying [100].) Stewart's wife had two young sons from her previous marriage; twin girls were born to the couple in 1951. The prewar image of Stewart as the shy bachelor beset, according to fan magazines, by predatory females, was replaced in the postwar baby and marriage boom by a mature, responsible family man, an image perhaps intensified by the prevalent TV images of the perfect American family, promulgated—by 1955—in such shows as "Father Knows Best" and "Make Room for Daddy."

Whereas Stewart's return from the war occasioned magazine articles about his bravery, his new parenthood brought on stories such as "Jimmy Stewart Tells What He Wants for His Family" (*Parents* 1952) and "The Pictures in Jimmy Stewart's Wallet" (*Modern Screen* 1956). Stewart even explained his heavy film output in the early fifties in light of his new family; "I sort of got this feeling that I hadn't had before that here I suddenly had a family to support, and I'd better get to work and get there fast and do a lot" (*Winchester '73* interview Side One 5:30).

The publicity about the star's return from the war and his family life centered around the theme of the "boyish" Stewart's maturation into manhood. Charles Wolfe wrote that after Stewart returned a war hero, "The question now remained: could he make the transition back to movie actor?" In his analysis of a *Newsweek* cover story tied to the release of *It's a Wonderful Life*, Wolfe sees the press treatment of Stewart's first postwar film as "the drama of a star's comeback—part of the fascination of moviegoing, and the calculations of movie marketing, since the days of Florence Lawrence and Carl Laemmle" ("Return" 48). The boyishness in Stewart's persona was identified by the *Newsweek* story as something that the army, as is its wont, had taken care of: "The word 'boyish,' in spite of its unfortunate connotation, was used more than any other to describe him, and was given credence by his addiction to model airplanes. The boyishness dwindled, however, when he bought his own plane, and vanished with his return from the B-24s, which left him with a few un-boyish gray hairs" (Wolfe "Return" 47).

As Stewart's acting career resumed, he was thirty-eight years old, and though *It's a Wonderful Life* proved an ideal transitional vehicle, he later described the difficulty of finding suitable roles in the late forties (Eyles 95). He might have had this problem even without the war. Stewart prewar could be described as a male ingenue, albeit an unusually successful one, but perhaps this is the "unfortunate connotation" of the boyishness to which the *Newsweek* story alludes. The graying, fuller-faced, and deeper-voiced Stewart had to become a bona fide "male star" around whom star vehicles that would acknowledge his passage into maturity could be packaged and marketed. The "Jimmy Stewart vehicle" was eventually found; it meshed with some of the safe genres the American film industry increasingly relied on in the commercially and politically treacherous 1950s. These included the biopic, the Hitchcock thriller, and above all, the Western.

Much has been written, especially by *auteur*ist and genre critics, about the five Westerns starring Stewart and directed by Anthony Mann between 1950 and 1955, mostly at Universal-International. Mann was one of the Hollywood directors who, though unrecognized in the United States, were hailed as *auteurs* by the young critics of *Cahiers du Cinéma*. Eventually it became axiomatic among American critics to describe Mann's films as Westerns that "modernized the genre, incorporating into it an increased violence and using it to express man's vision of self, the conflicts of his inner psychology" (Basinger *Anthony Mann* 84). The

Mann/Stewart protagonist was seen by film critics and scholars of the 1960s and 1970s as revising into ambiguity the once-clear opposition between hero and villain, making problematic the motives of the hero and revealing, as Basinger explained, the psychosis underlying such conventions as the gunfight and the reach-and-draw ritual.

These films were initially received as efficiently made entertainments brought through the assembly line by movie-makers with a sharp eye on the bottom line. A 1953 *Life* article explained:

> [In 1949] U-I was knee-deep in prestige from movies based on foreign novels (*Letter from an Unknown Woman*) and Broadway plays (*Another Part of the Forest*). But its ledgers were deeply dyed in red. Out the window went prestige, and the Universal program was aimed at a more universal appeal. One surefire formula was to get a big-name star who would forgo salary for a percentage of the profits, cast him in a colorful, well-made, down-to-earth American adventure story, and publicize it to the hilt with the willing help of the profit-conscious star. Biggest success with this formula has been made by the trio . . . of Jimmy Stewart, Producer Aaron Rosenberg and Director Anthony Mann. ("The Universal Appeal" 103)

The Westerns and thrillers that Stewart made at a rate of two or three a year in the first two-thirds of the 1950s settled into what audiences and the industry now knew as "just" Jimmy Stewart movies. They were the films that established him as an "adult" male star.

However, Stewart's gender ambiguity, which deepened as he aged, contrasted with the star's new tough veneer, resulting in Westerns that complicate the premises of the genre. The first thing one notices about Stewart's acting in the Westerns is a new restraint. His voice is mostly low and even, with few of the forays into the upper vocal registers familiar from the younger Stewart—side trips the voice still makes in comedies and in his "average man" Hitchcock roles. The delivery is level and direct. There is no stammering or hesitancy; he employs the harsh quality of his voice to rasp out lines, suggesting brusqueness and impatience passing for toughness. Similarly, Stewart restrains his face and body far more than usual. His frame, which can still seem gangling in other films, looks wiry and hard in the Westerns.

Stewart sometimes seems an exception to a general rule whereby the star underplays (Ellis 104, Naremore 224), emoting less than the supporting players do. In Westerns underplaying is essential to the cool, competent hero who gives nothing away. The rule applies in the Mann Westerns, but Stewart's restraint serves as a contrast to the moments when the character "cracks," revealing the toughness as a construction. Stewart compensates for this restraint by finding in his voice a low, insinuating purr that complements the often-impressionistic Technicolor photography whose colors seem to blur into one another. Stewart's rightness for such films demonstrates the truth of Jacques Rivette's remark in *Cahiers* in 1957 that "Anthony Mann's *mise-en-scène* is definitely influenced by James Stewart's style of acting" (Bazin et al. 37).

In *Bend of the River* (1952), in which Stewart plays a former Kansas border bandit trying to put his past behind him by working as a guide for a party of settlers, he saves a stranger (Arthur Kennedy) from hanging. The two engage in some wonderfully suggestive dialogue. McClintock (Stewart) tells Cole (Kennedy) that he aims to try "*farmin'* . . . or *ranchin'* . . . if I can get some *cattle*," his voice going up on each key word, drawing it out indecisively and turning the end of each phrase into a question, as if McClintock questions his own resolve. After McClintock tells his companion about the "real good biscuits" the settlers make, the man whose life he just saved reveals himself as the apparently infamous Emerson Cole. This happens in front of the innocent settlers, who know nothing of what's happening between the two men, so that Stewart/McClintock's reaction, made "in public," must be secretive and for the spectator's eyes alone. He turns toward his companion in quiet alarm and says, "Yeah, you're gonna like these biscuits," insinuating through the small talk an unspeakable understanding.

Stewart uses his drawl to imply breathily what the Western Man of Few Words cannot come right out with. He doesn't quite enunciate his most pointed lines, as if he's still "chewing them over" and dare not pronounce what he's actually thinking. In the day-for-night lighting of these scenes, the whites of Stewart's eyes glare out startlingly from the mottled dark greens and purples, blending with them into a *mise-en-scène* of contained hysteria.

Even more than usual, Stewart's body is effaced, with a major exception addressed by Paul Willemen in a well-known short article on Mann. Willemen stresses that the Mann Western turns on "the look at the male figure. . . . The viewer's experience is predicated on the pleasure of seeing the male 'exist' (that is, walk, move, ride, fight) in or through cityscapes, landscapes, or more abstractly, history" (16). The male spectator is implicated in homoeroticism on the visual level, which Willemen states is more important to the Mann Westerns than the narrative.

Homoeroticism is subtextual in a genre that celebrates men without women, poses women as threats to man's independence, and depicts relationships between men marked by unspoken bonds of affection. For instance, in *The Far Country* Jeff Webster/Stewart is a hard, self-centered man who considers it foolish to open himself to others or to help them. However, he cares about his pal Ben (Walter Brennan), lighting his pipe for him as a ritual gesture of endearment, and dreaming of "settling down" with him on a Utah ranch. The two virtually act out a conventional male-female relationship. Stewart/Webster is the breadwinner and decision maker; Brennan/Ben minds the home, provides his partner with food and coffee, and, "just like a woman," talks too much, a habit that gets him killed.

There is a sadomasochistic chemistry between the Stewart character and the smiling, manupulative villains. *The Far Country* features a love-hate relationship between Webster and Mr. Gannon (John McIntyre), an elegant bully in top hat and tails, whose often repeated line to the hero is a warmly spoken, "I'm gonna like you. I'm gonna hang you, but I'm gonna like you." In an over-the-shoulder shot from Gannon's point of view, Webster/Stewart replies softly, "Thank you, thank you," looking at him fixedly, projecting the wariness of one adversary toward another but also the guarded appreciation of a suitor's compliment. The film ends with Stewart once again headed for the altar with a perfunctory love interest who is the least threatening of all possibilities, after a range of sexual "types" have been killed off—Ben, the "feminine" half of a "male/female" gay relationship; Gannon, the foppish gay suitor; Ronda Castle (Ruth Roman), the sexually aggressive businesswoman who is Jeff's female double, and must die along with the selfish, aggressive side of him, which she represents and which is intolerable in a woman. This leaves Renée Vallon (Corinne Calvet), a tomboy type whose childish asexuality is mocked by Jeff, who calls her "freckle face." Renée represents Jeff's social conscience, and he grudgingly accepts her as an inevitable mate as he reluctantly accepts his responsibility to protect the fledgling community of Dawson against the dominance of outlaws.

The Western's containment of homoeroticism is complicated in these films by Mann's deepening of the convention whereby the Western man is more comfortable in nature. In Mann the wilderness could be said to double for the unconscious; it is the primal scene, the site of the return of the repressed. The male is not the "figure in a landscape," in Mulvey's phrase, but a figure *of* the landscape. Basinger notes the double entendres of many of the films' titles, which refer both to geographical places and to the psychological struggles of their heroes: *The Far Country*, *Bend of the River*, *The Naked Spur* (*Anthony Mann* 83–84). *The Naked Spur*, a film that draws on Stewart's talent for projecting masochism and hysteria, has only five characters, all of them social outcasts. It takes place entirely in forests and on riverbanks and mountain trails, without a glimpse of towns, wagon trains, or other signs of civilization. The protagonist is all alone with himself; even the conflicts with the villains, who are usually likable, self-satisfied men, are brought on by the hero, the consequences of his obsessions and compromises.

Thus, while the notion of "winning the West" is turned inward—man must clear his own wilderness—the spectatorial look at the vistas and horizons is also a gaze at the male body. While in the prewar films Stewart's body is either emphasized for comic effect or ignored while the camera dwells on the "earnestness" of his face and voice, Stewart's costuming in the Mann films deemphasizes the body's awkwardness while highlighting his masculinity in ways that make him an erotic object. His costume is virtually the same in each Western: a wool or buckskin trail jacket, a cotton shirt and neckerchief, and a sweat-stained tan Stetson (the same one worn from film to film). No doubt Stewart and Mann settled on this costume for its authenticity. The soiled hat removed thoughts of glamorous movie cowboys like Tom Mix or Roy Rogers. It gave the films a feeling of "realism" but also symbolized the moral state of the protagonist: There are blots and blemishes on this good guy's "white hat." It also became Stewart's signature in the Westerns, a reminder of the actor and persona behind the often unpleasant characters.

The crucial parts of the costume, however, are the blue jeans and the leather chaps that cover the fronts and sides of his legs from about the calves up, pulling up around his crotch. In the four color films, especially, the chaps noticeably encircle Stewart's genitals, highlighting them in ways that lead to questions about the ambivalence of the look at the male. There are scenes in which the highlighted genitals are unmistakably foregrounded just when the character is at his most vulnerable, for example, in *The Naked Spur* after Kemp (Stewart) writhes on the ground in agony after burning his hands trying to climb a rope up a mountain ridge. In *The Far Country* a full-body view of Stewart is followed by a shot of Ronda looking him up and down, focusing on one spot in particular. The active female gaze is made plain so that it can be punished later for the threat it poses. The transgression represented by a female or gay male look (the two are certainly equated when it comes to the gaze—both are forbidden) at the man's body is very clear. Moreover, the male body itself is punished and mutilated for posing as an object for both male and female gazes.

Stewart's performances in the Mann Westerns undermine the power of the Western protagonist. However, it should not be forgotten that in these Westerns an actor with a "feminine" image proves that he can act "masculine" enough to be credible in a male genre. Screenwriter Borden

Chase reported that when the first Stewart-Mann Western, *Winchester '73*, was sneak-previewed, "the minute Jimmy Stewart's name came on the screen, everybody laughed" (Eyles 102). This laughter must have been quickly dispelled by Stewart's convincing performance, since the film went on to be a great success.

Therefore there is a question of which matters more—Stewart's ability to show that he can project "masculinity" sufficient to calm nervous studio executives, satisfy scoffing audiences, and become a star of Westerns, or the capacity of the actor and persona to inject a complex gender dialectic into a definitively male genre. The studio chiefs who worried about Stewart's credibility in Westerns missed the point; the man's-gotta-do-what-a-man's-gotta-do determination of the archetypal hero creates dramatic conflict with the "weak and irresolute" tendencies projected by Stewart as actor.

The Mann Westerns invert the Stewart persona. Rather than give himself over to an ideal of the common good, a character such as Howard Kemp in *The Naked Spur*—the film that develops most fully the themes of these "adult" Westerns—shuts out all interests but his own in response to a past disillusionment. Kemp starts at the point where Mr. Smith and George Bailey are in their darkest defeats. True to generic conventions, the Stewart protagonist has been betrayed by a woman. His response to betrayal is not despair but a resolve to stay free of the entanglements represented by women, with money as his motive.

Some years before *The Naked Spur* begins, a woman has done the unthinkable—refusing to keep the home fires burning when her man goes to war, betraying him after he has committed to a life of domesticity and responsibility. Thus, in becoming a bounty hunter and bringing back a wanted murderer, the male protagonist acts against his conscience and principles. Like *Winchester '73* this film reverses the narrative pattern of classic Westerns, beginning (before the film opens) with home and a personal crisis, going far from home in search of a resolution, ending with the Love of a Good Woman and a return to home, wherever it can be found. The narrative in the end restores the male to his necessary place at the center of a benign patriarchy. The woman also must be returned to her "proper" place by his side. The man comes to see the betraying woman as an aberration. Moreover, the hero's actions are pathological, not befitting a "decent" sort like him. The drama involves conflict between what Freud termed "two opposing affects" in one subject, which manifest themselves in symptoms of hysteria.

In the character as scripted, a driving, relentless quest after a goal (a wanted outlaw becomes "a sack of money," as one character puts it) requires him to ignore moral principles. Through the deliberate effort to be amoral, however, breaks the affect of a gentle, decent person. With Stewart in the role, the conflict becomes a painful but manageable moral dilemma involving elements of the Stewart persona—the propensity for (and ability to project) self-punishment, the gentle visionary, the sensitive soul on whom masculine dominance and aggression do not sit "naturally," the idealist who gravitates to just causes and has no patience for compromise, and the romantic who gives himself over to his love object. In short, the Western hero is problematized by the actor's performance of these various "Jimmy Stewarts."

Naremore calls Stewart "an expert pantomimist," having defined pantomime, quoting John Delman, as "bodily action, simplified by selection, moderately exaggerated, [providing] a language of expression more universally intelligible than words" (64–65). We've seen in the Lincoln Memorial scenes in *Mr. Smith* Stewart's talent for miming emotional reactions. However, in *The Naked Spur* Stewart plays a character who shows desperation beneath the mask while masquerading as a tough Western man. In the opening scene the camera follows from behind the as-yet-unidentified Stewart as he rides to a place where he sees smoke from a campfire, ties up his horse, draws his gun, and walks up carefully. An old prospector (Millard Mitchell) is shown standing by his burro as Stewart's voice is heard: "Don't move. Turn around." As the prospector raises his hands, we see Stewart for the first time, pointing the gun, his eyes vigilant and steady, his voice and face unexpressive and authoritative. Later, in a full shot, the prospector, Jesse, bends down to tend his fire and coffee in the right of the shot while on the left, Stewart/ Howard Kemp remains standing, looking around impatiently. When Jesse asks if the man Kemp is looking for is a "friend of yours," Kemp produces a wanted poster, which we see in close-up, and barks, "He killed a marshal." On Jesse's line, "Kansas. You've come a ways," the camera returns to the earlier position and Jesse, not looking at Kemp, says, "It's not every peace officer that'd do that." On this line Kemp/ Stewart is momentarily arrested in his action of stuffing the paper back into his pocket and looks off guiltily.

The hysteria and moral masochism that underlie both the character's masquerade and his quest for money become as inextricable from this film's spectacle as Smith's martyrdom (Christian masochism) does from the spectacle of the filibuster. Mann often emphasizes this hysteria visually. In one scene in which Kemp confronts the others, Stewart is framed alone against a pale blue sky that precisely matches Stewart's watery blue eyes so that they seem to disappear, making him appear "blinded" by his obsession.

After Kemp/Stewart sustains a leg wound, which he carries with him

4. *The Naked Spur*. Stewart projects paralysis beneath the male masquerade.

through the film's middle section as virtually a scarlet A, a day-for-night scene begins with the camera slowly craning down from the trees; the soundtrack is silent. Suddenly a raving Stewart bolts up into the shot, shrieking, "Where are they?" as he is overcome by a memory. When Lina (Janet Leigh) soothes him with water, Kemp/Stewart lapses into a different memory, mistaking Lina for an unseen "Mary," and tenderly makes the arrangements to leave her with the ranch and come back after the war. Stewart's voice is heard in its familiar gentle register for the first time in this film. This scene can be understood as a popularization of Freud and Breuer's descriptions of hysterical symptoms.

The hysterical symptom "exhibits the hallucinatory reproduction of a memory which was of importance in bringing about the onset of the hysteria—the memory of either a single major trauma . . . or a series of interconnected part-traumas." The trauma has been repressed by the subject and brought back by an unconscious memory, leading to the reenactment of the traumatic event, marked by "motor phenomena . . . such as kicking about and waving the arms and legs as even young babies do" (*Studies on Hysteria* 15). The refusal of physicians to listen to Freud's early claim that men could suffer from hysteria shows the classic male displacement of disturbing phenomena onto the female. Jean-Martin Charcot, with whom Freud had studied in the 1880s, included male patients in his groundbreaking work on hysteria. Charcot found, as Lynne Kirby points out, "the astonishing appearance of hysterical symptoms in very virile, working-class men" (123). These men, Charcot discovered, were "emasculated"; "cultural displacement . . . made of its traumatized victims something like female hysterics" (Kirby 124).

The repressed, tense affect that Stewart projects, while showing the trauma and the hysteria into which it erupts, approximates what Freud and Breuer called "a splitting of consciousness," whereby "hysterical attacks and normal life proceed side by side" (*Studies* 16). In *The Naked Spur* the memory of the trauma intrudes at Kemp's moments of most exquisite pain. Stewart acts out what—if it weren't "too much"—could be read as male aggressiveness. Kemp's aggression tries too hard and seems overcompensation for weakness. We must ask whether the hysteria critiques the general meaning of the Western hero archetype or simply marks this character as not "having what it takes."

Freud and Breuer discuss ways in which a trauma can be "abreacted" or "corrected by [the subject's] putting the facts right, by considering his own worth, etc." (*Studies* 9). Kemp's self-justification about the need to retrieve his life before the trauma by whatever means necessary is a thin cover for the mythic Western man's inability to work through a personal problem by any means except external action, a hindrance traditionally portrayed as a virtue.

Notions of male hysteria usually assume that, like masochism, the condition puts a man in a feminine position. After his studies with Charcot, all Freud's celebrated cases of hysteria concerned women; "read socially, hysteria was an appropriate reaction against the oppressive roles women were expected to play as wives and mothers" (Kirby 122). Furthermore, Luce Irigaray suggests that women should subvert their positions as putative hysterics by means of mimesis. Since a hysterical attack virtually *is* an act of pantomime—a staging of the repressed memory—and since the "normal" feminine identity has conventionally been seen as a series of roles, mimicry of the masculine becomes a subversive act, a way to gain admission to male society while parodying it (*This Sex* 76–77).

Male hysteria also works as mime. Stewart shows Kemp as a hysteric and a mime; "unmanned" by the loss of his ranch and fiancée, he must regain his sense of masculinity by mimicking the lawful authority of a sheriff, the ruthlessness of a bounty hunter, and the moral outrage of a righteous citizen. In the terms of Joan Riviere's argument, he compensates for his loss of manhood by masquerading as masculine authority. He is unmasked by his masochism, his need to be punished for the chain of hatred and destruction that his moral compromise brings with it. Conventional male subjectivity does not tolerate awareness that masculinity is not a natural standard for a man to rise to but a role to be performed. As Lynne Kirby writes, "What male hysteria shows us is not so much the coding of men as women, but the decoding of men as men" (124).

In genres such as the Western and the detective film, which arbitrate masculinity, mimicry is conventionally the stuff of comic relief (such as the Mischa Auer character in *Destry*, a Russian who wants to "be a real cowboy and wear my own pants!") or of ill-fated minor characters (a "little guy" such as the Elisha Cook, Jr., character in *Shane*, who mimics the self-confidence of stronger men and confronts the villains, his demise telegraphed by the script long before it occurs). The ninety-eight-pound weakling who gets sand kicked in his face seeks to become more powerful by mimicking the masculinity that treats him with such contempt; Stewart/Ransom Stoddard's attempts to become a gunman against Liberty Valance in Ford's film exemplify this. Mimicry is at the heart of the Oedipus and castration complexes, which perpetuate the definitions and codes of masculinity.

While the film dramatizes male hysteria, it is through Kemp/Stewart's spectacular masochism and his submission to the "love interest" that the character works through to his redemption. Willemen states that the spectator's "experience is predicated on . . . the unquiet pleasure of seeing the male mutilated (often quite graphically in Mann) and restored through violent brutality" (16). Although Paul Smith has emphasized the masochistic hero's recovery from his wounds and his weakened position, I feel that in the Mann Westerns, as in the Hitchcock films, much of the spectators' interest and pleasure are based in the character's suffering and pain themselves. The perversity that pierces through the classical form in the work of both directors would be less disturbing without the

5. Dragged through the campfire in *The Man from Laramie*. Pleasure in pain as a drawing card.

palpable anguish that was actually a selling point of many of Stewart's films in the fifties. One has only to think of the famous publicity shot from *Vertigo*, of a terrified Stewart hanging from a roof gutter, or the image used in the advertising for *The Man from Laramie*, of Stewart's face in agony as he is dragged through a campfire.

While the Westerns refuse to permit the ironically civilizing moral codes of the genre John G. Cawelti describes, they assume a common moral standard. For instance, in two of the Borden Chase–scripted films, there is a similar line: In *Bend of the River*, when Cole keeps on shooting at adversaries after they have clearly been beaten and McLintock/Stewart orders him to stop, Cole's question, "Why?" brings the answer, "If you don't know, I can't tell you." In the later *Far Country*, it is the Stewart character who has the line spoken to him by the moralizing female figure, Renée. In the films beginning with *The Naked Spur*, the Stewart heroes lose track of common morality. It falls to women, in their traditional roles as soul savers, to guide them to humanity and its assumption of a common moral standard.

This secularized common morality, which before the twentieth century would have been connected to Christianity, may have been associated with femininity and thus trivialized, but it leads straight to patriarchy, to the father. It is the father whom Freud's moral masochist envisions as the administrator of pain. This masochist

> creates a temptation to "sinful acts" which must then be expiated by the reproaches of the sadistic conscience . . . or by chastisement from the great parental authority of Fate. In order to provoke punishment from this last parent-substitute the masochist must do something inexpedient, act against his own interests, ruin the prospects which the real world offers him, and possibly destroy his own existence in the world of reality. ("Economic Problem of Masochism" 200)

The moral masochist craves suffering for its own sake, holding "out his cheek wherever he sees a chance of receiving a blow" (196). This is seen when Kemp's sadism gives way to masochism during the massacre of the peaceful Indians who are after Roy, the dishonorably discharged army lieutenant, for the rape of a squaw. As Kemp sees an Indian tussling on the ground with the shackled Ben, he runs over, a panning camera following his movement, and fights off the attacker, repeatedly pistol-whipping him with more frenzy than the occasion warrants. The sound of the pistol striking the Indian and of Stewart/Kemp's heavy breathing in rhythm with the blows dominates the musicless soundtrack. Finally an oncoming war whoop sends Stewart/Kemp lunging headlong across the frame, as he is hit. In another ecstatic Stewart fall, he is caught in midstride, his head jerking back and his body arching across the entire frame diagonally as he plummets. As Lina helps Kemp to safety, a long shot of the clearing, littered with the corpses of the Indians, quietly shows the aftermath.

Later, after the five mount up and ride out together, the camera lingers on Kemp/Stewart as he painfully manages to mount his horse. He is shown in the foreground of a long shot, framed to the left as he faces the consequences of one of the first Western scenes to suggest that Indian fighting was slaughter. From the back his body is slumped as he looks out at the corpses; then he turns only partly around, shown in the kind of side-angle look that often signifies a privileged look at a character's private reaction. The glimpse of Stewart's face combines horror at what he's just been through, disgust at a massacre he is responsible for as a result of the unsavory alliances his bounty hunting has required, and the agony of the painful leg, which is unmistakably a punishment for destructive, "inexpedient" choices.

The guilt Stewart telegraphs in the film's opening scenes culminates with the slaughter of the Indians and the wound that Kemp/Stewart carries through much of the rest of the film. The scene that plays out on a mountain ridge after Ben loosens the straps on the suffering Kemp's saddle puts the spectator in an ambivalent position. As in *Mr. Smith* we know—and the Stewart character doesn't—of his imminent victimization. When the saddle finally falls and so—spectacularly—does Stewart, Mann cuts to a mortified Lina. Once again the "love interest" shares the hero's pain, but whereas Mr. Smith becomes Saunders's conscience, the woman's compassionate conscience takes over from the parental conscience to whose torments Kemp had submitted.

Lina functions in the familiar role of woman as mirror. In his scenes with her in the second half of the film, Kemp shows a gentle wistfulness as Stewart peels off the masks of hysteria and gruffness to reveal the "real" personality—the hopeful idealist of other Stewart films and the "nice guy" of his off-screen persona. The voice wanders into its familiar mistiness, with a note of anxiety, on a line such as, "Do you ever think for a minute Ben had the temper to settle on the *land*, to clear it, to build on it, to bring in the cattle and nurse 'em through the winter, round up *strays*. . . ," his voice growing more distant on the last phrase, his eyes wandering aimlessly, before returning to the character's studied gruffness.

The Naked Spur's didacticism leads to tension between sadism and sentimentality. Kemp arduously defeats Ben, matching him for brutality (Ben kills Jesse, then shoots the heels off Jesse's boots for target practice; with his spur Kemp chips his way up the rocks to where Ben is perched and then throws it in his face). But the "battle of will and

6. Woman as the mirror reflecting "Jimmy Stewart" the wistful idealist. With Janet Leigh.

strength" of the goal-oriented narrative is nullified by the immorality of the goal (dirty money for a dead body). The heroine persuades the hero to give up the goal in order to hold on to some remnant of his "decency." Jim Kitses, seeing the narratives of the Mann Westerns as directed toward the hero's reentry into society, writes: "Entry into the community can . . . feel like *defeat*, the hero not so much integrated as exhausted by his compulsion to pursue an unnatural course, not educated so much as beaten by a struggle against profound forces that operate as a kind of immutable law" (43). What this interpretation misses is that the Stewart character gives in to the *woman* who represents society's guiding morality. Moreover, he is forced to surrender to the woman precisely because she surrenders to him, forcing him to see good in himself but also compelling him to surrender. The final sequence of *The Naked Spur* features a major male star playing most of a scene with his back to the camera and then turning to weep lustily in close-up. It forces a final Western show-down between "male" goal orientation and "female" sentimentality, the latter signified by a filtered close-up from below of Lina/Leigh set against a billowy blue sky as a sweet string rendition of "Beautiful Dreamer" overlaps onto Stewart's sobs. Hence the first half of the film sets up the hero to be beaten by his own determination to "do what a man's gotta do." The second half depicts his capitulation at the feet of the noble "feminine" social conscience, part Janet Leigh, twenty-five-year-old ingenue, and part Eleanor Roosevelt.

Stewart/Kemp moves meekly to bury Ben's body rather than cash in on it; the shot in which Stewart looks up submissively at Leigh after giving in to her moral blandishments repeats almost exactly Smith's ex-pression on looking up at the encouraging vice president at the climax of his filibuster. The resolution of the Stewart character's masochism avoids recognizing the male pathology that drives him to make up for past humiliation by gaining mastery over another and then punishing himself. It may seem to resemble the masochistic subject's capitulation to the "oral mother" in Gilles Deleuze's writings on masochism, which Gaylyn Studlar has used in a controversial article and book on the Die-trich/Sternberg cycle of the 1930s. Studlar sought to introduce a model of spectatorship based on a pleasure in passivity and submission and a pre-oedipal identification with the mother as an alternative to the Mul-veyan paradigm of sadism and the oedipal centrality of the father ("Mas-ochism" 609).

Inevitably mixed up in Stewart's surrender in defeat (far different from Smith's passionate, willing surrender) are mythic notions—especially strong even in the many 1950s films that showed women as agents of humanity and social responsibility—of woman as sapper of man's strength, literally a domesticator (and thus slayer) of his wildness. Women in films like this one, as well as more "socially conscious" movies such as *On the Waterfront*, *Giant*, and *A Face in the Crowd*, might be compassionate, liberalizing influences, bringing men down from their selfishness and their power trips, but they are compelled to want marriage. They move men into their proper places in patriarchy so that they can assume their own. What Kemp/Stewart surrenders to at the end of *The Naked Spur* is the law of the father. In the guise of woman, however, it does not carry the transporting imaginary allure that history and patriotism have for Mr. Smith, for the same reason that George Bailey would rather sail away and "see the world" than succumb to Mary Hatch and stay in Bedford Falls. Social responsibility involves not the fulfillment of masculine dreams but the regretful abandonment of them.

If strength, will, control, and freedom do not equal justice but indeed defy it (thus the scant difference in Mann between the hero and the "savage"), what, then, is masculinity? What man appears to want in this film is anarchy, only because it's all there is, short of surrender to the real enemy of the Western man, femininity. However, Howard Kemp is Jimmy Stewart and thus evokes home, maternity, sincerity, and, as the villain in *The Far Country* sarcastically says, "public-minded"-ness. He is not John Wayne, who as Ethan Edwards at the end of *The Searchers* is excluded from the home and left to "wander between the winds" like the "savage" Native American. This difference makes the surrender somewhat conventional in that it fits the familiar contradictions of Stewart's persona. The ending also restates the ambivalence of a star persona slightly out of step with "masculine" values, compatible with the "feminine" but enshrined in official masculinity.

6

Hitchcock and Biopics

□□□

In an early critique of Laura Mulvey's theory of the active male gaze, Marian Keane made a case to which this chapter is sympathetic. Finding Mulvey's argument about male desire to be monolithic, Keane countered her reading of *Vertigo* by stressing James Stewart's screen presence and the actor's "capacity for suffering," which, quoting Stanley Cavell, "would admit him to the company of women" (233–234). Along similar lines, in discussing the "inherent and inexplicable" psychosis that Stewart projected in the Mann Westerns, Jeanine Basinger saw among Stewart's films "a direct linear relationship (Capra to Mann to Hitchcock)" (*Anthony Mann* 101).

With a star persona as contradictory as Stewart's, concentrating on a single element is sure to lead to trouble. To base an argument about Stewart on "suffering" is as simplistic as to consider only "boyishness" or "all-American-ness." Furthermore, it may seem reasonable to assume that Stewart's three performances for Hitchcock in the 1950s took off from the inner pain of the Mann heroes and their evidence of a "new" side of Stewart's persona and acting range; after all, Stewart's one pre-Mann Hitchcock film (*Rope* [1948]) is something of a miscast calamity. Here, however, criticism is inconvenienced by facts: Stewart said that Hitchcock did not see any of the Westerns (*Winchester '73* interview). Closer attention to the Hitchcock films of the 1950s and other Stewart vehicles of the time shows influences nearer the heart of the star's persona in a decade of conformity.

While not well remembered now, Stewart's biographies of American heroes were among his most popular postwar films. *The Stratton Story* (1949), a biopic about the disabled baseball star Monty Stratton, and *The Glenn Miller Story* (1954), an atypical Stewart-Mann collaboration, both costarred June Allyson as his wife, as did a Stewart-initiated project, *Strategic Air Command* (1955), a military drama set in the present day that put on the screen Stewart's devotion to flying and the Air Force. The fact that Stewart played married men in only six of the twenty-two films he made in the fifties (the others were *The Jackpot* [1950]; *Carbine Williams* [1952], a biopic; *The FBI Story* [1959]; and Hitchcock's *The Man Who Knew Too Much* [1956]) makes the Stewart-Allyson pair a kind of cinematic Ozzie and Harriet, a fantasy of normality. They exemplify the Anglo middle-class couple who transport the white-picket-fence ideal of marriage with them wherever they happen to go, be it an Air Force base or a struggling musician's Manhattan studio. Additionally, the actor's love of flying and perhaps his right-wing politics led him, at age forty-eight, to campaign for the role of the twenty-five-year-old Lindbergh in *The Spirit of St. Louis* (1957), which inexplicably proved a rare Stewart commercial failure.

The complaint of contemporary reviewers that Stewart was usually "just himself" in movies might have disqualified him from playing well-known people. Given the exigencies of the "biopic," however, the reverse is true. In his study, *Bio/Pics*, George Custen outlines the ways in which stars and biographical subjects were matched up. Custen finds that often the subject had to be "adjusted" to fit the star persona, especially when the star was a limited actor who could play only certain types (for instance, Betty Hutton in biopics of Pearl White and Annie Oakley [Custen 45–46]). Sometimes the star departed from his or her persona when the actor-subject combination was extraordinarily compatible physically and temperamentally (Kirk Douglas as Vincent Van Gogh [197–199]). In other cases actors "could 'tone down' their star image (that is, they could act), and critics would remark favorably upon this muted star energy as inspired casting" (Frank Sinatra as Joe E. Lewis [199]). In still other biopics the spectator's impression of the biographical subject rested on what he or she knew about the real life of the actor playing him (for instance, a dissolute late-career Errol Flynn as a dissolute late-career John Barrymore [46–47]).

The only one of these that never applied to Stewart was, not surprisingly, physical and temperamental compatibility; Stewart was invariably more personable than the original. He underplayed in the biopics, investing the subject with the Stewart charm while having learned to perform the subject's skill (baseball for *Stratton*, miming trombone playing for *Miller*). Like most biopics dealing with male subjects, Stewart's are about confidence, pluck, and determination, not about suffering— but not necessarily about ambition, either. These films display a sunny side of "male" aggressiveness and will in which the subject's drive to succeed looks as natural and involuntary as a nervous tic. As a consequence Stewart "acts" less than in most of his other films.

If the Westerns and Hitchcock films challenged the off-screen Jimmy Stewart persona, the biopics played to it. Casting Stewart as American heroes of the recent past provided a way to make box office out of his reputations as war hero and family man without exploiting them directly. It was probably impossible for a spectator in 1954 to watch the sequences showing Maj. Glenn Miller in World War II without thinking of the actor's war service. Although *Spirit of St. Louis* was not planned as a Stewart vehicle—Billy Wilder and producer Leland Hayward cast him after failing to find a suitable younger actor—it was infused with the star's well-known knowledge of flying.

Furthermore, the Stewart-Allyson "marriage" was screened in the context of magazine articles about Stewart's actual marriage. The 1955 *Look* profile ran a photo of Jimmy and Gloria Stewart beneath a production still of Stewart and Allyson in *Strategic Air Command* (95). Hence the biopics did not stress a separation between actor and persona but seemed smooth extrapolations of the "Jimmy Stewart" who was profiled in magazines, guest-starred with his wife annually on Jack Benny's TV program, and narrated Air Force documentaries.

Stewart's screen persona and acting style were well suited to the biopic. As Custen elaborates, the studio-era biopic boiled down the lives of the "great" into a formula that celebrated fame for its own sake, normalized the exceptional, and downplayed both labor and the possibility that the person who achieves fame might be a part of his or her time and culture rather than a magical gift to the world. Exceptional talent is treated as a seed that, planted in the brain of the subject at birth, must burst forth and blossom, no matter how many shortsighted people get in the way. Thus the genre drew on Stewart's capacity for projecting a vision.

Anthony Mann, who brought none of his revisionism toward the Western to the biopic's conventions, opens *The Glenn Miller Story* with a striking shot. A shiny trombone dominates the left half of a shot taken from inside a pawnshop window. A trolley car (establishing the period) occupies the right side; it is soon obscured by Stewart, who walks up wearing period garb. Mann holds the shot of man and trombone, with Stewart never looking away from the instrument, grinning warmly as if encountering an old friend. The film establishes Glenn Miller–as–Jimmy Stewart by drawing on the familiar fixity of the Stewart gaze, a look that here indicates desire and possession.

The motif of vision is fully articulated, characteristically for Stewart and for the genre, in a perfunctory love scene with Helen/Allyson, the woman-as-mirror. In that familiar dreamy tone used to describe "angry little mountain streams" (*Mr. Smith*), "rounding up strays" (*Naked*

Spur), and "lassoing the moon" (*Wonderful Life*)—always with a woman as listener—Miller/Stewart says, "I know exactly what I want and where I'm going." While such reveries in the Mann Westerns and the Capra films mark the character as a sad naïf whose ideals set him up for disillusionment, the biopic takes such lines straight, as symptoms of a drive that, as in myths about male sexuality, the subject can scarcely be expected to control. Talent and vision take Miller/Stewart and all who follow him toward the light of accomplishment and fame, the latter signified here by songs that are, to the spectator, already famous. Thus the presumption that allows Miller/Stewart to call and propose marriage to a woman who hasn't heard from him for a year is erased by the quest for "the sound," which makes Miller/Stewart both an irresistible force and an innocent figure of destiny.

Thus, beneath the droll distractedness of the "boyish"-though-forty-five-year-old Stewart, an image that was becoming a tired cliché by 1954, runs the familiar egoism of the male subject. Such social processes as courtship and weddings, designed to place heterosexual drives under the control of the community (and to rule out other drives altogether), were coded by the 1950s as rituals of "feminized" civilization. Miller's immediate marriage runs roughshod over the "feminine" rigamarole that is seen to complicate needlessly the man's quest for his goal.

One obvious difference between the biopic and most other classical genres is that while the prototypical Hollywood film fades out once the goal of a wedding has been reached, many biopics take place within marriages, which are often portrayed as years of bliss interrupted only by outside forces. Behind every successful man was indeed a woman, according to these films. The bourgeois marriage is celebrated as an apparatus designed to smooth the progress of the man in the world. In *The Glenn Miller Story*, marriage appears as virtually a business arrangement essential to the hero's fame, as the wife becomes the practical repository of the husband's drive, leaving the dreamy hero untainted by such worldly traits as ambition.

Unlike in the Western and in Stewart films from *It's a Wonderful Life* to *Rear Window*, marriage is not construed as domestic confinement and the end of the man's freedom. Clearly, however, it is the end of the woman's. *Miller* casts marriage for the woman as a no-contest choice between obscurity and a globe-trotting, upwardly mobile marriage with the all-American average man. Thus Helen/Allyson's wifely job of pleasing a successful man glamorizes the lot of the housewife in the 1950s. This glamorization extended to the film's publicity and commercial tie-ins: A 1954 ad in women's magazines showed Stewart as Miller swinging on the trombone. Posed below was a smiling Allyson shown

7. With June Allyson in *The Glenn Miller Story*. The biopic man of vision and the determined wife, repository of his unseemly ambition.

next to an equal-size bowl of Campbell's Soup, with the tag line, "The Man-pleasers." The hearty soup and the glowing wife who prepares it combine to produce the spectacular performance of the working male.

Furthermore, Allyson's diminutive stature (five feet one) made her appear all the more an appendage of the towering Stewart—the "little wife." She is the apotheosis of the wife as mirror, organizer, and loyal supporter of her spouse's projects, though never her own. When Miller/Stewart and his pals need $1,800 to start their band, Helen/Allyson produces a bankbook showing the magic amount, saved from money removed from her husband's pockets. When Glenn summons Helen from Boulder to marry him in New York, she drops family, fiancé, and roots to join him. The film fixes on Helen/Allyson as the hero's fated mate, and she falls under his possessive gaze as inevitably as does the trombone in the pawnshop window.

All this ensues despite the patronizing air the hero shows toward the heroine in their early scenes together, a condescension Stewart's addle-pated charm is clearly meant to contain. Fixing his will and desire on the female object, the Stewart figure stops just short of a later character's exclamation, "Judy, it can't matter to you," just as his distraction and vision do not move him to insist that women color their hair to re-create the lost object. Later in the fifties, Stewart will show the short space between the controlling vision as man's charming prerogative and as oppression and disease.

In a hotel room in a distant country, an American tourist is about to break some terrible news to his wife. A full shot takes in the couple as they enter the room through a corridor, then dollies back to show the woman sitting on one of the twin beds as the husband remains standing. When the woman reaches for the phone to make a call the husband testily snaps at her to stop. As she asks, "Are we about to have our monthly fight?" there is a cut to a slightly low-angled medium close-up of the man, who mutters, "I hope not," looking at something off screen; with his back to his wife, he enters a space all his and the camera's own. He looks stealthily out of the corners of his eyes as the camera moves in the downward direction of his gaze. His look is so guilty and secretive that students to whom I have shown this clip guess that he must be about to reach for a gun or a blunt instrument. His method of coercion is indeed blunt, though all too civilized.

The camera shows his hands as they open a drawer and pull out a small travel case containing vials of drugs. As the wife continues to protest, the hands pull out one vial and remove some pills. A cut returns to the earlier close-up as the man again looks furtively, then turns and walks toward the woman. The camera shows them both in the composition, him with his back to the camera, moving with his long neck slightly stooped and his head cocked, saying, "Take these—they'll relax ya." The woman protests that six months ago her doctor-husband told her she took too many pills. The man insists that she take the pills because "You're tense. You've been talking a blue streak." Thus he displaces his own "female" symptoms onto his wife, as she observes: "I think maybe *you* need them." It is almost as if the man's wife gets "excited and nervous," as he puts it, because he has decided that she will. He seems to fear losing what little control he has of the situation if his wife is in possession of her faculties.

"If invited to picture Stewart in a Hitchcock film," writes Robin Wood, "doesn't one (unless one thinks of *Rear Window*!) see him shot from a low angle, towering over someone (usually a woman), looking at once dominating and helpless, out of control, near hysteria?" ("The Men Who . . . " 202). In this scene from *The Man Who Knew Too Much* (a remake of Hitchcock's 1934 British thriller), Dr. Ben McKenna/Stewart needs to drug his wife, Jo (Doris Day), before he can tell her that their

8. "Are we about to have our monthly fight?" When Jo (Doris Day) looks up at Ben, it is with suspicion, which is mutual.

ten-year-old son has been kidnapped to keep Ben from going to the police with what he has learned in Morocco about an impending assassination in London. The scene is a primer in the use of classical composition, shot–reverse shot, and subjective perception, not to mention star persona and performance, to make ironic gender power relations (Wood "The Men Who . . . " 202). All the signifiers of dominance and passivity are present: the mobile, protective male in a visually superior position looking down on the seated, immobile female; his and the spectators' knowledge of the situation versus her ignorance; the classic relationship of the female patient and the male doctor (Freud included) who knows what's good for her.

Hitchcock, largely with the help of Stewart, uses the patriarchy and the cinematic system that supports it against themselves. Low-angle shots convey dominance as well as threat. Day is bathed in light, the elaborate wood scalloping on the windowpanes behind her casting artful but not sinister shadows on her. She is surrounded by plenty of space on both sides in the VistaVision frame. Ben/Stewart, on the other hand, is framed in front of darkness and shadow; a mirror behind him reflects the room in jagged diagonals and dark blues and grays. His dark blue suit

9. McKenna's inflexibility is contrasted with his wife's calm adaptability.

contrasts with her off-white dress. Thus the shot–reverse shot creates a contrast between relative light (Day/Jo) and relative darkness (Ben/Stewart). Stewart's head, shoulders, and arms are thrust forward into the shot. In another Stewart film such dominance would code assertiveness and leadership (one thinks of the early scene in *It's a Wonderful Life* in which George gives an impromptu speech to Potter in defense of his dead father); here in the context of the other elements it makes him overbearing.

Hitchcock takes full advantage of Stewart's tall, spindly frame. In the scene in the Moroccan restaurant in *The Man Who Knew Too Much*, for example, Ben/Stewart proves to be inflexible in both body and spirit, showing his inability to sit on a divan or eat according to local custom. It also shows his refusal to consider adjustments, such as practicing medicine in New York, which could allow his wife to keep her stage career and thus might make their marriage a partnership rather than a patriarchy. The scene takes off on the spectators' familiarity with Stewart's ungainly physique while probing the narrow-minded, parochial dimensions of his small-town persona. (Stewart may well have modeled the character after his father, who despite a Princeton education, remained a small-town merchant and was suspicious of the world his son inhabited.)

Whatever else he may have been, Hitchcock was a master of the dichotomy in mainstream film whereby conservatism and subversion exist side by side. Ina Rae Hark alludes to this, noting that when Hitchcock remade *The Man Who Knew Too Much*, he assigned the woman a more passive and maternal role than in the original and returned the husband to his rightful male place as active agent. Hark points out, however, that having restored patriarchy, Hitchcock showed it riddled with tensions (218–219). Thus the typical mid-fifties American couple comes outfitted with the codes of magazine spreads on "Jimmy and Gloria" and of the exemplary Stewart-Allyson screen couple. But to Hitchcock "typical American couple" means something distinctly sinister. Here it means that the woman, an accomplished musical comedy star, has given up her career to be with her husband, that he has insisted upon her subservience to him, that they live in Indianapolis, and that there is oedipal conflict brewing over their ten-year-old son, who threatens to emulate his mother more than his father.

In short, this is a marriage that, to a nineties spectator, appears headed for divorce sometime in the sixties. The fact that Hitchcock and the screenwriter John Michael Hayes give Jo a career that brought her a great deal of prestige and personal satisfaction, and that outshone her husband's, underlines the patriarchal marriage model as obsessively male-centered and designed to suppress the woman. This point is driven home, so to speak, by Ben's emphatic introductions of his wife as "Mrs. McKenna," his characterizations of her as "a doctor's wife," and his explanations of her name, Josephine; "I've called her 'Jo' for so long nobody knows her as anything else," he says, recalling Tania Modleski's citing of the line "Men have named you" from the song "Mona Lisa," heard in *Rear Window* (*The Women Who Knew Too Much* 84). However, the naming is in his imagination; her fans knew her as "Jo Conway" before she and Ben met, and her London friends even assume him to be "Mr. Conway."

The Stewart "average man" plays here as a narrow-minded provincial. He is the serviceman who was stationed in Casablanca during the war without learning anything of Middle Eastern culture; the Midwesterner whose only frame of reference is his home (he says that a Marrakech bazaar "reminds me of county fairs when I was a kid"); and the colonizer who expects to import his culture wherever he goes—"Glenn Miller" as the ugly American.

Stewart's performance combines his small-town-family-man image with the harsh demeanor of his Mann Western protagonists, resulting in a subversion of the masculine prerogatives celebrated in the biopic's rendition of the can-do American hero. Miller knows he has a new sound, and Lindbergh knows he can cross the Atlantic but, in the sense of knowing as an activity, Stewart's McKenna knows too much. He knows that his son has been kidnapped, knows "when and how to administer medicine," knows that they should go to London to look for Hank and later that they should go to the assassination target's unnamed embassy. In a broader sense he knows that his boy "will make a fine doctor," that his wife's place is in the home and not on a stage, and that he should be dominant in the marriage. Far from making him competent and strong, this "knowledge" makes him irrelevant. Unlike his wife, he doesn't know that Ambrose Chapel is the kidnappers' hideout, that Louis Bernard the Frenchman is acting suspiciously, or more crucially, that his wife is unhappy and that his son prefers his attentive mother to his restrictive father. This father knows most but doesn't know best, because his insistence on mastery keeps him from listening to others and learning from experience.

As we've seen, Stewart is often identified with excess; the actor whose performance style was "too much" for Jean Arthur here plays the Man Who Knows Too Much. He acts out an excess of the very masculine aggression and dominance that run counter to the surrendering, suffering Stewart and that are repressed by the "natural" achievers of the biopics. Stewart's McKenna has to work too frantically to maintain masculinity for it to be natural. Stewart's other genres and directors draw out certain categories of the Stewart persona and combine them with generic archetypes. In Capra's films Stewart adds the mama's boy, the look of surrender, and the Christian masochist to a jaundiced view of American frontier myths; in the Westerns he crosses the classical Western hero with the male hysteric and moral (sado)masochist; in the biopics the visionary, the war hero, and family man match perfectly and without irony the genre's success myths. The three Hitchcock films of the fifties, however, refuse to allow the contradictory categories of Stewart's persona to remain separate, lacing them together, with Stewart's all-American persona as their basic archetype.

A line like "I want a woman who can go anywhere, do anything, and love it" would sound straightforward enough in a biopic. In *Rear Window* Stewart delivers it while being therapeutically slapped by a nurse played by Thelma Ritter, punctuating the statement with an under-his-breath "Hold it" as he catches himself from falling backward into his wheelchair. The line now sounds like the egoistic fantasy of a helpless man denying his immobility and reliance on women; it is as if Lindbergh were shown what his life would be like as George Bailey. *Rear Window* virtually parodies the daring-but-modest biopic subjects, their offhand derring-do curbed by confinement to a tiny city apartment in

August, their gallant arrogance toward women exposed as dread, fear, and fetishism, their lofty visions diminished to voyeurism, and their achievements reduced to the photographer's exploitations of human suffering as spectacle—prize-winning photos of fires, car crashes, and atomic explosions.

In addition, the fifties Hitchcock films bring out an unspoken underside of Stewart's war-hero persona: the uneasy readjustment of World War II veterans to civilian and domestic life and the renewed misogyny that the war's years-long separation of the sexes appeared to have brought to a number of the Allied countries. Psychologist Lynne Segal reads the strict separation of male and female roles and characteristics in the fifties against men's common experience of the war:

> Army training relies upon intensifying the opposition be-
> tween male and female, with "women" used as a term of
> abuse for incompetent performance, thereby cementing
> the prevalent cultural links between virility, sexuality, and
> aggressiveness. Such practices serve not only to discipline
> men, but to raise "masculine" morale in the face of a more
> typically "feminine" reality—the enforced servility and
> conformity characteristic of army life. "Effeminacy,"
> as [Trevor] Royle observes, "was the ultimate soldier's
> crime" and "to some people, carrying a gun was like hav-
> ing a permanent hard-on." (18–19)

The phallic values of the military are effaced in much postwar publicity on Stewart, such as the 1946 *Newsweek* story in which the designation "war hero" manages to connote both "loyal, clean, and reverent" virtue and "war is hell" world-weariness. The phallic aggression of the military subculture is repressed by Stewart in the war-effacing *It's a Wonderful Life* and in his refusal to discuss his war experiences. However, the postwar misogyny that dominated American life and film representation in the fifties mingled with the effeminate elements of Stewart's persona. For Stewart's career the "official" values of war hero and family breadwinner kept at bay the "femininity" of his persona. While the latter could be used to revise the monolithic masculinity of the Western archetype, Stewart's own archetype was revised by the condescension and arrogance toward women that emerged in many of his postwar films. In Hitchcock this complacency doubles back onto Stewart's emotionality and masochism in order to show the impatient, sexist war veterans of *Rear Window* and *The Man Who Knew Too Much* as men whose loathing of femininity and insistence on male prerogatives, reinforced by the memories of their military experience, mask swollen egos and deep insecurities.

Hence the male protagonists of the fifties Hitchcock films seek to control and contain women. This and the fact that they work in what were, for the era, decidedly male occupations (news photography, medicine, law enforcement) led Laura Mulvey to define the Stewart-Hitchcock characters—specifically Scottie Ferguson in *Vertigo*—as "exemplary of the symbolic order and the law" and of "the power to subject another person to the will sadistically or to the gaze voyeuristically" (312). Without mentioning him Mulvey could be explaining Stewart's work for Hitchcock vis-à-vis his off-screen image when she writes that *Vertigo* takes the (spectator) position "normally associated with ideological correctness and the recognition of established morality and shows its perverted side" (312).

Tania Modleski, who also does not mention the actor, sees the Stewart-Hitchcock protagonist caught in a dialectic between control of women and confrontation with his own bisexuality. She finds the greatest collision of these in *Vertigo*. In Modleski's analysis Scottie's desire to cure Madeleine stems from a need to ensure that the mysterious "eternal feminine" exists by making her mirror male reason, turning her away from the omnipotent "dead mother" Carlotta Valdez and toward him as reassurance of his sufficiency as a subject. However, Scottie's investigation of Madeleine gradually leads him to identify with her, a point made by the famous mirror shot in the flower shop, in which a standard voyeuristic point-of-view shot is shown to include Scottie, who peers in through a crack in a door with a mirror in back, thus virtually appearing as Madeleine's reflection (*The Women Who Knew Too Much* 92). To Modleski "Scottie's failure to cure Madeleine deals a mortal blow to his masculine identity" (*The Women Who . . .* 95); in his dream he sees Madeleine's hallucination of her empty coffin as his own, an abyss into which his disembodied (castrated) head plummets, ending in an image in which he "dies Madeleine's death" from the bell tower at the mission.

Modleski sees the film's last forty minutes as a trajectory in which Scottie acts out the tragedy of "the mad Carlotta," searching the streets for Madeleine as Carlotta looked for her child. Spectator identification with Scottie's quest to re-create the ideal image of Madeleine, who never existed, out of Judy, "the original woman" (*The Women Who . . .* 96), is destroyed by Judy's flashback, which reveals Madeleine as the creation of another man who victimized Scottie as he will victimize Judy. Scottie makes the humiliating discovery that in his ultimate conquest he was "caught up in repetition," with its Freudian connections to "unfreedom, masochism, and death." Even this is dwarfed, however, by the realization that in exploiting his "weakness" Elster has equated him with the feminine, and that Scottie has all-too-automatically lapsed from his presumed male power into an acting out of the "feminine" role of the other.

As Marian Keane implies, film criticism's failure until recently to take into account acting and stardom sometimes leads critics to miss part of the meaning. Keane points out that the presence of Stewart, with his "capacity for suffering," problematizes Mulvey's claims for *Vertigo* as a rehearsal for her paradigm of an active, sadistic subjectivity. Modleski's analysis of the film's play on male fear and dread of femininity raises questions about how much the critic is reading "the character" and how much she is reading "Stewart." For in *Vertigo* Stewart's masculine and feminine sides meld, as if the ironic and inevitable result of a male subject's quest for masculine viability were reunion with his lost femininity.

Thus, even while acting as investigator and seeking to put Madeleine under his control, this Stewart character nevertheless gives himself over to the object of his gaze. He looks at Madeleine Elster in the red-and-black, womblike setting of Ernie's restaurant and later at Carlotta's grave. His look is stealthy, out of the corner of his eye, but strong and searching. The camera, craning from Scottie/Stewart's position at the bar and ranging over the diners at Ernie's, moves as if sent out by Scottie's gaze to find the object. The instant it finds her, the high-pitched and delicate violin romance of Bernard Herrmann's score fairly swoons, undercutting any notion of male control by echoing Stewart's own exquisite talent for swooning, which he reprises in *Vertigo*. This sublime love-and-death theme music is repeated at the moments of Scottie's other early point-of-view-shot discoveries—the portrait of Carlotta at the museum and her gravestone.

While Jeff Smith's fainting signifies martyrdom, and the Mann heroes pass out from self-punishment, Scottie faints, literally and figuratively, from fear of falling—falling back into the womb, falling down from the exaggerated height of "masculinity," and falling back into original bisexuality. However, violins swoon at the very moments when Scottie displaces feminine surrender to the object onto masculine possession of it, revealing Scottie's fate in a rapturous expression of the desire to be the other sex.

As has been widely noted, the phrase "power and freedom" recurs as a keystone in the film's dialogue and refers to myths of unrestrained exercise of male prerogatives in a preindustrial America. Scottie, in the person of James Stewart, is virtually the antithesis of such mythology. He embodies a desperate tension between power—the power of patriarchy over femininity and that in men which is feminine—and freedom, the unconscious desire to be free of ideologically constructed gender identity and the terror that blocks this desire from consciousness. The mingled terror and fascination of *Vertigo* stems from the exposure of the voyeur's objects as representations whose revealed artifice shows power and freedom to be illusory.

Scottie's discovery of the deceit constitutes a rupturing of the illusion of identification with Madeleine and mastery over Judy/Madeleine. Forced to abandon what Modleski calls her "original" femininity and return to the role of actress, Judy cannot help but put on Carlotta's necklace, so thoroughly is she "in character" as Madeleine. Armed with the truth about the necklace, Scottie is released from his role as "spectatrix," who—like the Mia Farrow character in Doane's reading of *Purple Rose of Cairo*—is incapable of telling representation from actuality. Scottie is restored to the deductive powers of a detective. Back in action, he sets out to win a final victory over femininity—a vanquishing of the vertigo and acrophobia that caused his "fall" from masculinity. But his triumph over vertigo returns him to sadism; immediately he slogs into the male role of victimizer. Dragging Judy/Madeleine up the stairs of the bell tower for the second time, he is still, as Modleski writes, "caught in repetition." In his willingness to break out of the pattern that disrupts masculine hegemony, he fails to recognize that the male role itself is a manifestation of repetition compulsion. He is now, like Elster, a slayer of women, one who uses and "ditches" them.

Scottie's final gesture, his walk onto the ledge of the bell tower with arms spread, reprises the position of his falling body in the dream and signifies his permanent fall from the illusion of masculine control. The gesture is outwardly an expression of loss (and the confusion of the male subject, whose only relationship to woman is one of control) and of a desire for completion that leads to death and in which a feminine position is equated with death. It could be said that in a Capra film nothing is truly private; the martyrdom of a figure such as Mr. Smith might be defined as the yielding of private feelings to public demands. By the postwar era this surrender to community values has given way to the biopic's public fulfillment of private needs; martyrdom degenerates finally in Hitchcock to a narcissistic death drive. In Hitchcock by the fifties, nothing is truly public, and the very idea of a professional, public-minded subject is reduced to nonsense. Male authority and power are revealed as unstable containments for a male subjectivity that threatens to become overwhelmed by its own internal tensions.

Given the all-or-nothing dualism through which patriarchy sees the opposition of masculinity and femininity, Scottie's gesture signals his entry into a netherworld of bisexuality wherein, to male subjectivity in the fifties, madness dwells. No wonder that even during the film's 1983–

84 reissue, Janet Maslin in the *New York Times* reported that audiences cheered at the climactic moment when Scottie appears to have conquered his vertigo and regained his love object, seconds before "the film's real ending left the audience gasping in disbelief" (Kapsis 50). The applause betrayed a desire for resolution and control, a recuperation of masculinity at the expense of the feminine.

In his "bio-bibliography" of Stewart, Gerard Molyneaux remarks that "Hitchcock was able to tap a vein of acting talent in Stewart that could reflect the psychological anxieties besetting post World War II Americans. . . . The fascination here is twofold: that the chosen vehicle would be the All-American boy and that through some professional prophylaxis the star image would stay untainted by these sordid roles" (24). Despite the customary talk about the *auteur* "tapping a vein" in the (bovine) actor, driving him like a "vehicle," and so on, these comments obscure how *Vertigo* and the other Hitchcock films might have been personal statements for the actor as well as the director. Stewart participated in plumbing the depths of his well-crafted persona. Hitchcock alone could not have moved Stewart to the resentful desperation of Ben McKenna or the emotion and hysteria of Scottie Ferguson. The question remains how the "beloved" Stewart and the militaristic, all-American Stewart keep body, soul, and persona together when the body is so fragile and vulnerable and the soul of a character's unexamined life is so often brought into the foreground of a Stewart film to suffer the consequences of a lack of self-knowledge.

Remembering
Stewart

□□□

In the early 1990s, two decades after his last starring film, James Stewart was still a valuable commodity. A survey by the American Advertising Council (AAC) in 1992 found that of all ad spokespeople, Stewart, whose uncredited voice had been heard since 1989 dishing up soup in an ad campaign for Campbell's "Home Cookin'," had the top "Q rating." He could be heard stammering his way through an anecdotal voice-over introduction to the video of *Harvey*, which was released in June 1990 and in six months became MCA's largest-selling "classic" title (Molyneaux 107). He could be seen receiving the 1990 tribute of the Film Society of Lincoln Center, on the *Tonight Show* reading his "homespun" verse, which was collected and published in the fall of 1989 as *Jimmy Stewart and His Poems*, and joining the cast (perhaps some of whom were under the age of eighty) of a 1991 "Bob Hope Special" welcoming home troops from Operation Desert Storm (Molyneaux 32).

Articles on him still appeared, usually in such nostalgia-driven magazines as *Life* and the *Saturday Evening Post*. A 1988 *Post* piece described the star as "a nice guy who's never had a scandal attached to his name" (Millner 60), repeating almost verbatim the statement from the *Look* profile 33 years before. The context was different, however. The 1955 story was written in the midst of Stewart's entrepreneurial successes. ("James Stewart—Highest Paid Actor" was its title.) His solid-citizen qualities were then seen in the context of the varied film roles that showed up on theater screens at the rate of two or three a year. His freedom from scandal was in the mid-fifties part of the developing persona of the hardworking, fabulously successful family man whose exemplary life left room for the serious actor. Thirty years later it was something of an article of faith for traditionalists as well as a qualification for sainthood (at least).

By the late eighties and early nineties, the "average-boy-next-door" image that harked back to the thirties had become enshrined as myth. A 1991 *Life* story heralded him, with some irony, as "just about all we've got left of a time when our ideals were clear and our purposes were certain" (Hendrickson 66), adding that the Hitchcock roles were "among the greatest Stewart performances, and yet it is as if we somehow forget them at least when imagining the man himself" (76). Thus the Stewart mythology changed with the market needs of each era. The emotional toughening and darkening in the fifties provided a mature touch when the middle-aged actor, who could not play forever on his "boyishness" and remain a box-office commodity, needed it.

However, those changes faded with time, and the image formed in popular memory finally is the "beloved" Stewart, a vague amalgam of the Capra films—remembered as sentimental Americana instead of the conflicted works that they are—and the years of association with patriotism and devotion to family and the small town. It was a sexually neutralized persona; Stewart became in memory what MGM's 1930s publicity had tried to sell him as before he had a body of films to his credit. Thus one writer in the 1990 *Film Comment* tribute sought to "take issue with the creeping canonization of James Stewart . . . as sweet bumbling eunuch, the all-American boy as gelding" (Murphy 35). Stewart's career ended as it had begun, with an affirmation of sanitized, nonthreatening masculinity and of the harmlessness of dominant ideology, or perhaps as nostalgia for a time when such myths were believed.

Stewart's legacy, then, is a lasting reminder of the dialectic of dominance and subversion. Stewart's secret lies in compartmentalization: In one compartment Stewart in the 1990s is sexless; in another he is the exemplary father, husband, small-town denizen, and servant of his country, a man beyond reproach; in a third he is a tortured, vulnerable emotionalist, a "feminine" hero albeit one who displays an inner pain in masculinity, a screen figure who proves the "manufacture" of the phallus and the illusion of idealism, the longer he appears in films. The first two compartments keep contained the secret that rages in countless forms and guises in the third compartment.

One film that embodies the remembered persona as well as the dismemberment it holds in check is *Harvey*, the 1950 film version of Mary Chase's 1944 Pulitzer Prize–winning stage comedy about Elwood P. Dowd, an eccentric, heavy-drinking, small-town-dwelling heir to a comfortable fortune; his invisible companion, a six-foot-three-inch rabbit named Harvey; and Elwood's sister Veta, who is determined to commit him to a sanitarium where he will not continue to embarrass her efforts to find a husband for her daughter, Myrtle Mae. Stewart was long identified with Dowd; he first played him on Broadway in 1947 (as a replacement for the actor Frank Fay, who originated the role) and in London later the same year. He revived the role in a 1970 Broadway production, which was restaged for television two years later, and he played Dowd for the final time onstage in London in 1975.

Dowd became a role some audiences had trouble separating from the actor. In his introduction to the video of *Harvey*, Stewart describes men "who hadn't shaved for a couple days, hadn't had their suit pressed for quite a while," who would stop him on the street and seriously ask if Harvey was with him. If I needed more proof that *Harvey* was very important in the popular memory of Stewart, none was necessary after hearing a local radio commercial for an Indianapolis gun show in which a Stewart impersonator describes the gun show to "Harvey." The ad points out the significance of the gentle Stewart as an icon for the culture's most violent orthodoxies; the next step must be a reproduction of the movie's painting of Stewart/Elwood and Harvey with a caption, "We are the NRA." That the commercial has an appropriately violent ending—Harvey gets run over by a truck—settles for the ad's "target audience" the Stewart persona's troublesome gender ambivalence in the same way that the studio executives put to rest their qualms about Stewart by recalling his bombing missions.

Given Stewart's ability to project a special sense of vision, it was logical that he would become well known for a role in which the costar was invisible and had to be suggested by the strength of the actor's gaze. Surreptitiously *Harvey* is one half of a male buddy film, with the missing half provided by the actor, the filmmaking, and the spectator's strongly encouraged imagination. This talk of missing halves and compensated lacks smacks, of course, of Lacanian psychoanalysis and the desire for the bisexual half who is separated from the subject at his or her entry into the symbolic. However, the key to the durable appeal of *Harvey* is the protagonist's complete absence of desire, a fantastic contentment that makes him convincingly insane but still an irresistible figure of fantasy.

Stewart's Elwood has in common with Eastwood's Man with No Name a preternatural self-sufficiency that rises above desire and puts a spectator in the bizarre position of desiring a life free from desire. Unlike Eastwood's, this Stewart fantasy promises freedom from sexuality and from gender and class differences. As radical as this may sound, however, one can be sure that the narrative itself maintains the very differences of which Elwood in his "willed madness" (Canby 20) divests himself.

As Vito Russo explains, the "buddy film" extends from silent films such as *The Flesh and the Devil* and *Wings* (1927), through the films of comedy teams—Laurel and Hardy in particular—and action-adventure films such as Howard Hawks's *Only Angels Have Wings* (1939) and *Red River* (1948), to the genre's reemergence with *Midnight Cowboy* and *Butch Cassidy and the Sundance Kid* (both 1969). "The primary buddy relationships in films," writes Russo, "are those between men who despise homosexuality yet find that their truest and most noble feelings are for each other" (70). Visually, the buddy film usually shows the two friends together in the frame; if one buddy is gone from a shot, his absence is represented as a void. Accordingly the visual conventions of classical *mise-en-scène*—the over-the-shoulder shot, two-shot, and *plan Américain* (a shot of the full human figure, from about the mid-calves up)—are composed and the actions within them blocked, as if Harvey were a visible figure within them.

Stewart delivers a line to Harvey, such as, "Veta wants to talk to us; I think she wants to congratulate us on the impression we made at her party," with a mixture of total sincerity and the detachment of the insane. What gives Stewart's *Harvey* its durable appeal is the star's ability to suggest a private world far more welcoming and comfortable than the one "we" (represented by the other silly, bustling, striving characters) inhabit. Thus, although Dowd has unwittingly demolished Veta's party, the spectator is moved to agree that Dowd and Harvey should be congratulated. Their male company is much more inviting than that of the pretentious, status-conscious women whom Dowd frightens off without meaning to; in fact, the novel that he takes off the shelf to read to Harvey—*Sense and Sensibility* by Jane Austen—more closely reflects his sister's society than a life of male companionship.

Elwood's invisible buddy relationship subverts a female-dominated world of society teas and pretentious musical programs. This is one Stewart "Smalltown U.S.A. picture" (Russo 72) in which the boy next door stays in his mother's house too long instead of lighting out for the territory, as George Bailey wants to do. "Female" domesticity drives Elwood into a mad world of his own. But if he's taken to the funny farm, the laugh is on . . . whom? Nineteenth- and early-twentieth-century writers such as Charlotte Perkins Gilman depicted madness as woman's only revolt against the gilded prison of patriarchal marriage and the home. *Harvey* subverts the trappings of domestic society by crossing it with a single man whose refuges from the world of women are withdrawal into a travesty of friendship with an imaginary buddy and the gregariousness that allows him to open the doors of the house to the lower-class denizens of bars.

By insisting on Harvey's reality, however, the film belongs in part to the comic genre in which the insane, those relieved from everyday norms, are the ones who know how to live. It is the intellectuals and socialites who are in need of treatment; Stewart's first film for Capra, *You Can't Take It With You* [1938], was also of this ilk. Thus, like a mad Huck Finn, Elwood brushes aside the maternal restrictions now embodied in his sister by charting a world of his own. Elwood, however, adheres to the social rules of decorum and etiquette; a more unintentional and civil disobeyer there could not be.

Furthermore, this buddy relationship is of a most nonphallic nature. Dowd is oblivious to domination, power, competition, fear, goal orientation, or ego. Although Elwood's inherited house has a plaster black servant in front of it, one senses that Elwood wouldn't mind a bit if a black family moved in next door, perhaps reason enough to brand him a mental case in the America of 1950. The image of Stewart as "sweet, bumbling eunuch" derives most of all from *Harvey*. Dowd represents a parodically destructive "boy next door," "a great home boy," as his sister describes him, whose refusal to leave his mother's house and strike out on his own prompts whispers about whether there isn't something a little funny about aging Junior.

In 1944, when the play opened on Broadway, to show an able-bodied man lingering in the neighborhood while there is a world war on was to imply "something funny" to begin with. In her article on *Mildred Pierce* (1945), Linda Williams noted that the men on Mildred's wartime homefront are shown as "sleazy no-counts . . . as if the real men . . . are elsewhere" ("*Mildred Pierce*" 22). The wartime variable intensifies the long-standing suspicion in American culture of unmarried men over the age of thirty. In an age when all homosexual men were effectively closeted and many took wives in order to "pass" (as well as to try to convince themselves that they were not really gay), just staying single was either a symptom of madness or an unheard-of act of defiance. The same would be true of nonphallic, nonegoistic, non-goal-oriented male behavior.

The play and film operate under conventions whereby "normal human beings" recoil from the mentally disturbed. What besides a man who introduces people to a nonexistent companion would white, heterosexual society in 1950 recoil from? Who else could Elwood introduce who would break up Veta's tea party? Certainly the dangerously violent, which Elwood emphatically is not. A black acquaintance would do it. So would a gay lover. And these two would have something in common with Harvey; in the 1940s and early 1950s they were invisible, a metaphor that both black and gay writers have used to characterize their position in the culture. While blacks and gays historically have been willed invisible, however, Elwood wills his pariah visible, and that makes him objectionable. "I sometimes see this white rabbit myself," confesses Veta, "and he's just as big as Elwood says he is."

10. Elwood/Stewart pointing out the invisible. What would polite society recoil from in 1950?

The buddy genre's loathing of women and the latent homoeroticism of its protagonists are perfectly in place in this "invisible buddy" comedy. Dowd is a spectator at *Harvey*'s romance, which takes place between a couple of bland minor characters, a doctor and nurse. Even though Chase's play describes Dowd as "a man in his late forties" and the film makes him forty-two, Stewart's age in 1950, it treats the character as a man without sexual interest or any possibility that women might be interested in him. The play casts Dowd in the role of a kindly matchmaker decades past his forties who appreciates the beauty of the young "love interest" but recommends her to Dr. Sanderson, an *eligible* bachelor. This is probably why no one called the actor too old for the role when he returned to it in his sixties; the character's apparent asexuality seems more appropriate to Stewart's grandfatherly persona in the 1970s than to a star who was playing romantic leads in other films of the time.

It follows masculinist logic that the gentle, nonphallic man be asexual. Since sexual intercourse, to Lacan, centers around the phallus, the very idea of nonphallic sexuality leaves the male emasculated, out of the running in the heterosexual sweepstakes, and feminized as gay men conventionally have been. Dowd/Stewart is given nowhere to turn but to the invisible partner, with homosexuality *as* invisibility, "homosexuals [being] just as invisible onscreen as they were in real life" (Russo 63). The invisible other is displaced onto "pleasantry," with the result that Elwood's little joke on the world looks preferable to the lives of "perfectly normal human beings—and you know what stinkers they are," as the cab driver at the end of the play exclaims.

Once again a Stewart film invites the spectator to revel in an alternative to conventional gender identity, but also to sense an underlying desperation. To tear Elwood away from his illusion would be to confront him with his misery, a prospect this light comedy spares its audience. Vincent Canby writes that "in Mr. Stewart's great performance, Elwood's optimism is always on a knife-edge. If Elwood didn't drink, he might just put a gun to his head" (2–20). Dowd's lapine apparition represents a compromise between the closeted world of repression and the forbidden option of an overt relationship with a flesh-and-blood "Harvey."

For me to suggest homoerotic subterfuge in the "beloved" *Harvey*, with its "canonized" all-American star is to put myself in the position in which Russo finds himself in his book. Russo begins with the assumption that to assert homoeroticism in Hollywood films is to work against America itself. He repeats a story about the producer Samuel Goldwyn: When Goldwyn was told that he could not make a film based on Radclyffe Hall's novel *The Well of Loneliness* because the main character was a lesbian, Goldwyn replied, "So what? We'll make her an American" (62). In discussing the "unmistakable" homosexuality in Laurel and Hardy's "sweet and very real loving dimension," Russo concludes:

> All of this is charming, sometimes very funny and certainly of no great consequence. Yet when one suggests that there may be clues to homosexual behavior in the ways that Laurel and Hardy related to one another, it is as though one were attacking America itself. . . . In pointing these things out, one attacks the American illusion—the illusion that there is in fact such a thing as a real man and that to become one is as easy as changing one's name from Marion Morrison to John Wayne. (73–74)

We've seen that the male club is not at all an easy one to belong to but a construction that must be arduously maintained. However, to bring out the seemingly infinite number of quiet challenges to accepted masculinity in Stewart's films comes to feel like "attacking America itself." Partly this is because, as we've seen, Stewart's essential bisexuality is covered first by his clean, boy-next-door prewar image and then by his wrapped-in-the-flag postwar persona—a patriotic image so pure that when Frank Capra found that he had been listed as a security risk during the anticommunist witch-hunt era, he named in his defense "[General] Jimmy Doolittle and Jimmy Stewart . . . among his friends" (McBride 597). Stewart was promoted to the rank of brigadier general in the Air Force Reserve on July 16, 1959, two weeks between the New York premiere and the national release of the racy *Anatomy of a Murder*, which Stewart's own father took out an ad in the *Indiana Daily Gazette* advising readers not to see (Robbins 96–97). Thus Stewart's official virtue continued to cancel out films that might contradict it.

Harvey and *Anatomy of a Murder* bookend Stewart's career in the fifties. They won him his only Academy Award nominations of the decade, and *Anatomy* won him his first New York Film Critics Award since *Mr. Smith* exactly twenty years before. They were eagerly anticipated, presold properties rather than vehicles; they have more of the feel of virtuosity and "performance" than Stewart's film roles usually do; and they are buddy films, without love interests for the Stewart protagonists.

Anatomy of a Murder marks a key moment in the breakdown of the Stewart persona's sincerity and idealism. Based on a best-selling novel by Robert Traver, the pseudonym of John D. Voelker, a Michigan supreme court justice, the film stars Stewart as Paul Biegler, a longtime district attorney defeated for reelection, who takes up private practice and in his first big case defends a young army lieutenant (Ben Gazzara) accused of murdering the man who raped his wife, Laura (Lee Remick). After the trial begins with the prosecution blocking the defense's attempts to include the rape in the case, Biegler/Stewart, in the foreground of one of Otto Preminger's characteristic deep-focus compositions, makes a passionate plea to the judge who occupies, during this shot, the essential position of the camera. The body language is Hollywood-statesmanlike. Bowed over, head thrust forward, hands open and outstretched, the lawyer gives the impression of an eloquent supplicant with deep convictions. The speech climaxes with these lines:

> The prosecution would like to separate the motive from the act. Well, that's like trying to take the core from an apple without breaking the skin [he mimes such a coring with his hands]. Well now, the core of our defense is that the defendent's temporary insanity was triggered by this so-called trouble with Quill and I beg the court, I *beg* the court, to let me cut into the apple.

11. An earnest Stewart makes "acceptable" a cynical view of the courts, but only by enacting it in the familiar idealistic codes.

The delivery is classic Stewart earnestness. The lines "I beg the court" come out in the misty near whisper of the idealistic Stewart, his face (which moves into close-up range) along with his whisper connoting intimacy and sincerity. No one could say no to such honest passion, and the judge overrules the state's objection. However, the issue is hardly the preservation of democracy or the future of intercontinental flight; it's a

defense lawyer's cynical ploy to get a rape ruled admissible in the trial of
an accused murderer who—after being acquitted due to the lawyer's
skill—is revealed to have beaten his wife, misled his attorney, and
duped the jury.

The open mention of rape was sensationally new in American film in
1959. Although the wife is played as a "loose woman" who flirts with
men a few days after her rape, the film leaves no doubt that it was rape.
There's also no doubt, however, that the rape is regarded as a violation
of the husband's property. The film suggests that the husband returns his
wife to a life of abuse while skipping out without paying his lawyer. The
lawyer, meanwhile, uses his first successful case as a springboard to a
promising new career. His buddy, an alcoholic, has-been attorney named
Parnell (Arthur O'Connell), rehabilitated by Biegler's confidence in him
as an aide on the case, is invited to become a partner. The film ends with
the two men, at the site of the couple's abandoned trailer, driving off
happily into the sunset. The camera holds on a shot of a broken high-
heeled shoe, sign of the woman who is victimized on all sides, by
a rapist, a violent husband, and an easily manipulated criminal justice
system.

Stewart plays Biegler as a hardheaded, expedient professional. However, the lawyer is written as a wily trickster who scrambles the codes of
sophistication and simplicity as Stewart himself does. *Anatomy* in fact
comes closest of all his films to unmasking the Princetonian, careerist
side of Stewart, which the star's various other masks obscure. A back-
woodsman (the film is set on Michigan's remote Upper Peninsula) who
often seems more concerned with fishing than with law, he is also portrayed as a hipster who relaxes by playing improvisational jazz piano and
even sits in with a jazz band led, in a cameo appearance, by Duke
Ellington (who wrote the film's score). He is also something like a biopic
subject in that he possesses a talent that he makes look easy and "natural."

The film self-consciously uses populist codes of city/country, sophis-
tication/simplicity. The district attorney is depicted as an ineffectual
Thomas Dewey to Stewart's Truman; Dantzer, the assistant attorney
general from the state capital (George C. Scott) is a smooth shark of a
prosecutor. In one irresistible scene, as Stewart/Biegler is about to bring
up a legal precedent for his defense of "irresistible impulse," the judge
(played by the affable Joseph H. Welch, a celebrated sixty-eight-year-
old Philadelphia lawyer who gained national fame by upbraiding Sen.
Joseph McCarthy during the televised McCarthy-Army hearings of
1954) asks about a fishing lure stuck in the lawbook Biegler brings him.
While the prosecutors wait helplessly, the defense lawyer explains the
fine points of frog-baiting to the plainspoken judge. When the judge

finally gets to the precedent, Dantzer recalls the case and concedes, "We're hooked, like the frog."

While the pleasure machine produces delight at the triumph of the "humble country lawyer" (as Biegler melodramatically refers to himself in court) over the "brilliant prosecutor from the big city of Lansing," the film makes troubling the populist codes and the polarities of Hollywood moralism. The childlike faith in the good motives of law that marked studio-era films like *Destry Rides Again* and *Young Mr. Lincoln* is difficult to sustain in the grown-up world. While the press in 1959 was reacting to the sensational first use of terms like *rape*, *panties*, and *sperm*, Preminger slipped past the rapidly loosening Production Code a film in which a likely criminal evades justice while the audience cheers the "homespun" trickster lawyer who gets him sprung.

Anatomy seems an example of a film's effect softened by star casting. Preminger said that Stewart's presence made "a delicate subject acceptable" (Robbins 96). The film blurs the difference between the calculation of a lawyer and the sincerity of an idealist. The courtroom lawyer defends a client despite his own doubts about his innocence and is shown to milk every advantage from the populist symbolism of the opposing attorneys; "I loved that 'humble country lawyer' bit," Parnell says with a laugh while the jury is deliberating.

Most important, the case turns on a principle that renders irrelevant the difference between right and wrong. The precedent for "irresistible impulse" overturns the legal notion that insanity does not depend on the accused's ability to know right from wrong. This might be the cruelest cut to the idealistic frontier mythos of classical Hollywood. One thinks of Henry Fonda's Lincoln reading lawbooks and murmuring, "So that's all there is to it—right 'n' wrong," or Saunders lecturing Mr. Smith on "plain ordinary everyday common rightness." Practicing the law is shown to have little to do with administering "commonsense" justice and everything to do with symbolism and appeals to emotion. When Biegler dismantles the convict's testimony, he steams that "the prosecution has seen fit to put a felon on the stand to testify against an officer in the United States Army."

This base appeal to emotion, of the sort often heard in political campaigns, was nevertheless unlikely to sound ironic or cynical coming from Stewart the Air Force officer. While another actor—say, Charles Laughton, in *Witness for the Prosecution* (1957)—might show more clearly the calculated emotional displays of a trial lawyer, Stewart seldom indicates the difference between sincere indignation and an attorney's "acting" for effect. Stewart had never before played a character who makes his living from public persuasion. We've seen that Stewart sometimes shows a character "acting"—Kemp in *The Naked Spur*, for example; however, he doesn't do so here. If he had, the film would have become the cynical comment on the American judicial system that it appears on closer inspection to be.

On the other hand, the eloquent Stewart idealist of the Mr. Smith model is based on persuasion of "natural" ideals and principles, not skilled calculation within institutional norms and routines. In *Anatomy* the homely, honest primitive melds with the cunning, fast-talking sophisticate. Stewart did indeed make Preminger's "delicate subject acceptable." His presence, along with the familiar codes of the idealistic amateur and the country boy who outwits the city slickers, fashioning fishing lures (as Destry carved napkin rings), supplies the film's "conservative" reading.

Thus a performative, strategic Stewart is nearly a corrupted one; Biegler may look like an older Smith or Destry, but the film is rife with the cynical realism of Senator Paine, Capra's "sold-out" senior statesman. It may well have been "a bit of a shock for some of Stewart's longtime fans to find him in such an adult role" (Eyles 145). However, on this rare occasion when Stewart plays "an adult" without illusions or special vision, a man who knows himself and enjoys his life, the character is a shrewd pro who knows how to manipulate the system in ways that would have sent a disillusioned young "Jimmy Stewart" home to mother.

Anatomy makes explicit the complexity and moral shades of gray that the Mann films injected into the Western. "As a lawyer," Biegler explains, "I've had to learn that people aren't just good or just bad, but people are many things." The film appears to perpetuate Stewart's screen image as a "forty-year-old virgin" (make that—by 1959—"a fifty-one-year-old virgin"), with the "buddy" relationship between Paul and Parnell—a visible Harvey—as loving as that between Glenn and Helen Miller, without the layer of resentment.

The Hitchcock films, which destroy the myth of the phallus, and *Harvey*, which fantasizes the "madness" of nonphallic male subjectivity, were in the 1950s neutralized if not recuperated by the image of Stewart himself. Stewart left the sets of *The Man Who Knew Too Much* and *Vertigo* each day an Air Force officer, and the spectator could leave the theater with the status quo similarly in place. The popular memory of Stewart is untroubled by performances that might seem to shake the sweet young/old man persona down to its bony knees. Ultimately, the *Saturday Evening Post* persona that renders rock-ribbed authority harmless and benign keeps the challenges to the persona from spilling across their celluloid—or videotape—boundaries.

If the Stewart persona is a complex discourse, therefore, why have readings of Stewart been so dualistic, so that to the public the exemplary "down home" Stewart obscures the Hitchcock Stewart and for critics the "dark side" of Stewart overrides the popular persona? Is this the result of a split between the popular and the "seriously" artistic, with a complex, textual Stewart for intellectuals and the nostalgia-driven "real person" for the public? I think not. Stewart's durability has to do precisely with his complexity, the contradictions that await beyond any single one of the star's various images. I return to Richard deCordova's notion that the fascination of stars resides in a "dynamic of secrecy and confession, concealment and revelation that supports discourse on sexuality [and] supports discourse on stars as well" (*Picture* 143). The secret is bisexuality, and the lack of ambiguity with which Stewart's quite ambiguous career presents itself shows how far dominant ideology will go to keep that secret from consciousness.

PART TWO
□□□

Jack Nicholson:
Performance Anxiety
and the Act
of Masculinity
□□□

Hollywood
"Epic"

□□□

There is a shot in *Broadcast News* (James L. Brooks) that got a laugh from an audience in Columbus, Ohio, the day after Christmas in 1987, even though there is nothing particularly funny at that moment in the script. The film, which narrates the operations of a fictional network news bureau, simply cuts to a monitor on which the anchor is giving his sign-off to the evening news program; in the anchor's chair, on an authentic-looking news set, is Jack Nicholson.

It is not my intention to confuse the responses of real audiences with the hypothetical spectator that I generally assume to be implied by the point-of-view structure of Hollywood film. However, the laughter seems to me to pose a number of questions about Nicholson's star persona as a signifier. What were they laughing at—the surprise of seeing a major star in a small, unbilled role; the incongruity of Jack Nicholson impersonating Dan Rather or Peter Jennings; a tacit recognition that Nicholson often plays characters who try to act out incongruous roles; or an awareness that the male "news anchor" himself wears an oversized mantle of authority and performs a presumptuous, impossible role?

Later in the film when this Nicholson/anchor arrives in the newsroom, his walk is heavy and ponderous, his voice low and authoritative. He appears in the Washington bureau on a day when the network plans to lay off a large number of the staff and states his position—well—authoritatively: "If we're not there for each other during the tough times, we're not a news organization." He punches the word "news" in a way that suggests that this man either takes his role too seriously or not very seriously at all; that is, this is not so much a man as a set of roles: anchor, network star, managing editor, formidable patriarch. Similarly, Nicholson is present in this film in the roles of this newsman, guest star, "Jack Nicholson," and working actor taking a part in the script.

The tone of the line reading and of the brief performance is irony.

Whose irony it is—the character's or the actor's—seems also to be an open question. At the same time that the line and the man's bearing are pompous, they have about them a feel of authenticity; one could imagine a network news anchor acting this way on a visit to one of the bureaus. The man's action of coming to the newsroom is clearly motivated and prepared for, although his absurd behavior somewhat undercuts the motivation and suggests the range of subtexts discussed above. The verisimilitude is undermined by an air of mockery that would be absent if the role were played by an actor long typecast as an authority figure, as Leo G. Carroll and Walter Pidgeon were for years.

Broadcast News, after all, is about a young anchor (William Hurt) who doesn't understand the news he reads but knows how to "sell" himself as an authority on it, a concept that illustrates Jean-François Lyotard's assertion in *The Postmodern Condition* that in postmodernity what matters is not the truth of a statement but how convincingly it is performed. In this context Nicholson's style of acting, in which a character's "truth" lies in his performance of an assumed identity, undermines the film's theme of solid competence versus hollow performance by exploding the difference between them. Nicholson's characters often mistake performance for competence, and their "failure," as Robert C. Cumbow describes it, tends to be overshadowed, in terms of spectatorial pleasure, by the actor's exuberant emphasis on performance. The spectator familiar with Nicholson might infer that this anchorman is probably more entranced with his narcissistic performance of an exalted role than he is involved in substantial work. However, the script emphasizes his competence as a managing editor versus the Hurt character's total reliance on "handlers." Thus Nicholson's performance knocks out the character's coherence, eclipsing motivational logic by a foregrounding of performance, ego, and a range of disconnected roles. Furthermore, Nicholson's appearance in *Broadcast News* undercuts the film's theme of substance versus performance by exploding the difference between them. If this film's idea of a journalist of integrity is a puffed-up Jack Nicholson as anchor, then Hurt's airhead newsreader seems just the next step in a rhetoric of simulation.

I've begun with the shortest of what Nicholson calls "short parts" because his style of acting is more easily introduced in a performance that makes a quick impression and is not sustained over the course of a film. When Nicholson plays a starring role, he italicizes the idea of himself as actor and of his characters as actors. His performances construct a seeming verisimilitude, or what Jean Baudrillard calls "the simulacra," whereby postmodern life turns the real into a series of simulations. Whereas in a realistic acting style like the Method an actor imbues a simulated person, a character, with aspects of the real and a belief in individual, liberal humanist subjectivity, Nicholson brings to his simulation a sense of the individual that is itself simulated. This creates an awareness of the character as a construction separate from the actor—who himself might be a simulation—and from concepts of unified male subjectivity.

Nicholson's characters often mistake performance for competence. Since competence, the ability to get things done, is key to male subjectivity, their identities depend on role-playing of the sort that masculinism generally represses and displaces onto woman. One of the functions of most film acting, like that of classical realist film, is to mask signs of its artifice. For the actor this actually means masking a mask, making stylization appear real. What Nicholson does is to deny the "naturalness" of masculinity and stress the mask. This choice caused a reviewer of *The Postman Always Rings Twice* (1981, Bob Rafelson) to complain that "Nicholson's face is becoming a Kabuki mask: it's those triangular eyebrows and the hair receding on both sides of his head and the stylized, leeringly evil expressions" (Kael "Chance/Fate" 179). Nicholson explained in 1983 that he wanted "to attempt the affectation of style within cinematic acting, which is something the audience heavily penalizes you for because they're stuck at the turn of the century; they're only interested in naturalism" (Wolf 36).

Such "affectation of style" allows Nicholson to superimpose awareness onto an unaware character. Nicholson's persona does not operate on the kind of Lacanian misrecognition that, as we'll see, sustains the relationship between film and spectator at Eastwood's films of the 1970s. If anything the Nicholson persona itself dramatizes, acts out, misrecognition, in that a little man thinks that his gender gives him special powers and abilities. The dialectic of James Stewart's persona allows male anxiety an outlet, while containing it within the hypernormality of Stewart's star image. Nicholson brings the anxiety to center stage, literally. By performing "masculine" aggressiveness, rituals, and self-presentation, Nicholson turns an individual man into a representation of "Man." This breaks down unitary masculinity, in Brechtian fashion, into "a series of comportments" (Dort 102), with the paradoxical result that "the coherence of the character is in fact shown by the way in which its individual qualities contradict one another" (Brecht 196). A character's traits are mediated, or "read," in Brecht's term, by the actor, rather than simply "portrayed" by him, emphasizing the character as a social and narrative construction.

In these ways Nicholson's performance strategy can be described as Brechtian "epic" acting. The actor presents himself and his characters as actors of ideologically assigned roles. He does this by "reporting on" a character rather than "identifying" and "emphasizing" with it and appearing to "become" it (Brecht 142). To Brecht acting that divorces the actor from the character separates character from liberal notions of the individual and establishes it as a product of ideological construction and cultural subjectivity. Such a male character would make a spectacle of himself, by experiencing himself as a "masculine" individual rather than the social construction the actor reveals him to be. Thus Nicholson makes a spectacle of himself and of the character. He also constructs a spectacle of masculinism as a set of assumptions about mastery and superiority. These result in a Brechtian *Verfremdungseffekt*, or "alienation effect," which presents character traits as symptoms of the character's conditioning in gender, race, and class, and of the base needs of the human animal.

Masculinity cannot be taken as implicitly understood in a "cinema" (to paraphrase Brecht's use of the word "theater") in which "everything to do with the emotions has to be externalized . . . developed into a gesture . . . must lose all its restrictions so that it can be treated on a big scale" (Brecht 139). This "big scale" refers to the Marxist project of getting the audience to recognize character traits not as motivated characteristics of a given individual, but as signs of ideological cultural construction without which the character is contradictory and incoherent. Thus, when Nicholson explains that "I wanted to be *bigger*" (Wolf 36, emphasis added), he is talking about nothing less than extending classical notions of an actor playing *a man* to implicate *man in general* (or at least white heterosexual American man) in his performance.

Brecht realized that stars could be useful in attaining the "alienation effect." About the first English-language performance of *Galileo*, which took place in Hollywood, with the film star Charles Laughton in the title role, Brecht wrote:

> The principle—that the actor appears on the stage in a double role, as Laughton and as Galileo; that the showman Laughton does not disappear in the Galileo whom he is showing; from which this way of acting gets its name of "epic"—comes to mean simply that the tangible, matter-of-fact process is no longer hidden under a veil; that Laughton is actually there, standing on the stage and showing us what he imagines Galileo to have been. Of course, the audience would not forget Laughton if he attempted the full change of personality, in that they would admire him for it; but they would in that case miss his own

opinions and sensations, which would have been completely swallowed up by the character. (Brecht 194)

Nicholson—quite consciously, if his many interviews are to be believed—moved from the margins of the film industry in the late 1960s to
the mainstream, with the intention of "pushing at the modern edges of
acting" (Wolf 36), introducing advances in postwar theater to Hollywood
film, just as new filmmakers, many of whom became his collaborators,
were integrating strategies of European "art cinema."

Nicholson's approach poses some contradictions to "classical Hollywood Cinema" as I treat it in this study. Many of his films, especially
those of the seventies, scrutinize and problematize male subjectivity.
However, two of the few that do not, *One Flew Over the Cuckoo's Nest*
(1975) and *Terms of Endearment* (1983), were unsurprisingly Nicholson's only "breakout" box-office hits before his guest-star villains of the
late 1980s and early 1990s. Many of the films also utilize identification
structures that are considerably more distanced than the Hollywood norm
as it's usually discussed in film studies. The films that take a subjective
approach vis-à-vis their protagonists, such as *Chinatown* and parts of *The
Shining*, do so ironically; rarely in Nicholson films does point of view
equal mastery, knowledge, or possession.

Nicholson's determination to "unmask" acting precisely by wearing a
mask gives the effect of watching the construction of male identity, and
seeing that identity being constantly "re-earned," in the way in which
Nancy Chodorow, for example, demonstrates that it must be. It may be
true, as Ron Rosenbaum wrote in 1986, that "few men between the ages
of 25 and 50 in America today have not delivered a line without some
imitation or caricature of Nicholson's trademark, mocking, deadpan
drawl" (15–16). However, they are delivering imitations of imitations;
to Brecht the actor "has to learn how to imitate; something that is dis-
couraged in modern acting on the ground that it destroys his individuality." The epic actor should represent "no longer himself as king,
scholar, gravedigger, etc., but just kings, scholars, gravediggers, which
means that he must look around himself in the world of reality" (142).

An example of an epic approach in Nicholson's acting comes early in
Batman (1989). In the Axis Chemical plant, Jack Napier, before he becomes The Joker, picks up his gun off the floor and whirls around to find
that his target, Batman, has disappeared. In facial expressions that describe rather than portray "surprise" and "suspicion," Nicholson's eyes
move deliberately and precisely. The facial expressions seem separate
from one another; each is virtually a mask on which an emotion or reaction is imprinted, as if the actor's face itself were a Delsarte chart from a

late-nineteenth-century handbook of outer movement and precise physical and facial displays of emotions. Thus the character in this film may soon wear a mask, but the actor certainly does wear one, setting up a self-consciousness and mediating the action marked as "present" with the audience's familiarity with conventions and archetypes. Rather than pretend, as realist acting generally does, that the character is a differentiated individual, the like of whom the spectator has never seen, Nicholson's performance puts quotation marks around the character; it recalls *every* character in a similar situation that the spectator has *ever* seen.

Admittedly I am arguing for a radical performance practice in the context of films that are essentially conservative. Indeed, by the time of *Batman* Nicholson's manner of performance had become little more than shtick, eccentric business that met rather than frustrated audience expectations—any radical potential there might be is easily recuperated by the film that encloses it, in this case one of its year's most visible artifacts of corporate capitalism on a massive scale. However, Nicholson became a star in the midst of new filmmaking, audiences different from any the American film industry had ever experienced, and a range of foreign influences not seen in Hollywood since the 1920s. Thus we should examine how Nicholson fitted into the encounter of modernism and classicism that was taking place in American cinema in the late 1960s and early 1970s.

The influence of the nonclassical postwar European "art cinema" on American film at this time has been taken nearly for granted by many film scholars and reviewers of the era and since. Nicholson's appearance on a December 7, 1970, *Newsweek* cover about the "New Movies" confirmed his identification with what became commonly known as "the new American cinema." The new cinema drew its impetus from a range of sources: the ideological meltdown the United States underwent in the wake of the Vietnam War and civil rights protests; Hollywood's awareness of a young audience that rejected the genres (Westerns, war films, romantic comedies, musicals) offered by an industry in severe financial straits; a young cohort of filmmakers excited about the European "art cinema" of the 1960s, especially the French *nouvelle vague* (New Wave), but who were eager to apply to Hollywood narrative the sensibilities of a generation weaned on old movies on television and "art films" in college film societies; a sense—spurred by the 1968 collapse of the Production Code and its replacement by the Ratings System—of a "new freedom of the screen," a feeling that the time had come for Hollywood to "grow up" (be like the Europeans); and a corps of film talents trained to work quickly, cheaply, and efficiently in the exploitation factory of Roger Corman and American International Pictures (AIP), on the fringes of the industry.

Before he happened onto stardom with *Easy Rider* (1969), replacing Rip Torn after the start of production on this genuine sleeper hit, Nicholson worked at AIP and environs for ten years in various capacities—as actor, director, writer, and editor. His early stardom drew on friendships from AIP: with screenwriter Robert Towne; director Bob Rafelson; cinematographer Laszlo Kovacs; and producer Bert Schneider. This group, along with critic-turned-director Peter Bogdanovich, became the nucleus of BBS Productions, "an ultra-hip collective of seasoned Hollywood veterans who introduced timely political concerns into their work" (Cagin and Dray 81). At BBS Nicholson appeared in *Easy Rider, Five Easy Pieces, The King of Marvin Gardens* (1972, Rafelson) and *Drive, He Said* (which he directed but did not act in, in 1971).

Many of the films, including the two Monte Hellman Westerns that Nicholson acted in and co-wrote and the AIP "biker" films, were infused with a romantic existentialism in which attractive young rebel heroes (and, much less often, heroines), faintly redolent of Brando in *The Wild One*, were pursued by an inescapable fate, in the guise of the Establishment. Such films put a spectator in the position of flattering masochism; the characters bear little responsibility for their actions. Like Meursault in Camus's *L'Étranger*, they are motiveless, doomed, and stripped of control by existence itself.

BBS Productions and the counterculture were finished by 1973 or so. "The new Hollywood cinema" began by the mid-1970s to fall victim to low box-office returns and renewed formulaic moviemaking. Nevertheless the cinema and currents of the 1960s continued to have a hold on Nicholson. He worked consistently with some of the era's innovative American directors, such as Arthur Penn and Mike Nichols, and was also drawn to such European "art cinema" directors as Roman Polanski and Milos Forman, as well as Stanley Kubrick, who is harder to classify. He turned down the roles that Robert Redford eventually took in *The Sting* (1973) and *The Great Gatsby* (1974) to work with Michelangelo Antonioni on *The Passenger* (1975) at a time when the Italian "master" was a pariah in Hollywood due to the debacle of *Zabriskie Point* (1970) (Shepherd 100). His interviews in the 1970s and 1980s are peppered with references to Godard, Brecht, and Beckett. He said in 1985, at the height of the space-film craze, that "I don't want to make a better 'alien' movie. If I did, it would probably reflect that period we're so fond of. I'd do it *Alphaville*-style: Take out all the art direction and mix in a little *Krapp's Last Tape*" (Walker 58).

"The New American Cinema," a loose designation like most of those applied to similar national and historical film "movements," attempted, as Robert Phillip Kolker explained in 1980,

> to come to terms with narrative itself, the story and its telling, and to realize the possibilities inherent in *refusing* the classical American approach to film, which is to make the formal structure of a work erase itself as it creates its content. These directors delight in making us aware of the fact that it is a film we are watching, an artifice, something made in special ways. (Quoted in Schatz, *Old Hollywood* 223)

David Bordwell and Janet Staiger more skeptically acknowledged that such films as *Easy Rider*, *Thieves Like Us* (1974, Robert Altman), *Sugarland Express* (1974, Steven Spielberg), and *American Graffiti* (1973, George Lucas) shared some of the characteristics of nonclassical films. Citing Thomas Elsaesser they noted that these films "revealed unmotivated protagonists, picaresque journey structures, and a self-consciousness that slipped into pastiche, parody, or 'the pathos of failure'" (373). They agreed that "in the classical film, the puzzles are born of *story*: what is in her past? what will he do now? In the art film, the puzzle is one of *narration*: who is telling this story? how is the story being told? why tell the story this way?" (374). To Bordwell and Staiger, who use Coppola's *The Conversation* (1974) as their case in point, stories in the "new cinema" still operate by means of a conflict-complication-resolution model; characters are causal agents and their traits consistent. Meanwhile, the films "absorb . . . narrational strategies of the art cinema," controlling them within "a complete conservatism of style" (375–377).

Nicholson then becomes a subversive force in 1970s films that adhere basically to the classical narrative paradigm but at least imply criticism of the dominant order, often largely through Nicholson's highly prominent role-playing. In *The Last Detail*, a convincing example of Nicholson's deconstruction of character and the masculinity that determines it, nothing besides Nicholson calls attention to its own production. However, the actor's performance, which in that film dominates virtually every scene, derails the naturalistic character motivation perfunctorily present in the script, showing an actor staging a man who is staging himself. Nicholson's performance shifts the film from a screenplay (based on Darryl Ponicsan's novel) that bemoans the male's restriction by the system to one that shows the man's desperate reliance on an oedipal system. By the end of the film, the hypermasculinist military man Badass Buddusky has been revealed as a robotized creation of dehumanizing institutional naval rituals, which he professes to loathe but without which—it has been revealed by the actor—he would have no identity. As he and his partner stride out of the film's last shot, muttering about their "chicken-shit" lives but headed, the viewer knows, to continue them, his lack of recognition recalls that of Mother Courage at the end of Brecht's eponymous play, continuing to push her cart and sell her wares even though the war she profits from has taken away all her children.

It can be said that Nicholson's initial Hollywood films, *The Last Detail* and *Chinatown*, set up a dialectic between the modernism of Nicholson's performance and the classical cinematic form that parallels the dialectic between subversion and restoration of gender and race issues. *The Shining*, on the other hand, does meet the definitions of modernist "art cinema" set by Bordwell and Staiger (374), and Nicholson's performance in it is by far his most purely "epic." Nicholson appears to want to synthesize a Brechtian awareness of ideology with the classical cinema's capacity for involving an audience. When he speaks of trying "to drip acid on the nerves" (Rosenbaum 49), he seems out to alienate the audience from the class complacency reaffirmed by classical film while still "immersing" them (in Brecht's term) in an affecting diegetic experience.

This synthesis, which the "new Hollywood cinema" in general did try to achieve in the 1970s, is basically unstable, ensuring—along with an increasingly conservative climate in America as the 1980s approached— that the movement would be relatively short lived (as the paradigmatic European ones had been). The gloomy air of Kolker's 1988 revision of *A Cinema of Loneliness*, in which he refers to films "that carry on an ideological debate with the culture that breeds them [but] never confront that culture with another ideology, with other ways of seeing itself, with social and political possibilities that are new and challenging" (10) sums up the failure of the possibilities briefly held out by the "new Hollywood" and sketches the outlines for the conventional course Nicholson took in the 1980s, a surrender for which he was well compensated.

All this will make my treatment of Nicholson's films different from those of the other actors in this book because Nicholson's performances turn character into a discourse on male subjectivity. For male spectators, to identify with *The Last Detail* or *Chinatown* or *The Shining* is, to paraphrase Christian Metz, to receive and to release an oddly parodic and ironic experience of self in a time period—the 1970s—marked by trouble for masculinism. These films cannot be treated in terms of how masculinist subjectivity or the male gaze is constructed; they must be analyzed in terms of how the characters are portrayed and how Nicholson often "narrates" rather than embodies characters, undermining male autonomy by revealing masculinity as an act. Furthermore, the films' view of masculinity is often self-reflexive, in that the movies themselves show how masculinity is constructed and maintained. They explore the conventions—social, narrative, and cinematic—that have kept the constructions viable.

Thus I sometimes need to discuss what goes on within the cinematic representation rather than simply to examine the means of representation. This may put me as a critic in the paradoxical position of discussing characters as discrete individuals in films that I see as deconstructing the notion of a discrete individual. In order to show the difference between the ways in which men in Nicholson's films model themselves on masculine notions of identity and the actor's demonstration of that modeling, I must play devil's advocate and discuss to a certain extent the representation of the representation, the "real people"—or, more to the point, the "real men"—whom the characters are represented as trying to be.

As we explore Nicholson's key films in the 1970s, the question to ask is whether Nicholson, by coyly undermining masculinism at a time when it perceives itself as under siege, is critiquing it or rehabilitating it, finding an alternate way for it to exist, fashioning the kind of fake self-consciousness that serves as a disclaimer, like the person who apologizes for being a racist before telling an ethnic joke. Can a commercial cinema turn masculinity into a discourse, without the "given" at some point reclaiming its accustomed position?

9

What Exactly Is "Easy"?: Nicholson at BBS

□□□

Nicholson in *Easy Rider* was already thirty-two in an era when the ad line for *Wild in the Streets* (1968), a youth-protest fantasy film from Nicholson's home studio, AIP, proclaimed, "If You're 30, You're Through!" Nicholson's age, his receding hairline, and his characters' sympathy with sixties youth culture dampened by their inability to be an actual part of it, made him a transitional figure. Like Clint Eastwood, his presumed polar opposite, Nicholson connected sixties counterculture to an older tradition. Eastwood managed to combine anti-Establishment impulses with the interests of the self-same Establishment, while Nicholson did the reverse, reviving the figure of the postwar "antihero" in its lineage through Garfield, Clift, Brando, Dean, and Newman, but revising genres and story structures that asserted the values and assumptions of the Establishment without rethinking patriarchy.

In his breakthrough performance in *Easy Rider* Nicholson plays George Hanson, the alcoholic lawyer son of an old Southern family who meets the young hippies Wyatt (Peter Fonda) and Billy (Dennis Hopper) in jail, where he's sleeping off a bender, and takes up with them on their motorcycle trek across the country. The role is a good example of the contradictions that keep Nicholson oddly ahistorical. Told to wear a helmet for motorcycle riding, Hanson brings his old high school football helmet. While Wyatt and Billy, obvious references to Western legend and all, are one-dimensional icons, Hanson conveys disillusionment ("This used to be a damn good country; I can't figure out what happened to it," he says), crossed with the sense of being stuck between two cultures. He belongs neither to disaffected youth nor to the indifferent middle class.

The sense of not belonging connects Nicholson's early stardom to a durable and ongoing type of male protagonist who began to turn up some twenty years earlier, shortly after the end of World War II. Usually categorized by an overused and underdefined term, antihero, this character is alienated by a confining world that doesn't accept him. In the Eastwood chapter I distinguish antiheroes from "anti-Establishment heroes." There are, however, two closely related types of antiheroes: those who cannot accept the lives that have been planned for them or who are rejected by others whose values the audience is led to criticize, and antiheroes of whom the spectator is invited to disapprove, despite the characters' attractive qualities. These latter protagonists overreach the bounds of morality and civilization or contemptuously reject the normative values of society and are left finally to stew in their own failure and bitterness.

What these two strains of antiheroism have in common is failure to complete the oedipal identification with the father and occupy a properly male role. These protagonists fail to move beyond the desire for the mother and join with a mate in a marriage that would perpetuate the traditional familial pattern. Jim Stark (James Dean) in *Rebel Without a Cause* (1955, Nicholas Ray), who is among the first type, escapes a domineering mother and a henpecked father to "play house" with a runaway "family" made up of a young girl who needs to learn her "proper" female role as wife and mother and a fatherless young boy who seems to act as Jim's "son."

On the other hand, Hud Bannon (Paul Newman) in *Hud* (1963, Martin Ritt) is coldhearted and unethical, while his father stands for old-fashioned values of integrity and hard work. Although, as his father tells him, "You got all that charm goin' for you and it makes the youngsters want to be like you," Hud's shunning of an honorable-father role model and his disinterest in monogamous heterosexual love relationships mark him as a lost man. The spectator is primed to reject Hud's hedonistic values because they go against the ideal of responsible manhood in a film coded as "realistic" (that is, such fantasy figures as James Bond or Dirty Harry are not held to these responsibilities but represent an escape from them).

Rebel Without a Cause and *Hud* exemplify the 1950s version of a subgenre that had long existed in American film, the "social problem drama." The subgenre's new success in theater and TV, as well as film, coincided with the new postwar predominance of the Method, or Stanislavski system of acting, which, simply put, sought to create "realism" and honesty by teaching actors to act "from the inside out" and to channel the characterization through their memory and emotions. The emphasis on behavior that is "natural" rather than "performed" lent itself to the "honesty" and "realism" of the new generation of playwrights (Tennessee Williams, Arthur Miller, William Inge) and filmmakers (Elia Kazan, Nicholas Ray, Sidney Lumet).

Bobby Dupea in *Five Easy Pieces* (1970), Nicholson's first starring role and the one that solidified his star status, seems cut from the antihero mold at which Method actors so excelled. Bobby is a musical prodigy turned prodigal, an unhappy young man who has fled his family of musicians to drift among the working class. When the film begins we see him working with the crew in an oil field, which is in CalforNia (although most of the accents sound Appalachian); he lives with a dependent, simple-minded waitress named Rayette (Karen Black) and hangs out with an equally simple-minded worker and drifter named Elton (Billy Green Bush). The film is divided into two sections. The first takes place among the low culture of oil fields, trailer parks, and bowling alleys, all to the steady twang of country music. The second concerns the high culture of the Dupea family compound on Puget Sound, a sterile environment on which the sun never shines, where glass doors wall people off from one another, and where Chopin and Mozart sound stark and arid and linger as oppressively as the Tammy Wynette songs of the first section.

The characters of these worlds are tailored to American stereotypes—the ignorant hillbilly and the repressed intellectual. Bobby's sister, Tita (Lois Smith), is a distracted and sexually frustrated spinster; his brother, Carl (Ralph Waite), a conceited prig who, literally rigid, wears a neck brace and walks stiffly. Most rigid of all is the patriarch, who has had two strokes, can't speak, probably can't hear or understand, and must be hand fed and pushed around in a wheelchair, virtually a stone statue of "the father."

Bobby is one of the few attractive characters we see; he conforms to the earlier antihero model as he has failed to grow up to the life marked out for him by his middle name—"Eroica"—a life of heroic musicianship. The hyperbolic polar alternatives, and Bobby's impossible relation to them, might appear to put the spectator in the familiar position of alignment with the protagonist in an attitude of superiority. However, the unacceptability of both worlds leaves the film without a moral position, unlike the earlier antihero films, and posits an existential hopelessness more typical of European directors such as Antonioni or Resnais. The last scene of *Five Easy Pieces*, in which Bobby leaves everything—his girlfriend, car, and jacket with wallet and identification—at a filling station and hops aboard a logging truck bound for Canada, seems to foreshadow Nicholson's film with Antonioni, *The Passenger* (1975), in which a man exchanges his clothing and passport with those of a dead man, taking that man's identity.

There are also strong hints of the nihilism and misogyny of the British "angry young men" of the late 1950s, not to mention the American Beat writers. Thus this film, which is so identified with late 1960s rebellion, actually has an oddly out-of-time aura that smacks as much of middle-aged male bohemianism left over from American literature of the fifties as it does of 1960s counterculture. The rancid odor of the *Playboy* Philosophy–Kinsey Report 1950s wafted even more strongly through Nicholson's next film, *Carnal Knowledge* (1971, Mike Nichols). *Five Easy Pieces* thus represses its own historical moment (as does a most classical Hollywood film, *Mildred Pierce*, according to Linda Williams). Bobby's escape to Canada resonates of the flights of draft evaders, even though the film makes no mention of Vietnam or antiwar protest. It is just as abstractly ahistorical as the conventional Hollywood movies *Five Easy Pieces* was supposedly counteracting.

A typical Hollywood film might pose the deadening influence of the symbolic order—of home, family, and responsibility—against the freedom of escape and wide-open spaces. In the postfrontier, industrial America of *Five Easy Pieces*, however, there is no escape. The fields of the imaginary are now pocked with oil derricks. Trailer parks contain drastically confined versions of home, family, and responsibility. Bosses—father figures with their own repressive laws—wield power. Palm Apodoca (Helena Kallianotes), a garrulous hitchhiker, appears to speak for the film when she rails against "all the crap" of the consumer society created by "Man"—a stinking, contaminated place one can only flee in the hope of finding a frontier somewhere, perhaps Alaska, where it will be, as she says, "cleaner."

The film's women function as mirrors for the male protagonist; in fact, it is in its sexual issues that the film shows confusion about its male protagonist as well as its roots in sexist ideology. The film uses the male fear of being confined, embarrassed, or disapproved of by women to demonstrate his impossible relation to both cultures. Rayette, alternately pathetic and smothering, is a male nightmare vision of intimacy, manipulative and dependent. Like Betty (Sally Struthers) and Twinkie (Marlena MacGuire), two women Bobby picks up in a bowling alley, Rayette is a childish sex object. Unlike the other two women, Rayette DePesto (as in "pest") has stayed around long enough to become a nuisance. Pregnant by Bobby, she becomes one of the responsibilities he looks to evade. The film attempts to render these women as sympathetic characters by pointing up their victimization. In the midst of a children's game, Banbury Cross, that Bobby and Elton play with a half-dressed Betty and Twinkie, Betty tells a story that indirectly indicates that she was neglected as a child. Rayette, too, becomes an object of pity, mixed with the contempt with which Bobby regards her. Furthermore, moments such as a full shot of the two of them, both clothed, Rayette wearing a skimpy minidress, cuddled on a bed with the camera in the position of

12. Nicholson channels his performance energy into Bobby's frustration; it then emerges as hostility toward women. With Karen Black and Billy Green Bush.

someone standing at the end of the bed, do nothing to break the Mulveyan model of the woman's mutual possession by male protagonist and spectator.

The women on the island—Tita, Bobby's sister, and Catherine (Susan Anspach), his brother's fiancée—represent different kinds of arrested development. Tita, overweight, awkward, and bespectacled, seems an incorrigible old maid (in her early thirties). Catherine, graceful and self-confident, would seem the hero's match in a conventional romance, but she serves to show Bobby's unsuitability for such a relationship; what he sees in the mirror she holds up is his own emptiness.

Nicholson's project of artistic risk taking and spectatorial self-examination still reproduces women's diminished role under patriarchy. The "second wave" of feminism came about partly as a reaction to the sexism of the antiwar and civil rights campaigns. "In . . . politically progressive movements . . . women were experiencing [a] discrepancy between male activists' egalitarian commitment and their crudely sexist behavior toward female comrades" (Moi 22). An irony of the male left, as reflected in postwar art especially, is that rebellion against the dominant order is too often blindsided by a misogyny and phallocentrism that ensure the order's continuation, a situation the Nicholson–Nichols–Jules Feiffer film *Carnal Knowledge* seems almost to recognize. Furthermore, the influence of European art cinema doesn't necessarily entail a more enlightened depiction of gender. "Sexist ideology," wrote Claire Johnston, "is no less present in the European art-cinema because stereotyping appears less obvious" (135). In short, although the "New American Cinema" aspired to revise and counter "classical cinema," it too is marked by contradiction, not to mention misogyny.

Of a(n easy) piece with the misogynistic treatment of women is the emphasis on Bobby's sexual conquests. A long scene shows Bobby and Betty having sex while moving around a room, finally landing on a bed. After they climax (simultaneously) Bobby sits up, revealing a Nicholson grin and a T-shirt that reads "Triumph," the word referring to more here than a make of motorcycle. Even though Catherine senses from the first that she and Bobby are all wrong for each other, on the force of Bobby's sexual prowess and spectatorial desire the plot at first overrules her, as Bobby overrules her objections in a bedroom scene that idealizes acquaintance rape; the man knows his desires, and the woman needs him to show her hers. The hero's forcefulness in the face of frustration (or at least every kind of frustration but sexual) was probably a key factor in making Nicholson a star in spite of the film's hopelessness. It also pulls the film into fantasy; it might follow that a man as lost and confused as Bobby Dupea would be impotent, but Bobby pulls women into bed as easily as James Bond.

If women show Bobby what has happened to him, his inability to adapt to his father's values and do what was intended for him to do *are* what has happened to him. The lack of paternal reconciliation or recognition leaves him without identity. The film was popular because it seemed to depict a generation's disaffection with the values of its parents. However, it locates rebellion and confusion in men alone, and shows how lost the male subject is when he abandons the subject position destined for him by the father. As Kaja Silverman writes about the Oedipus complex, "the 'normal' Western subject is fully contained within a predetermined narrative" (*Subject of Semiotics* 136); there really is no other option. Although many of Stewart's films for Mann, Hitchcock, and Capra show the problems and difficulties of an oedipal reconciliation with the father (which Capra's and Mann's films do eventually force into being), this "new Hollywood" film depicts a hopeless universe by showing no alternative to the symbolic and little recourse for the subject in the imaginary; in fact, Bobby seems to act out the confusion of the subject "trapped within that order [the Imaginary]."

> Unable to mediate between or escape from the binary op-
> positions which structure all of its perceptions, [the sub-
> ject] will fluctuate between the extremes of love and hate
> toward objects which will undergo corresponding shifts in
> value. Moreover, the subject will itself be capable of iden-
> tifying alternatively with diametrically opposed positions
> (victim/victimizer, exhibitionist/voyeur, slave/master).
> (Silverman *Subject of Semiotics* 158)

Moreover, with its patriarch (who resembles Johannes Brahms) the
film poses a quandary, since music is a form that—like film—combines
the symbolic values of language, form, and rationality, while appealing
to the imaginary. Thus one of Bobby's few moments of liberation comes
when he bolts from his pal's car in a freeway traffic jam and plays a
Chopin étude on an upright piano on a flatbed truck. In this instance
music is subversive, celebrating freedom from social restrictions; however, the concept of classical music itself as a feminizing "civilization" is
subverted as well.

Nicholson's acting at this time is mostly naturalistic and understated.
While his even, reedy voice might seem to lend itself to a calm placidity,
it almost never does. Instead there is a vocal tension that the character
can be heard trying to keep under control. The face, similarly, is often
kept impassive, as the character tries to maintain an even temperature
while he's boiling. Accordingly Nicholson shows an impressive range in
this film, notably at times when the character's attempt to be calm and
civil won't hold and he breaks into a rage, as in a shot in which, after
trying to stay calm with Rayette, who is passive-aggressively trying to
goad Bobby into taking her to Puget Sound with him, he gets into his car
alone and explodes into a flailing, inarticulate fit, or in the famous scene
in which he carries on a desperate, tearful monologue with his father.

The ironic, self-aware style Nicholson developed later can be seen in
its early stages here. The character performs one role in the working-
class milieu, affecting a southern drawl, whose artifice the spectator discovers only gradually, and another way on the island, where he at least
tries to behave with cultivated civility. But the spectator who knows
Nicholson's later, stylized acting might be surprised to find that an often-
recalled scene—the "chicken salad" sequence at a diner, in which Bobby
antagonizes a waitress while trying to get his order the way he wants it—
is played rather quietly; its effect comes from the intensity of Nicholson's vocal inflections and the accelerating rhythm of his diction. This

outward calm should not be taken to connote a macho strong silence. Rather, Nicholson, by the film's end, conveys the feeling that the character keeps himself from constant explosions of anger or despair by affecting an even disposition, just as he affects a dialect and behavior to fit his surroundings.

Nicholson's style is eclectic, although explicitly Brechtian and absurdist from the mid-1970s on. He has never been a Method actor, although he attended classes at the Actors Studio for a short time in the mid-1970s; Jeff Corey, one of Nicholson's two acting teachers (the other was Martin Landau), says that he teaches the Delsarte chart and that he also took elements from Brecht, Peter Brook, and Stanislavski/Strasberg (McGilligan 38). Nicholson's career has reflected this eclecticism; this might explain why one of the few references to Nicholson in Naremore's *Acting in the Cinema* comes in a discussion of the Method. Referring to the scene in *Five Easy Pieces* in which Bobby talks to his father, Nicholson told an interviewer that he drew on the same sort of "affective memory" that is at the heart of Method acting (203).

Five Easy Pieces draws its air of hopelessness from the male oedipal compulsion to identify with the father and the impossibility of a man's living as a unified subject if he refuses. The inadvertent affirmation in *Five Easy Pieces* of the patriarchal identifications at which the film lashes out shows that the "new American cinema" was not so new. The movie provides a textbook demonstration of why second-wave feminists needed to rebel against the established order that the men *thought* they were rebelling against (it also shows why little about the culture changed in the long run). Ironically, Nicholson needed to enter the belly of the Hollywood beast in order to develop a true subversive streak. The problem of Nicholson's next important characters, Buddusky in *The Last Detail*, Gittes in *Chinatown*, and Jack Torrance in *The Shining*, is not that they haven't identified with the patriarchal system that holds them. The trouble is that they have.

10

"A Staging of the Father": Nicholson and Oedipal Narrative in *The Last Detail* and *Chinatown*

□□□

Many feminist writers have acknowledged the patriarchal role of woman as "actress." Male fears of acting as unmasculine have their basis in the patriarchal notion of femininity as a series of roles and of woman herself as "actress." Luce Irigaray posits femininity as an elaborate role that must be played, one in which "the woman loses herself, and loses herself by playing on her femininity" (84). Lucy Fischer writes that women "have been urged to embody a wide range of dramatis personae: from earth mother to temptress, from madonna to whore" (64). However, patriarchy's posing of feminine performance against masculine nature is a displacement onto woman of the notion that male gender identity might also consist of playacting, and a denial of any quality of constructedness or "performance" in masculine identity. This leads to a paradox. On the one hand, in patriarchy men *act*—they do things—while women *are*. On the other, male identity is seen as natural, while female identity is capricious and defined by a series of acted-out roles. Indeed, several key Nicholson films reveal the patriarchal masculine role itself as one that must be put on and performed.

Far from being static and stable, masculinity is in constant danger of slipping away, of losing its coherence; thus it must be repeatedly reearned (Chodorow 33). We can see examples of this in male genres such as the Western, in which courage, stamina, and prowess with guns must be proved again and again. While woman, assigned to her passive position, need only stay "in her place" to keep her gendered identity, man must "act" in order to keep his. This dialectic of "doing" and "being" goes further; as Silverman bluntly puts it, "men can only be aggressive and potent if women are passive and impotent" (*Subject* 140). Moreover, the oedipal complex of identification with the father is so fragile that the male subject repeatedly convinces himself of its efficacy by reenacting as drama the process by which manhood is earned and retained.

In the politically retrograde 1980s, for Hollywood narratives ceaselessly to repeat the oedipal process was to reassert the dominant order. One example out of many is *Field of Dreams* (1989, Phil Alden Robinson), a restorative film in which the 1980s atone for the 1960s across the common ground of a baseball diamond. The "field of dreams" condenses male aspirations and self-idealizations; all struggles, father-son or black-white, can be leveled. The whispered phrases "If you build it, he will come" and "Ease his pain," whose pronouns turn out to refer not to a baseball hero but to the protagonist's dead father, move Ray Kinsella (Kevin Costner) from being a somehow still anomic sixties rebel to becoming a fully integrated traditional male whose wife watches from the porch as father and son finally learn to play ball with each other. George Hanson or Bobby Dupea at last turns into George Bailey or Jeff Smith as each era plays out its conflicts about masculinity in terms of the male subject's relation to his father.

The "benign patriarch," Robert Kolker's term for an implied figure who predominates in films of the 1980s (255), represents only one side of the oedipal coin. It is a fearsome, primal father with whom the male child bonds in the Freudian scenario, but the male subject represses those negative elements and reconstitutes them as positive values in order to complete his identification process. "The means by which the male subject 'dissolves' his Oedipal desires are important" (Silverman *Subject* 141), these desires being the subject's transformation of the mother into his object of desire and a "cultural imperative to *be* his father" (140). As Silverman says:

> If everything goes according to cultural plan, he identifies with his father by internalizing the latter's authority or "voice." This operation is in essence an assimilation of cultural prohibition, and it forms the superego. The male child will henceforth measure and define himself in relation to this repressive paternal representation, and thus to his society's dominant values. (*Subject* 141)

Much of the instability in male subjectivity lies in this concept that a subject identifies with a figure who represents law and restriction, a figure toward whom the subject holds deeply repressed resentments. This volatile relation gets acted out in narrative. Hence Roland Barthes refers to "the pleasure of the text" as "an Oedipal pleasure (to denude, to know, to learn the origin and the end), if it is true that every narrative . . . is a staging of the (absent, hidden, or hypostatized) father" (10). So the drama of male subjectivity is a struggle to bond with an authority figure whose hostility and benignity exist implicitly in a perpetual dialectic. "Death of the Father," writes Barthes, "would deprive literature of many of its pleasures. If there is no longer a Father, why tell stories? . . . Isn't story-telling always a way of searching for one's origin, speaking one's conflicts with the Law, entering into the dialectic of tenderness and hatred?" (47).

Stewart's films tend to emphasize the bond with a benevolent symbolic father (think of Jeff Smith's compulsion to emulate his saintly, slain father). Eastwood's films eradicate the conflict with a repressive father by having the subject take on himself the characteristics of the Law against an authority defined as feminine. Nicholson's films express a loathing of oedipal identifications but demonstrate the male subject's inability to get beyond them.

As I've mentioned, the "new Hollywood," like the *nouvelle vague* in France a decade before, sent dozens of young first-time directors behind the camera, where most of them rapidly self-destructed (including Nicholson, whose *Drive, He Said* [1971] was barely distributed). However, as an August 1974 *Time* article, issued in the flush of *Chinatown*'s success, noted, Nicholson survived the demise of the "new Hollywood" and transferred his power from the offices of the short-lived independent, BBS, to the boardrooms of the major studios ("The Star with the Killer Smile" 44). When Nicholson shifted to "Establishment Hollywood," one might assume that he "sold out," acquiescing to making conventional films while cashing in on his commodity value as a star.

However, the situation was not nearly so simple; it took at least a decade to close the deal on the sellout. On the face of them, the new films *were* conventional commercial products. He went from an existential identity-crisis drama with heavy overtones of the Beat writers, and an examination of sexual mores written by a *Village Voice* cartoonist (*Carnal Knowledge*) to his first major-studio projects, both released in the first six months of 1974, a military comedy-drama in which he played a sailor, and a private-eye film.

Of course, such oversimplification overlooks the fact that both *Chinatown* and *The Last Detail* were written for Nicholson by Robert Towne, his longtime friend from the Corman days. But perhaps because Nicholson was now in the mainstream industry, he played characters who were at the same time generic types and fully formed individuals who are the plot's causal agents; this is a change from the lost drifters of *Easy Rider* and *Five Easy Pieces*. However, it is just at this time that one notes a definite change in Nicholson's acting style, away from naturalism and toward a multilayered stylization. Through this stylization Nicholson shows up, as it were, man's "growth rings"; like the chart showing the phases in a tree's life that Madeleine shows Scottie in *Vertigo*, these are the stages and layers that make up a character's construction and self-delusion.

Identity construction in Western culture conditions the white male to think of himself as master of his destiny. At the same time he represses the fact that his father and other father figures are his masters. As he molds himself by emulation into a perception of himself as master of others, he must forget that other subjects, who have been conditioned as he has, can be master of him. He does this by setting himself up as superior to some, such as women, who reaffirm his masculinity, and male members of other races and groups, who validate his racial and class superiority. He does it by engaging in competition with "peers," glorifying any mastery over others as some sort of great accomplishment. And he does it by keeping the cycle going, setting up himself as "father" to "sons" whom he will ridicule and belittle (castrate) if they fail to cast themselves in his image.

Billy ("Badass") Buddusky, the protagonist of *The Last Detail*, is a sailor who seems never to go to sea but awaits his orders on a naval base in Norfolk, Virginia, and, in the action of the film's plot, escorts to military prison in New Hampshire a hapless young seaman who's been sentenced to eight years for the trivial but politically sensitive crime of stealing forty dollars from the polio contribution box, a favorite charity of the base commander's wife. At first Buddusky talks his fellow escort, Mulhall (Otis Young) into racing the prisoner up to Portsmouth and taking five days to spend the rest of the week's per diem allowance on the way back. However, when he sees the pathetic callowness and naïveté of Meadows (Randy Quaid), their eighteen-year-old prisoner, Buddusky takes it upon himself to "show him a good time." This means initiating him into "manhood"—teaching him how to assert himself, how to ask for and get what he wants (which in this case means insisting on having the cheese melted on his hamburger the way he likes it), getting drunk, holding his own in fights, and having his first sexual experience (with a prostitute).

In a film starring a father figure such as Eastwood or John Wayne, a young boy might be guided through similar rituals, but the stakes would be life or death—the completion of a massive cattle drive, the crucial support for the older man in a desperate gun battle, even a last chance at Grand Old Opry stardom (in Eastwood's *Honkytonk Man*). The rituals might also involve a temporary separation from the father, as if the youth's "wild oats" have to be sown in an uncontrollable burst of nature which defies the restrictions of the father, or at least pretends to, even if the father gives his tacit approval.

In *The Last Detail*, however, the triviality of the rituals, as opposed to the weight they are given by Nicholson/Buddusky, calls them and the "manhood" they ostensibly signify into question. Even though it could be said that behind the entire plot is a feminized chain of command, caused by "the old man's old lady's favorite do-gooder project," the film spends most of its time on the pointlessness and emptiness of masculine hegemony. Mulhall, the more practical of the two escorts—perhaps because he is black and knows better than Buddusky how much there is to lose—insists that taking the kid through male rites of passage will "only make it harder" for him to spend eight years in the brig, a line that turns prophetic when Meadows's newfound assertiveness gives him the nerve to try to escape, the acquisition of "manhood" proving a futile accomplishment contradicted by the rules by which these three are bound.

Buddusky's stake in the passage-into-manhood rituals are high. He needs to prove that the steps do "make a boy into a man," that they work. His adamant insistence reveals a desperate insecurity, the need to have his way of life validated. At one point Mulhall upbraids Buddusky for "turning that boy's head around to prove what a fuckin' big man you are. You're a lifer like me." This seems to be the film's point: that displays of masculine prowess and, indeed, masculinism itself, are meaningless when the constraining social apparatuses of modernity confine and virtually negate male autonomy. "Military discipline" depends on the harnessing of phallic ego, aggression, and energy.

This is not to suggest that the film sees authoritarian structures the way Eastwood's Dirty Harry series does, as feminizing. Rather, the film shows the military as an institution of the repressive father. It does this in the way that it shows the navy holding up methods of threat and intimidation to be emulated; for example, consider this tirade, which the executive officer at the Norfolk base (Clifton James) gives Meadows while introducing him to his escorts: "Do you know why they are taking you to the brig? Because they're mean bastards when they want to be and they always want to be, and you can take my word for it, they aren't about to take any shit from a pussy like you. If they do, they'll get reamed out and they know it." During this speech, the camera, which holds on a two-shot of Buddusky and Mulhall, shows them looking at the floor in embarrassment and rolling their eyes at each other. These "lifers" know that they're being billed as "mean bastards" for the purpose of intimidation and humiliation. The speech shows that all meaning here comes around to the institution: "they'll get reamed out and they know it." They are "mean bastards," "badasses," at the pleasure and for the purposes of the navy. Furthermore, the Ex. O. has been shown in the previous scene with the two escorts as a nice guy when at ease, so his speech itself is

13. "The Badass." An actor's demonstration of an elaborately constructed masculinity. With Otis Young.

clearly an act, an expression of his "public" persona as opposed to his "private" personality.

Buddusky, however, doesn't separate so easily into public/private. His public side (which seems conflated with Nicholson's performance of it) is an expression of bravado and toughness that he has internalized to the point where there is no interior, no "private" that the character knows or understands. The private side of Buddusky that Nicholson does show is uncontrolled, debilitating rage; this is a man who, for all his (or Nicholson's) charm, can get abusive. We see this three times in the film, once with a surly bartender who won't serve the underage Meadows; once in a beer-soaked hotel room scene when he tries to get the lamblike (and appropriately named) Meadows to "take a poke at me," Meadows's refusal launching Buddusky into a snarling, inarticulate rage during which he punches a lamp and smashes his fist against the wall; and at the end, when he frenziedly pistol-whips Meadows and needs to be pulled off by Mulhall. These frightening outbursts of anger set a pattern in Nicholson's films, of definitive moments when the character becomes an embarrassment, when one would like to look away but can't, moments that eventually become knitted into an entire film, *The Shining*, in which Nicholson shows how short is the space between man's elaborate civilization and his evolution from violent, primal origins.

It's hard to know immediately if the film attributes Buddusky's violent rage to his subservient position within the massive structure of the U.S. Navy or to man's persistence, in trying to embody an image that cannot be lived up to, in pumping himself up into a replica of the Father who oppresses him. I vote for the latter, although the film could be accused of reflecting the views of sociologists who theorize a "crisis in masculinity," a result of modern bureaucratic structures that negate individuality, challenges from women and other "marginal groups," and loss of economic power to serve as the "provider." "The concept 'crisis,' " according to Arthur Brittan, "involves the realization that [men's] power and authority can no longer be taken for granted" (183).

But such a notion of male "crisis," with its attendant ideas of trivialization and impotence, assumes constructed masculinity as an intrinsic good, not as something that itself needs criticism in order to change. *The Last Detail*'s "crisis" stems from the exposure of masculinity as a measure of man's capacity to bend things and people to his will. Eastwood films in the early seventies justify and rehabilitate male egoism. This contemporary movie rather gently shows the rites of masculinism that allow man ignorantly and complacently to continue to assume his superiority, and that such ignorance and blindness keep the dominant order moving on its implacable way.

Accordingly Buddusky grabs at any victory, such as correcting a marine at Portsmouth for forgetting to "pull a few goddamn copies" of paperwork, and "hustling" some men in a bar at darts, propping up his self-image as "the badass." The U.S. military, probably the safest target for a leftish Hollywood film just after the U.S. withdrawal from Vietnam (right-wing stars like Wayne and Eastwood stayed away from military topics during this period), may oppress and demean its members, but the white male keeps himself going with lies and male fantasies that, the film and Nicholson strongly suggest, he must know but still can't admit aren't true.

The blue language that made the film a minor cause célèbre on its release gives the men a kind of verbal power, as if by surrounding themselves with a shield of constant obscenity they construct a private language that keeps intruders out. But, as I found during my undergraduate years, when I worked summer jobs in factories where the *f*-word was used in practically every sentence and as every part of speech, profanity and obscenity lose their shock value after a while. With overuse they become as banal and humdrum as the rest of Buddusky's and Mulhall's

14. "Doing a man's job." Nicholson playing Buddusky playing "the Badass," with the naval signifiers "guaranteeing" masculinity and the cigar thrown in for (extra) good measure.

lives (they actually become a kind of jargon, and we know how deadening that can be).

The film has few close-ups, little subjective or point-of-view work. Ashby favors group shots and, in some important moments, such as the climactic one when Buddusky and Mulhall chase the fleeing Meadows in the snow, long shots. The spectator is posed as a fly on the wall, a position not of involvement but of interested, distanced behavior observation. The group shots emphasize Nicholson's small stature, especially when he is shown between the much taller Quaid and Young. Combined with his military-shaved head and the dark blue uniforms against his pale, almost pink skin, amid gray winter landscapes, this makes Buddusky comically scrawny and pallid, especially compared to the machismo ("I am the badass!") whose would-be embodiment he is.

The kidding showmanship for which Nicholson later becomes well known really shows itself here for the first time, perhaps the BBS outsider's response to working in Hollywood. Nicholson plays Buddusky as an actor, intent on attracting attention and approval. The ads for *The Last Detail* showed a bare-chested, tattooed Nicholson, wearing a mustache and a sailor's flat hat and pointing a cigar. The pose, like so many of Nicholson's performances, suggests something a bit off balance, since the signs of masculinity are so overdetermined as to suggest parody. Part of this feeling of things being not quite on the level comes from the fact that the ad image is so self-consciously a pose. And poses are exactly what Nicholson's Buddusky continually strikes. He appears variously as a concerned (but not too openly concerned—that would be unmanly) father figure; authoritative professional (as when he manages an unconvincing straight face and asks Meadows if his "trouble with the cops" was "in the nature of a serious offense"); signalman instructor ("Some people have a flair for this sort of thing," he pronounces. "I, for instance, I have a flair for this sort of thing"); and dashing would-be seducer of a young woman (whom he bores to distraction) at a party ("There's nothing like being on the sea. Doing a man's job," he mock-solemnly intones).

Furthermore, each of Buddusky's "accomplishments"—his demonstration of the signals, his fight with the marines in the men's room, his confrontation with the surly bartender—is carried out with a flourish, with "a flair for this sort of thing," and followed by Buddusky's own (highly favorable) critique of his performance. With his eyes, his slightly exaggerated facial expressions, and stylized "Gestus" (Brecht's appropriation of a German word meaning both gesture and gist, "an attitude or a single aspect of an attitude, expressible in words or actions" [Brecht 42]) Nicholson adds the actor's layer of self-awareness to the character's behavior. He contributes an element of criticism to Buddusky and italicizes the sailor's efforts at machismo. This is Nicholson's first strongly Brechtian performance, or what Brecht called "acting in quotation marks" (Esslin *Brecht: A Choice of Evils* 115), in which "the character who is being shown and the actor who demonstrates him remain clearly differentiated. And the actor retains his freedom to *comment* on the actions of the person

15. Buddusky's performance impresses mainly himself. With Nancy Allen.

whose behavior he is displaying" (Esslin *Brecht* 116). It is this "quoting" that qualifies the customary softening of an unsympathetic character by the charm of the star who plays him. On the other hand, Nicholson actually invites the spectator to imagine the unpleasant character apart from the charm of the actor. Bernard Dort cites Walter Benjamin's comments on epic acting as "as series of comportments . . . both concrete and discontinuous." These comportments could be contradictory; the actor "could at one moment be as playful and light-hearted as a comedian in the silent cinema, and at the next be as contorted and self-absorbed as a product of the Actors Studio. . . . It is the spectator who is astonished, and who is compelled to understand and contemplate it. Character is a result of this; something shared between the audience and the actor; not a given" (101–102). The illusion involved in acting is not effaced; rather the actor's awareness of the illusion calls attention to the character's masks, his illusions about himself as an individual.

Accordingly the change in Nicholson's roles as he moves into mainstream film is not only that he now plays men who have completed the oedipal separation from the mother and identification with the father, but that—unbeknownst to them—the resultant male identity is a cage these men are now stuck in. The image of the father is so imposing and unreal that the subject, no matter how hard he tries, can never match it. The character never recognizes that the power he craves is also the power that oppresses him. Eastwood in the 1970s indulges the spectator in fantasies that close the gap between the subject and the idealization. Nicholson highlights a lack, whose negotiation is the preoccupation of dominant male subjectivity (Silverman *Acoustic Mirror* 2), and shows the difference between the "badass" Buddusky wants to believe he is and a frustrated, subordinated man. Although much of this awareness is conveyed comically, the spectator laughs with Nicholson at Buddusky, in the kind of laughter akin to criticism.

Nicholson's next film, *Chinatown*, carries even further the concept of the Nicholson male as one who acts out a masterful role, this time using much-vaunted intelligence, experience, and logic as his tools. He is a private eye in late-thirties Los Angeles, a role and milieu that put him in a familiar place in myth and genre. J. J. ("Jake") Gittes (Nicholson), heaving a world-weary sigh, tells his "associate," "Walsh, this business requires a certain finesse." *The Random House Dictionary* (1980) defines "finesse" as "delicacy or subtlety in performance . . . skill and adroitness in handling a highly sensitive situation." Nothing could better describe the self-image of Nicholson's Gittes, a careful, self-confident, glib detective who dresses immaculately, parts his (sparse) hair down the middle, and does business in a smartly furnished office, with Venetian blinds (one of the film's many nods to older crime-film styles) that were "just installed on Wednesday."

Gittes's demeanor suggests that he has seen and done everything, an attitude that contrasts with the warning of the wealthy Noah Cross (John Huston): "You may think you know what you're dealing with, but believe me, you don't." By the end of *Chinatown*, a bitterly revisionist "hard-boiled" detective film, the cool Gittes is shown up as a kind of prize fool, with virtually every deduction he's made proved disastrously wrong. His mistake, like that of Stewart and Hitchcock's Ben McKenna, is that he "knows" too much. While Hitchcock and Stewart show Ben's uncertainty, in Roman Polanski's Eastern European fatalism/absurdism Gittes is never uncertain for a moment.

In an article in which he contrasts *Chinatown* with the figure of the "hard-boiled" detective as developed by Dashiell Hammett, Raymond Chandler, Ross Macdonald, and others, John G. Cawelti describes the archetypal detective

> not only as a figure outside the institutionalized process of
> law enforcement, but as the paradoxical combination of a

man of character who is also a failure. . . . He is the most
marginal sort of lower-middle-class quasi-professional.
Yet unlike the usual stereotype of this social class, he is a
man of honor and integrity who cannot be made to give up
his quest for true justice. He is a compelling American
hero type, clearly related to the traditional western hero
who manifests many of the same characteristics and conditions of marginality. (561–562)

In addition Cawelti writes that "one of the most deeply symbolic clichés
. . . is the hero's refusal to do divorce business, in fact one of the primary
functions of the private detective" (565). Gittes, on the other hand, does
what he euphemistically calls "matrimonial work," terming it "my
métier."

Nicholson and the script entangle Gittes in a mass of contradictions
between the character and the archetype and within Gittes himself. Cawelti calls Nicholson's Gittes "a character who is not quite what he
seems" (564), but the characterization is more complicated than that.
Take, for instance, the scene just quoted above—a conversation with
Mrs. Mulwray (Faye Dunaway) in an expensive restaurant. The look of
the scene evokes Hollywood glamour. Mulwray/Dunaway, just wid-
owed, is lit softly from above as she wears an elegant black mourning
dress and hat with a veil. Gittes/Nicholson wears an impeccable dark
blue pinstripe suit with white silk pocket handkerchief and showy print
tie. The lighting is classical; while the woman is lit to look alabaster and
ethereal, the man's look is warmer, tanner, and earthier. "The Way You
Look Tonight," a song Astaire sang to Rogers in a musical, issues di-
egetically from an unseen piano as the two converse warily.

Even though Polanski's intention to make the film in *noir*ish black and
white was overruled by Evans, the scene, like much of the film, could be
in a forties romantic thriller; Nicholson and Dunaway seem stand-ins for
Bogart and Bacall. However, subtle differences jar the spectator's perceptions. Throughout the film the detective's "finesse" is undercut by an
errant vulgarity that Gittes seems helpless to control. The women in the
film (Mrs. Mulwray and the actress [Diane Ladd] hired to "play" her)
seem posited, as in Westerns, as arbiters of civilization, and also as
mirrors in which men see their true selves. Gittes makes his slips in front
of them, the most spectacular one (which makes a spectacle of him)
being the long dirty joke that Gittes tells Duffy and Walsh as Evelyn
Mulwray (in Dunaway's entrance into the film) appears behind Gittes in
a deep-focus shot. While the women, like the victims and *femmes fatales*
of "hard-boiled" novels and *films noirs*, are mysterious and hide secrets,

Gittes himself is something of an enigma—a smooth-talking, suave detective who seems oddly unable to control himself and winds up overtaken by forces beyond his understanding.

This film is famous partly for Nicholson's appearance in the middle third of it with a large white bandage taped across his nose. This renders the glamour treatment distinctly ridiculous. The gauze-covered nose is often mentioned by critics as proof of Nicholson's willingness to do whatever a part requires and of his lack of the narcissism popularly associated with actors. It is Gittes's narcissism, however, of which the bandage seems a mockery, one that goes directly to a quasi-comic exhibitionism and narcissism that mark many Nicholson characters, beginning with these two written by Robert Towne. The archetype, described by Cawelti, of the private eye as a relatively poor man is violated, introducing an element of class envy and insecurity. Gittes's suits and ties are meticulously stylish and manage to seem both fussy and gaudy, showing a concern for haberdashery that is heard even in Gittes's complaint about the "goddamn Florsheim shoe" that he loses in one of his late-night stakeouts of the Los Angeles riverbed. In fact, the Nicholson characters in both *The Last Detail* and *Chinatown* act very concerned with their appearance and do a lot of preening. The payoff of the montage with Buddusky and the woman at the party is that he likes the way the navy uniform "makes my dick look." At another point Buddusky is shown slicking back his hair and touching up his mustache with great flourish. His sailor's flat hat, which he habitually rolls up, adjusts, and refashions, serves as what Naremore calls an "expressive object" for Nicholson throughout that film.

The moment in which Gittes/Nicholson is first shown with the bandage on his nose can nearly be viewed as an enunciation, which sets up the character as an object of spectacle. The back of Gittes's head is unfocused in the foreground, with his associate Walsh focused in the background, talking about something else but reacting with dismay to what he sees. A cut then reveals the object of dismay—Gittes's nose. Gittes in close-up rolls his eyes as if exasperated and embarrassed by something in the conversation, although the spectator reads it as a reaction to the tape on his nose.

This shot makes clear what has been implicit before in the film—that Gittes/Nicholson's body is on exhibit. The bandage obscures the actor's face so much that it serves as a mask. The theatrical mask, far from hiding a character's identity, exaggerates and abstracts a particular aspect of identity. In this case it serves as a reminder of Gittes's vulnerability and frailty—in several scenes it actually is a bleeding wound. However, I don't mean to suggest that it signals castration but rather that it embodies a return of the male repressed; it is a marker of fragility that contradicts and undermines Gittes's slick male logic and self-confidence. Like a more urbane Buddusky, Gittes seeks to forget how powerless he actually is; the bandage that glares from the center of his face makes such forgetfulness impossible.

As I suggested earlier, the bandage calls an unusual amount of attention to the actor behind the character; the spectator can't help but think of Nicholson the star not caring how *he* looks, daring to appear ridiculous. However, as soon as one is tempted to think of Nicholson, the actor-as-hero, one is reminded that it is a problematic hero who comes dressed in adhesive tape and gauze, dripping blood from a nearly surreal attack. Again, in commenting on a character by telegraphing the fragilities and undermining the facade, Nicholson recalls Brecht. It's as though, as in Brechtian theater, the actor came on screen accompanied by a banner explaining his character's condition.

Of course, Nicholson has been commenting on Gittes even earlier. As Cawelti mentions, the "hard-boiled" hero is best known to popular audiences from the screen versions of *The Maltese Falcon* and *The Big Sleep*. Any actor who takes on such roles also takes on the icon of Bogart, an association of which Nicholson and the film are entirely conscious. In the very first scene Gittes responds with extreme boredom to the traumatized reaction of a client to photos of his wife having sex with another woman, as if Gittes believed no one with class would get upset over a spouse's affair. Without getting out of his swivel chair, Gittes/Nicholson puts a cigarette in his mouth, turns to a liquor cabinet in back of him, gets out a bottle, and pours. In close-up he is shown with a heavy-lidded squint like Bogart's; he finally lifts his eyebrows, the cigarette in his lips giving him a Bogartian sound as he says, "Down the hatch." Only once more, late in the film, does he perform a specifically Bogartian gesture. In his first close-up as Gittes, however, Nicholson has done enough to code the character as "Bogart" that the spectator may be prompted to "read" the character as being "like Bogart" or of the same type as Bogart. It is as though the character idealizes himself as Bogart and has internalized some of his mannerisms.

Such an association, especially in the nostalgia-mad early 1970s, works to undercut the character. Anyone would suffer in comparison to Bogart's Marlowe or Spade, and so Nicholson is signaling, in Brechtian fashion, that he knows that Gittes is bound to fail. More important is the fact that in 1937, when the film is set, Bogart was still a fourth- or fifth-billed Warner Bros. contract actor, playing supporting parts as heavies and mob henchmen; he starred as Spade in 1941 and Marlowe in 1946. So Gittes could not have seen Bogart's iconic detectives, making Nicholson's mediation even more obvious; Nicholson plays on the audience's and the actor's perception of him in a way that makes Gittes the object of an audience that may also recall the Belmondo character's conscious emulation in Godard's *Breathless*.

This is another way in which Nicholson isolates his acting from the character, a separation that reveals both the character's behavior and the acting as performed constructions. Even Gittes's name, which comes from that of producer Harry Gittes, a mutual friend of Nicholson's and Towne's who would later coproduce *Goin' South* (Shepherd 102), serves to undercut the myth—the name of a crony (especially in light of articles such as the 1974 *Time* cover story about Nicholson's penchant for teasing his friends with pet nicknames) substituted for names with legendary connotations. (Cross's thug Mulvehill is also named for a Nicholson-Towne acquaintance.) Furthermore, in light of Nicholson's unusual propensity for characters with his first name (in *The Shining* and *Batman*), J. J. ("Jake") Gittes is very close to John Joseph ("Jack") Nicholson. Thus Nicholson personalizes the icon and quietly banalizes it, stripping it of its mythic import.

Gittes's gashed nose objectifies the character/actor in another way as well. The thug who cuts his nose is played by none other than the film's director, Roman Polanski. In his article "Hitchcock the Enunciator" Raymond Bellour analyzes the opening scenes of *Marnie*, in which the director's on-screen look toward the heroine in his trademark cameo seals the enunciation of her as the object of the film's gaze. If the need to set up others as objects in a narrative is fueled in the theories of Mulvey and Bellour by sadism, Polanski's on-screen violence literalizes even more than Hitchcock's coercive on-camera gaze the protagonist's visual objectification. This is especially true since the look in films is often the starting point for violence, even if it is a desire for sex confused with a desire for violence.

Polanski's slash diminishes Nicholson-slash-Gittes's two most attractive traits—his wisecracks and his mastery as a detective, as seen in his ability to look and investigate. ("You're an awfully nosy fella," says Polanski/thug. "You know what happens to nosy fellas? They lose their noses.") If the detective's nose—the figurative site of his ability to "snoop," to "sniff out clues"—is thought of as connected to vision in his capacity for investigation, then Gittes's lacerated nose undermines the heroic mastery that could give pleasure, shifting it from Nicholson/Gittes as subject to the star/character as something of an object who goes on acting the part of subject.

Cawelti notes that the ending of *Chinatown* is "almost contrary to that of the myth. Instead of bringing justice to a corrupt society, the detective's actions leave the basic source of corruption untouched" (564). He also calls "the potent perversity embodied in the figure of Noah Cross . . . reminiscent of the primal father imagined by Freud in *Totem and Taboo*" (567). The revelation of Cross's incest with his daughter Evelyn is the second-to-last layer of the narrative that Gittes/Oedipus unravels; the final one is the fact that the primal father controls all the apparatuses (governments, courts, police) that could possibly put a stop to him.

The presence of John Huston as Cross, even though he has only about 15 minutes of screen time in a 130-minute film, carries enormous resonance. According to Nicholson:

> "There was a kind of triangular offstage situation. I had just started going with John Huston's daughter [Anjelica], which the *world* might not have been aware of, but it could actually feed the moment-to-moment reality of my scene with him. '*Are you sleeping with her?*'" intones Nicholson, in an unmistakable imitation of John Huston's line from that scene. (Rosenbaum 17)

This subtext, which involves Huston as an intimidating father figure on screen and off, puts Nicholson at a vague disadvantage that adds to Gittes's distinct powerlessness in the face of Cross's money and power. This is compounded by the fact that Huston was, of course, the director of *The Maltese Falcon* and a friend of Bogart's.

It seems appropriate that one of the fathers of the genre being "revised" should be unveiled as the sire of a bottomless evil that devours everything in its wake. Huston's screen presence is so overwhelming that it almost obliterates a strong personality like Nicholson. Not only do Gittes's claims to myth diminish in its shadow, but Huston's ripe, hammy delivery, his deep facial pouches and lines, and his satchel-like mouth suggest in Cross an atrocious malignancy. Yet Gittes's struggle against him is not a fight of good against evil, but one of dueling male egos. A long climactic scene between Huston/Cross and Nicholson/Gittes in Evelyn's backyard, a Panavision two-shot in one take, opens with Gittes confronting Cross with the evidence—a pair of Cross's glasses Gittes found at the bottom of Mulwray's saltwater pond—that he killed Hollis Mulwray—and with his knowledge that he is the father of Evelyn's daughter. It ends with Cross disarming Gittes and making him take him to the girl, in Chinatown. Huston delivers the line to his henchman, "Claude, take those glasses from him, will you," with a kind of nonchalant authority that is chilling in its presumption.

But Nicholson/Gittes has delivered lines with the same presumption of knowledge and rightness throughout the film; Nicholson's reading of lines like "C'mon, Mrs. Mulwray, you've got your husband's girlfriend tied up in there" shows Gittes's assumed mastery of a situation; it also refers back to the genre, in which such detectives, and in particular Bogart, delivered lines with the subtext "Don't kid me." So sure is Gittes that Evelyn is lying to him that "Mulwray's girlfriend" is actually her sister that he bullies her into telling the truth, as detectives traditionally revert to force when deduction fails them. Nicholson bites on a cigarette, evoking Bogart's slurred speech: "I'll make it eashy for ya," he snarls—and slaps her with each of her "lies."

At the end of this scene, not only has Evelyn revealed a worse corruption than Gittes could have detected but he has just added to her brutalization; he is one more male beating and abusing her. Ultimately both he and Cross try to master and control people; Gittes just isn't nearly as good at it. Once again the attempt at identification with the father only brings a demonstration that what the male has identified with and perpetuates is a talent for oppression, a fact that the white male in his complacency discovers only when some of the oppression rubs off on him (as it did on American men during the Vietnam War, which provides a thinly veiled subtext of this and other generic revisions of the late 1960s and early 1970s).

Garrett Stewart, comparing *Chinatown* to *The Long Goodbye*, Robert Altman's 1973 Raymond Chandler revision, calls both films "highly centripedal . . . taking their focus and emotional center from the mentality of their heroes, who appear in nearly every scene" (27). The consequence of this is that the spectator becomes trapped into accepting Jake's lower-middle-class white male perceptions, perceptions that might approximate a spectator's own. To Gittes, Cross's money and status make him "respectable." Evelyn's aloofness casts her as a *femme fatale* whose mystery translates as deviousness and destructiveness. As Virginia Wright Wexman points out, Gittes's prejudices about gender cause him to make the common male mistake of tagging the female victims of crimes as their perpetrators (*Roman Polanski* 98). Similarly Hollis Mulwray, an upright, conscientious man, appears from the "centripedal" viewpoint as a pale, scrawny Milquetoast, a utilities nerd with "water on the brain."

Most centrally, Chinatown to Jake is "a subjective locale, a ghetto in the mind" (Stewart 28), the white male's landfill for social ills and imagined wrongs, site of everything that such men are incapable of understanding or doing something about. Jake's return to Chinatown for the plot's disastrous climax is an acting out of his compulsion to repeat. He has said earlier in the film that when he worked in Chinatown before, he "tried to keep someone from being hurt, and instead ended up making

16. An overshadowed Gittes. The discovery that the male has identified with a talent for oppression.

sure that she was hurt." With his beating of Evelyn and misinterpretation of her victimization until it's too late, we see how that earlier tragedy happened. Jake is too busy trying "snidely to outface and so beat the system," as Stewart puts it, to recognize that he does its bidding (27). The line represents an unconscious prophesy, just as Chinatown represents for Jake the return of the repressed.

Wexman sees the film as a upside-down rendering of the classical spectator-protagonist relation. The film's many shots of Gittes peering in from the far edge of the Panavision frame encourage a structure whereby the spectator follows the detective hero into the scenes of crimes, gaining with him a kind of mastery over them. Finally, however, Gittes is exposed as a spectator rather than a causal agent of private-eye myth. The movie's spectator is left to sort out the bigotry of the genre, the presumption and brutality of the mythic hero and American capitalist culture's confusion of moral hierarchies. For Wexman, Gittes's "culturally conditioned displacement of guilt onto the weak" causes the otherworld of Chinatown actually to embody his own guilt and degradation: He finds himself in "a world in which the individual is helpless in the face of the complex intrigues surrounding him" (99).

Chinatown and *The Last Detail*, Nicholson's formal entries into mainstream Hollywood stardom, elegantly dismantle the central classical principle of the protagonist as individual and causal agent. Moreover, they do so with a purposefulness and precision not even attempted by the BBS films, which in some ways were more conventional. Buddusky and Gittes fail to recognize the subjectivity that cancels their vaunted individualism. Ironically Jack Nicholson rides these vehicles to stardom in a system that elevates the concept of the individual to exaggerated, all-encompassing importance. Thus Nicholson as star actor enters a collision course on which the contradictions of spectatorial expectations and his star persona are forced eventually to confront each other and themselves. Nicholson was able to make *The Shining*—the culmination of his effort to push past the humanism and naturalism of Hollywood—before the contradiction caught up with him.

Masculinity
and Hallucination:
The Shining

□□□

Patriarchy is born!
—Overheard at a screening of Kubrick's *2001*, as the ape-
man finds that he can use a bone as a weapon

We have seen in *The Last Detail* and *Chinatown* the difference between
how characters view themselves and what Nicholson shows, setting up
tension by giving subtly Brechtian performances that open a space between character and actor. In Stanley Kubrick's *The Shining* (1980)
Nicholson plays out a more abstract, less differentiated idea of the male
subject, but one as dependent as the others on role-playing and illusion
and as specific about the construction of white male masculinity.

The difference between actor and character in *The Shining* is paradoxically both more and less distinct than in the earlier films—more distinct
because the more insane and robotized Jack Torrance becomes, the more
one is aware of the histrionic heights to which the actor is pushing himself. At about this time the phrase "over the top," meaning beyond conventional limits of naturalism, humanism, and mimesis, becomes regularly
attached to descriptions of Nicholson's style. Nicholson does not forget
Brecht's dictum that "even if [the actor] plays a man possessed he must
not seem to be possessed himself, for how is the spectator to discover
what possessed him if he does?" (193). Nicholson's "bigger" style often
contradicts a scene's ostensible action, making his broadly visible "acting" a definite distraction. For instance, Nicholson often performs in a
way contrary to what "Jack Torrance" is saying, as in the very threatening scene in which he tells his son, Danny, that he loves him while
looking as if he might break his neck. Brecht wrote: "When [the actor]
appears . . . besides what he actually is doing he will at all essential
points discover, specify, imply what he is not doing," so that "the alternative emerges as clearly as possible" (137).

On the other hand, the difference between character and actor is less distinct than before because Jack Torrance melds with a star persona and mannerisms that by 1980 are very well defined—the arching eyebrows; the smirking, electric smile; the insinuating, nasal voice. As with James Stewart in the 1950s, Nicholson's star persona is fully implicated in the character in a way that it wasn't in his earlier films.

The close connection between actor and character is literalized, as in *Chinatown*, by the character's name. The name originates in Stephen King's novel and Kubrick was reported to have worried that having Nicholson play a character with his own first name would be "distract-ing" (Wilson 54) (not the first or last time that Kubrick in interviews has seemed [pretended?] not to understand his own films; the purpose would seem to be to *have* it be distracting). The effect is an estrangement of usual star/character dichotomies, as if "Jack Torrance" were—ab-surdly—impersonating "Jack Nicholson."

Furthermore, in doing what he calls "pushing at the modern edges of acting" (Wolf 36), Nicholson adds a strong element of the absurdist style of acting, in which the self, as Virginia Wright Wexman explains,

> contains no core of authenticity but rather is constituted out of a series of roles. Absurdist actors dramatize the ab-sence of a center out of which these roles are generated by using the occasion of their performance to problematize the relationship between role-playing and identity. The ab-surdist emphasis on the self as a series of roles parallels poststructuralist notions of fragmented subjectivity. ("House of Games" 3)

Obviously the distinction between the two projects is fine, since both attack the ability of the actor to project—and the audience to believe in—the notion of identity as coherent and unitary. While Brecht sees identity as an illusion engendered by capitalism and class systems, Beck-ett or Ionesco would see the self as a product of man's useless insistence on imposing meanings and "essences" where there are none. Indeed, while absurdism in general has been seen as deriving from a range of sources, from Rabelais and *commedia dell'arte* to German expression-ism, Martin Esslin saw Brecht's "alienation effect" as actually working much more effectively in the antirational, motiveless absurdist theater than in Brecht's didactic theater (*Theater of the Absurd* 360–361).

Accordingly Jack Torrance instinctively puts on and takes off roles assigned to him as a male in society—the eager and obsequious job interviewee, loving husband and father, family breadwinner, loyal employee, hardworking writer, and hail-fellow-well-met with Lloyd, the bartender, sophisticated man of society.

Jack seems a pastiche of Nicholson characters, a term Fredric Jameson uses to characterize the film as a whole. Like George Hanson, the out-of-sync rebel who wears a football helmet on a motorcycle trip, Jack Torrance is an out-of-sync sophisticate who wears an old faded jacket at a society ball. Whereas Bobby Dupea was an alienated musician, Jack is a frustrated writer. His attempts at rationality and deduction, like his speech to Wendy about ethics and principles, and his triumphant recognition of Delbert Grady as the caretaker who murdered his wife and kids, recall the insecure detective Jake Gittes. His male bravado covering limitless anger recalls Badass Buddusky. Perhaps most important is a quality that Rosenbaum sees in a performance I haven't discussed—Nicholson's R. P. McMurphy in *One Flew Over the Cuckoo's Nest*—"a pathological impulse behind the drive for pure liberation, a self-absorbed quality that ignores the destruction that 'liberation' can bring upon more fragile souls" (17).

Nicholson does not abandon Brecht's concept of the actor as one who shows character as an ideological construction. As he falls deeper into madness and the manipulations of his ego by the patriarchs of the Overlook Hotel, Jack comes to illustrate a remark by Earl Jackson, Jr., that "phallocentric culture is a hallucination," that is, a vision the male subject wants to have because it shows him a gratifying image of himself as powerful, important, and autonomous. At the same time the patriarchy encourages the self-image because it perpetuates the dominant order. Nicholson appears in this film as a kind of Nicholson-cartoon character (while *The Shining* itself asks to be seen, on one level, as a cartoon), as a composite of his overconfident, self-destructive characters of earlier films, and as a prototype of the husband/father in American capitalism. He also comments on the horror movie madman, in effect helping Kubrick put quotation marks around a genre.

If much classical narrative can be seen as a reaffirmation of values and of an order endangered by events in the story, Stephen King sees horror working in a similar way:

> Monstrosity fascinates us because it appeals to the conservative Republican in a three-piece suit who resides within all of us [sic]. We love and need the concept of monstrosity because it is a reaffirmation of the order we all crave as human beings . . . and let me further suggest that it is not the physical or mental aberration in itself which

horrifies us, but rather the lack of order which these situations seem to imply. (Quoted in Carroll 199)

Similarly, when he was making the film, Kubrick is said to have phoned
King to ask, "Aren't all ghost stories fundamentally optimistic?" because
they assume a life after death (Wilson 42).

Noel Carroll in his book *The Philosophy of Horror* construes horror as
confronting its spectators with a being, a monster, which is shown to
possibly exist, to threaten, and to be impure (27–28). Under King's
terms Carroll's monster would be a threat to our established notions of
existence, order, and propriety. In the novel the monstrous results from
an inversion of the accepted order: The father is supposed to be the provider and protector of the family. When he turns on those whom he
should protect—the wife and child—and becomes the threat to home
and security, the effect is horror (as it would be in life; David Cook calls
the film "an account of America's long-concealed history of domestic
violence and child abuse" [*A History* 882]). What is then required is for
the male child to reclaim the mother and subvert the horrific father by
summoning Hallorann, who is black and fits perfectly the stereotype of
the loyal servant who saves his master's child (Shirley Temple established the same sort of bond with the "uncle" types in her films). This
formulation may sound simplistic, but King's novel does work a variation on a formula whereby "the humans regard the monsters they meet as
abnormal, as disturbances of the natural order" (Carroll 16), the latter
being in this case the "natural order" of the family.

Robin Wood in "The American Nightmare: Horror in the 70s" sees
horror as based on concepts of repression and the other, especially as
they are contained in the family. He finds some seventies horror films
"progressive" because they bring out horrors that society represses in
order to maintain such institutions as monogamous heterosexual marriage and capitalism. Both of these theories have major problems, however. Carroll, in the early chapters of his book, appears to posit horror
fiction as a usually restorative kind of narrative (the kind that Wood calls
"reactionary"), but in a later chapter, entitled "Horror and Ideology," he
backs away from ideological implications like those to which King
frankly admits, offering examples of horror stories that do not end res-
toratively and sometimes missing even the ideological undertones in
those. In *Rosemary's Baby*, for example, "Satan is birthed" (201) indeed, but the ultimate horror is Rosemary's mother instinct, which
proves stronger than her revulsion at discovering that she has given birth
to the devil's son. As for Wood, the fact that he offers as his model of a
progressive, antirepressive horror film *The Texas Chainsaw Massacre*

(1973), in which a young woman is prolongedly tortured and hacked to death, tells us all we want to know about the gaps in his thinking, a point made by Tania Modleski in an article, "The Terror of Pleasure," about which I'll have more to say later.

Carroll's and Wood's theories are of interest in that they help show how the film of *The Shining* works against conventional definitions of horror. Kubrick subverts the restorativeness of King's plot so that whereas in the novel the hotel wanted Danny's powers, in the film it wants Jack to carry on its history of murder and oppression. The novel operates on the feeling, redolent again of the Oedipus myth, that something is wrong, with the something becoming more and more threatening as its shape becomes clearer. In the film it is very hard to pinpoint what is wrong. As many commentators have noted, Jack seems crazed from the beginning; "something wrong" seems a normal state for the Overlook and the Torrances. The only real change is that the stilted, deliberately pleasant manner that Jack, Wendy (Shelley Duvall), and Ullman (Barry Nelson), the manager, affect around each other in the film's first half-hour perceptibly falls away after the Torrances begin their isolation together.

The "order" of which King and Carroll speak seems shaky in the film. Danny has his premonitions of blood and terror even as Jack is at his interview; Wendy nonchalantly explains to the pediatrician (Anne Jackson) about how Jack, in a drunken rage, had dislocated Danny's shoulder. This trouble in the family is there in both versions, but in King's it foreshadows and sets up motivations for Jack's later attacks on his family, establishing the eventual conflict between Jack and the Overlook against Wendy, Danny, Hallorann, and "the shining." In the film this disorder is covered over by an aura of normality; Wendy describes Jack's dislocating Danny's shoulder as "just the sort of thing you do a hundred times with a child in a park or in the street." However, in Jack's retelling to Lloyd, the bartender, what emerges, absurdly mixed up with the father's expressions of love and duty, is contempt—"I wouldn't hurt one hair on his goddamn little head. I love the little son of a bitch!" In Jack's version the dislocation incident occurred three years before; in Wendy's it was only five months earlier; men's tendency to consign their violent episodes to "history" becomes one of the film's central issues.

It is with revelations such as these, which the film presents in such deliberate but unexceptional ways, that every event seems part of a normal continuum, that the film reverses Carroll's and King's notions of order and Wood's notion of repression. In addition, a concept explicitly central to Carroll's argument and implicit in Wood's is that of "affect." "The genres of suspense, mystery, and horror derive their very names from the affects they are intended to promote—a sense of suspense, a sense of mystery, a sense of horror" (Carroll 14). Linda Williams asserts further that the most disreputable genres are those that elicit from their spectators/readers the same base physical responses they draw from the characters: in horror, screams; in the woman's picture or "weepie," tears; in pornography, orgasm (*Hard Core* 5).

To Wood disreputability, affect, and repression are bound up with one another. The horror film exposes hostility toward others (of race, nationality, gender, sexuality, and class), which—even though repressed—drives the operations of society. According to Wood horror films are subversive because they do violence to established institutions of order and show the tensions within them. The problem with this idea, as Modleski shows, is that in such films "the female is attacked not only because . . . she represents sexual pleasure, but because she represents a great many aspects of the specious good—just as the babysitter [in *Halloween*] quite literally represents parental authority" ("Terror" 163). Modleski worries that it is the slashing, bloodletting, and killing that appeal to the horror film's audience, and that the desire for these exists outside a desire for narrative, connecting the terror(ism) to an ego gratification like that served by Eastwood's quasi vigilantism. Horror may exist (at its most benign) for its reaffirmation of order, but it surely also exists for its "affect." Kubrick's film subverts both of these functions on one level, in order to lead the spectator to deeper horror on another.

The horror *is* the order. As I mentioned earlier in this chapter, Robert Kolker theorizes a guiding patriarch in eighties cinema; in criticism indebted to Lacan and Metz, Kolker writes that the "hailing of the subject into the imaginary realm . . . reverses the Oedipal process. The subject is not cut off from comfort and sustenance, he is offered them. He is given an illusion of power. Rather than being positioned against or at the mercy of the patriarchy, the subject is put under and made witness to its protection" (255). In a chapter on Spielberg Kolker refers to films that operate under such a system, not those that make it their subject matter as Kubrick's film does. In *The Shining* the apparatus of society is treated as unconscious. This is why the film shows effects but not their causes. A key to this approach is the "narration" within the film of Mr. Ullman, the hotel manager. Ullman, a pleasant but completely impersonal man, interviews Jack and later leads the Torrances—and the audience—on a tour of the hotel. Among the little tidbits of history that he mentions, in the offhand manner of a tour guide, is that the hotel was built on an Indian burial ground, "and I believe they actually had to repel a few Indian attacks while they were building it." He says this only a few minutes after he has drawn the Torrances' attention to the "Navajo and Apache motifs" in which the lounge was decorated. Thus the hotel's (the country's) past is built on the conquest of others, whose culture it then appropriates and assimilates into the mainstream. Similarly the fact of oppression is repressed and assimilated into an ordinary life (plain, unexceptional, according-to-the-order) as bland as the film's conversations between people, that David Cook likens to the inane chatter that passes for conversations heard by news anchors and disk jockeys on TVs and radios during the film.

Moreover, Kolker identifies the eighties' "benign patriarch" as a specific personage. "The patriarchy," he writes, "assumes a maternal position, of care, rather than of authority. . . . Ronald Reagan (re)enters cinema as the guiding patriarch offering maternal care" (255). Accordingly Stuart Ullman sits concernedly in his office explaining to Jack about the caretaker who had slaughtered his wife and children and says "I can't believe that actually happened here." Reagan in his 1980 debate with Carter said that "We didn't know we had a race problem." He went on genially to lead the country through eight years of willed unconsciousness and denial, not believing that any dark doings in our history actually happened here or that they could have "left traces behind," as Hallorann explains to Danny.

In the same way the Torrances have repressed their own history, as Wendy begins her explanation of Jack's abuse of Danny oxymoronically, as " . . . purely an accident. My husband had been drinking." The Torrances deny their problems, calling each other "hon'," "babe," and "darlin'," and generally acting as a married couple is expected to act.

Furthermore, the film is studded with mirrors into which people look and don't see themselves (but an idealization?) A mirror, after all, shows the referent, but backward. As Danny/Tony shows with the "redrum"/murder scrawlings, a referent, paradoxically, must be backward in order to be recognized—and Jack and Wendy appear to themselves deceptively straightforward. As the film goes on, when Jack looks in mirrors, he doesn't see himself at all; the naked woman who rises from the tub in Room 237 is alluring when gazed at voyeuristically from across the room (Nicholson's leer in the reverse shot parodies the desiring male gaze, thus breaking the spectator's pleasure in voyeurism); when he looks in the mirror, he sees a rotting crone, his identity embodied by the dread of woman, just as the fantasy woman embodies his fetishism. Still later in the red-and-white bathroom with Grady he sees Grady, his ancestral "double," not himself. As shown in "William Wilson," Edgar Allan Poe's classic doppelgänger story, to gaze into a mirror and see the Other is to be mad.

The hotel's "Overlooked" history of class oppression ("all the best people" stayed there, according to Ullman), murder, and violence ultimately mirrors Jack's violent tendencies, which seem based on an unconscious frustration with his position as an "ordinary" male in society. David Cook refers back to the film's opening scene, the interview, calling it

> a typical job interview, with the candidate grabbing for the brass ring he both *desires* out of his socially conditioned sense of competition and desperately *needs* because of the ruthless competition built into our market economy. Jack Torrance is in a classically defined position—that of an American male who both *wants* and *needs* to support his family and who, we soon learn, deeply if unconsciously resents the fact. The interview is successful (as how could fraudulence fail to appeal to fraudulence); Jack will sell his labor to a corporation and move his family to a new job in a new town. It happens every day. (3)

The film fuses two entities that would seem to be opposites—maternal care and patriarchal law. The combination sets up a Brechtian difference between how the character acts and how the spectator responds to him. Jack's insane exhilaration at his (he thinks) newfound murderous freedom and power (it's as if Jake Gittes unconsciously wished he were Noah Cross, as well he might) may be experienced by the spectator as exhilaration at falling back into the womb—which, according to Freud, is a secret desire of men, often associated with water (hence the number of key scenes in bathrooms). The womb is evoked by the motherly way in which Jack is treated by Lloyd and Grady: Grady cleans off Jack's jacket and tells him, "You're the important one." Lloyd nurtures Jack with a soothing presence and drinks that look like mother's milk in the white light of the Gold Room bar. Jack reads these encounters as male camaraderie, while the *mise-en-scène* absorbs Jack into womblike settings from which he is not always distinguishable.

There is a debate, which I think will grow more heated as study of acting and stars becomes more important to the field, over the place of the actor in the film apparatus. Formalist critics Bordwell and Thompson see the actor as an expressive figure in the *mise-en-scène* (*Film Art* 4th ed. 157–163). Others argue that actors' presences are so strong that they themselves can be *auteurs* whose styles and personas transcend and define the *mise-en-scène*, even if they are technically inside it. I tend toward the latter view, but *The Shining* provides brilliant examples of why both should be taken into account.

Nicholson told an interviewer: "I complained that he [Kubrick] was the only director to light the sets with no stand-ins. We had to be there even to be lit" (Kroll 99). The film reveals that what Nicholson must have seen as eccentric obsessiveness on Kubrick's part produced a startling effect. In the scenes showing Jack's "possession," the lighting on him matches a warm, glowing background that makes it hard to see where the illusory surroundings end and Jack, the equally illusory human subject, begins.

In the first scene in which Jack conjures up Lloyd (in a very offhand way; the camera is on a medium close-up of Jack as he, under his breath, offers "my goddamn soul for just a glass of beer," the most unconscious Faustian pact in cinema), Jack covers his face with his hands, looks up, and says "Hi, Lloyd." Lloyd is then shown, completing the eyeline match. The amber light of the ballroom is so warm and intense that it envelops Jack, too; the only contrast comes from the white of Nicholson's teeth and eyes. Jack's ravings and his chummy confidentiality with Lloyd make him part of the spectacle, rather than the individual that the character thinks he is. The music throughout the film (by Bela Bartók, Krzysztof Penderecki, and György Lygeti) does not call attention to itself as the music in Kubrick films often does. Rather, it seems one long primal scream issuing from (or toward) the Overlook. And the (false) aura of the womb enfolds even more the conversation in the white-and-blood-red bathroom where Jack in effect seals his inevitable fate with Grady ("You have always been the caretaker here," Grady tells him), the lighting again blending Jack with the surroundings, not so that he is lost in them, but so that they seem an organic part of him and he of them.

This feeling of enclosure by the womb is not treated with the dread one might expect, especially since it may be Jack's and the spectator's secret desire and may explain why Jack so welcomes his fate. It is treated with irony because once again a Nicholson character does not recognize the real object of his drives. This double presence of patriarchy/maternity pervades the film visually. In the opening shot the (apparently helicopter-borne) camera advances on an island in the Rockies. The island is tiny, and it is surrounded by water, but it is so verdant, with a large pine tree and overrunning foliage, that it doesn't appear to know that it's an island. Jack doesn't appear to know that he is bonding with the primal father, as his descent into its control resembles a fall into the warm, welcoming womb.

The gaze that advances on him repeatedly as he types away in the cavernous Colorado Lounge becomes his undoing when he tries to appropriate it for himself, evidence that the male subject can never really take the father's identity as his own, but can only serve its purpose. The

17. The lord and master overlooking an enveloping womb.

best example of this is the shot following the well-known one in which Wendy discovers Jack's "All Work and No Play Make Jack a Dull Boy" manuscript. The massive camera movement from behind the outside pillars of the room and through them into it is one that we have seen before in the film. When we see it here, from Jack's point of view, it is clear that Jack is both encouraged to take the hotel's position, to do its bidding, and doomed by his presumption in taking the controlling position of the father unto himself.

Therefore the dichotomy of patriarchal authority and maternal care is expressed visually. The patriarchal gaze shows itself in its voyeuristic "peeks in" on Jack and in the tracking camera's relentless monitoring of him. The maternal side is shown in the warm, enveloping lighting of the scenes in which Jack is being enticed but also absorbed. The paternal camera represents (literally) what is happening to Jack; the maternal camera shows how the fantasy works. The spectator is distanced and unnerved by both because they put him or her in an uncomfortable, unaccustomed position—Danny (on his Big Wheel, for instance) and Wendy are the pursued, but they usually move *toward* or with the camera. Jack is the pursuer, but the camera usually moves toward him like a predator. Furthermore, the scenes of Jack's welcoming into the fold of patriarchal history, which take place in the Gold Room and red-and-white bathroom, are startling in their unconventionality. At once chilling and warm, comforting and indefinably strange, they suggest unmistakably notions of the *unheimlich*.

Diane Johnson, who wrote the screenplay with Kubrick, told a *New York Times* reporter with the doubly uncanny name of William Wilson that while preparing the script they read Freud's "The Uncanny" (1919) (Harmetz 72). "Uncanny" is an imprecise translation of the German word *unheimlich. Heimlich* originally meant "familiar" or "homelike," from the word *heim,* or "home." However, Freud notes, in everyday usage *heimlich* denotes its opposite—"concealed, kept from sight, so that others do not know about it, withheld from others" ("The Uncanny" 25). Eventually Freud traces the ways in which the subject represses some things that are *heimlich,* in the etymological sense of "familiar," "friendly," and so on, into things that are *unheimlich*—eerie, strange, taboo; thus *heimlichkeit* unconsciously contains its opposite.

Beneath "the uncanny" lies the principle that horror is the order underlying the male subject, inside him waiting for release. When it is released, however, the subject will not recognize it as horror but as something familiar and friendly—like Lloyd, the bartender—or the womb, which Freud says is an object pertaining to the home and therefore familiar, which men construe as *unheimlich* ("Uncanny" 51). "The uncanny" then begins to account for one of the many things that bothered reviewers in 1980 about the film: that the narrative does not take Jack through a rational process to madness (nonsensical as that sounds); that he seems mad to start with. Hence the interview scene, in which Nicholson twitches his eyebrows and flashes his devilish grin, prompting some to think that the actor is just indulging in unmotivated mugging, is the character's unconscious responding to the *unheimlichkeit* of the hotel while his conscious obsequiously grins and glad-hands in order to get the job. This scene is important because from the beginning we have another Nicholson character, like Gittes, whose outward attempts at decorum cannot master his unconscious drives and responses.

Freud writes that "the uncanny is in reality nothing new or foreign, but something familiar and old-established in the mind that has been estranged only by the process of repression" ("Uncanny" 47). Jack finds long-buried animosities, recalling Robin Wood's discussion of the centrality of the other in the horror genre. In the dialogue with Grady (from the novel) Jack is asked if he knows that his son has made contact with "a nigger." Jack lowers his head, pauses, and asks incredulously, "A nigger?" as if not only to reorient himself to the idea that his wife and his son "interfere," but to retrieve from history the buried idea of black people as "niggers." In contrast, the spectator recalls the 1980 Jack's studied handshake and hello to Hallorann in the first part of the film.

The 1921 Jack, however, would not have repressed such racism, not in a place—and a state of mind consigned now to the past—built on an Indian burial ground. The 1980 Jack has repressed his racism but finds it familiar and comforting to know that, like Jake Gittes, he can displace the feelings of inadequacy evidenced by his writer's block onto racial others, just as he has displaced them onto his wife. Nicholson's perform-ance has often been called "mechanized" and in a sense, Jack does call to mind HAL the computer in *2001*. Where HAL's handler dismantles his memory in order to bring him under control, Jack's handlers activate his. The hotel's treatment of Jack rests on a process of getting him to remem-ber repressed attitudes of resentment, hostility, and murder. Freud writes: "An uncanny experience occurs either when repressed infantile complexes have been revived by some impression, or when the primitive beliefs we have surmounted seem once more to be confirmed" ("Un-canny" 55).

The key event in Kubrick's *oeuvre*, the one to which all of his films inevitably return, is the moment in *2001: A Space Odyssey* in which history continues in a simple graphic match from the prehistoric age to the age of interplanetary travel with the toss of a weapon into the sky. History and male identity (the "man" in "the dawn of man" is gender-specific, I believe) are shown to be built on violence and the domination of others. In addition it is a short space between man's advanced civiliza-tion and his most primitive instincts; a good example of this is Jack's description of the yanking of his son's shoulder out of its socket as "a momentary loss of muscular coordination—one extra foot-pound of en-ergy per second. . . . " Man's advancement permits him mostly to coin better-sounding euphemisms and craft more technological justifications for his brutalities.

Kubrick would certainly say that attention should be called to dialec-tics, but he appears to believe even more that differences should not be overemphasized. His project is to collapse such dualisms as reason and madness, past and present, self and Other, horror and normality, strength and weakness, knowledge and ignorance. As with the double meaning buried in *unheimlich*, the favored side easily turns into its opposite through a repression. This film seems to agree with Michel Foucault that "we have yet to write the history of that other form of madness, by which men, in an act of sovereign reason, confine their neighbor, and commu-nicate and recognize each other through the merciless language of non-madness" (*Madness* ix).

An effect that this film seems to have had on Nicholson is that his acting moves much more quickly between the opposites the farther he gets from realism/humanism. His performance also left Nicholson with a reputation for playing insane characters, or perhaps more precisely, for playing insanely. Kubrick's previous film, *Barry Lyndon*, used an unreliable voice-over narrator, subtly inappropriate music, and an odd ensemble of clashing, nonnaturalistic acting styles to set up a problematic relation between the ideological content of narrative conventions and the values that the conventions assume; the signifier and the signified never match.

In *The Shining* the inversion of the affect of horror comes from the fact that the signifier (Nicholson's performance) never matches the apparent signified (Torrance's madness and menace). Jack/Nicholson is funny when he should be frightening and self-destructive when the character acts other-destructive. Nicholson acts out this misfit between genre convention and the film's affect. It is the sense of role-playing, and of Jack Nicholson self-consciously playing a character who self-consciously plays a horror movie villain from Nicholson's AIP period, that takes over. The film shifts to Santayanan horror, men's forgetfulness of the past assuring not only that they will repeat it but that the patriarchy supported by the forgetfulness will continue.

Nicholson *as* the System:
The 1980s and Early 1990s

□□□

I have concentrated my discussion of Jack Nicholson on the movies that problematize male subjectivity—films that, as we've seen, stem from the mixture of late 1960s radicalism and European influence that enjoyed a brief but intense vogue between about 1967 and 1975. However, in keeping with Nicholson's self-perpetuated reputation for perversity, it seemed for a while in the late 1970s and early 1980s that the farther the country—and American cinema—moved from the influence of 1960s counterculture in an increasingly conservative climate, the deeper Nicholson's acting delved into experimental styles.

His experimentation culminated in a trio of stylized, antirealistic performances—in *Goin' South* (1978, directed by Nicholson), *The Shining*, and *The Postman Always Rings Twice* (1981, Bob Rafelson). These non-naturalistic performances brought about his rejection by the journalistic critical establishment that had celebrated him in the *Easy Rider*–through–*Cuckoo's Nest* period. In addition, the commercial failures of the three films, plus those of *The Missouri Breaks* (1976, Arthur Penn), *The Last Tycoon* (1976, Elia Kazan), and *The Border* (1982, Tony Richardson), nearly spelled his extinction as a bankable star. In 1984 *American Film* suggested that one of the reasons Nicholson accepted his "comeback" supporting role in *Terms of Endearment* (1983, James L. Brooks) was that he had become practically uncastable for lead roles.

The popular success of *Terms* was accompanied by rapturous reviews for Nicholson, even by critics such as Pauline Kael and Andrew Sarris, who didn't care for the film. The reviews welcomed back a prodigal actor who had learned "restraint" (the operative word in many reviews) and gotten over his "self-indulgence." Critics had taken a punitive attitude toward the stylization of *The Shining* and *Goin' South*. This "punishment" of Nicholson for going beyond codes of realism and humanism the mainstream knows how to read is oddly matched by the course of the narratives in many Nicholson films. A number of films require that the Nicholson figure "go too far" and thus "lose," that his transgression from decorum, whether it be patriarchal (*Five Easy Pieces*, *The Last Detail*, *Chinatown*) matriarchal (*Cuckoo's Nest*), or a Freudian kind of social repression (*Carnal Knowledge*, *The Shining*, *Postman*), brings about his downfall. Just as the dissipated Garrett Breedlove in *Terms of Endearment* is rehabilitated by taking his proper male role in a relationship with a woman his own age (who, the film suggests, needs a man in order to fulfill her), so Nicholson the actor may show glints of devilishness and unruliness, but the characterization must nonetheless put down roots in rational motivation. The rewards for conventionality, moreover, were high, higher than Nicholson could have known in 1983.

The key to Nicholson's appeal even in the films critical of male role-playing is the sense that he breaks the standards for acceptable social behavior. It is as though a spectator recognizes that when Gittes scoffs at the cops and Water Department thugs; when McMurphy outsmarts Nurse Ratched; when Torrance giggles over his own menace; when Charley Partanna loses himself in love, over the disapproval of his Mafia godfathers; and when the Joker gleefully overruns Gotham City, their carelessness and lack of male self-control assure their ultimate failure. Many of the films may be critical of patriarchal roles, but the childish abandon of the Nicholson figure is often suicidal—"Sometimes I just kill myself," as the Joker says—because it leaves him open to the strictures of the symbolic, which cannot allow irresponsible behavior in grown men.

At the same time that the figure's childish abandon of rules and mores, his play-acting, and his loquacious misappropriation of symbolic language must be reined in, even while the films appear to disapprove of such restraint, the crossing of behavioral boundaries gives pleasure in Nicholson's films. This is established early in his star career, in the best-remembered moment in *Five Easy Pieces*, the scene at the diner in which Bobby Dupea tries to get around a rigidly made-up menu in order to get a few pieces of toast, finally elaborately ordering a chicken salad sandwich, and telling the waitress (the source of withholding maternal authority) to hold the chicken salad "between your knees." The next scene, back in the car, shows Palm Apodoca, the hitchhiker, saying, "Fantastic that you could figure that out and lay all that on her as a way to get your toast. Fantastic!" "Well, I didn't get it," answers Dupea/Nicholson. "No, but it was very clever." The "cleverness" that exists for its own sake expresses a repressed male desire for the Fall and for another kind of "imaginary signifier," a desire to descend to a state of mess and disorder. The difference between this and the model of an "imaginary signifier" in classical cinema is that many of Nicholson's 1970s and early 1980s films make a spectator conscious of the imposition of "invisible" symbolic structures.

One film that doesn't is *Terms of Endearment*. Garrett Breedlove's unruly behavior is explained by Aurora (Shirley MacLaine) as the actions of "a man who has achieved his ambition and is now and forever a spoiled child," another way of repeating the "boys will be boys" defense. Breedlove/Nicholson's leering delivery, arched eyebrows, and lilting, insinuating line readings are neatly motivated and excused. The script later turns him into Aurora's faithful helpmeet—"Who would have thought you'd turn out to be a nice guy?" she says when he turns up halfway across the country, where Emma, Aurora's daughter, is in the hospital with cancer. It even suggests that he will take his proper place as father figure to Emma's orphaned children.

Furthermore, Nicholson, the role-playing oedipal subject, is now posited (as he was once before, in *Cuckoo's Nest*), as the "natural man" in a way that redounds to the actor's honesty and the star's daring. It is Aurora Greenway who role-plays, wearing blond wigs and frilly, impractical dresses that overemphasize femininity. Breedlove, despite a string of pointless romances with women less than half his age, is supposedly frank about his middle age. The then-forty-six-year-old Nicholson told interviewers that he wanted to dispel the notion of "midlife" crisis, and that while the pudgy actor usually loses weight for a film, he didn't for *Terms*. So in the bedroom scene in which Nicholson and MacLaine stand at opposite sides of the bed, the actor/character's paunchy belly sticking out, attention once again goes past the character to Nicholson the comic actor, who now dares make a spectacle of his middle-aged spread. This exhibitionism runs counter to the tradition of actors such as Cary Grant, Gary Cooper, and to some extent Clint Eastwood, who continued their careers while seldom calling attention to their advancing ages. These actors played the same sorts of roles at fifty-five as they had at thirty-five, with results like *North by Northwest*, in which Grant's mother is played by Jessie Royce Landis, born the same year as Grant. Cooper at fifty-seven starred as the hero in an Anthony Mann Western, *Man of the West* (1958), with the plot's villainous father figure played by the forty-eight-year-old Lee J. Cobb.

After *Terms of Endearment* Nicholson, who had never been a physical actor—his face and voice having served as his expressive focus—calls increasing attention to his body as a point of spectacle and mortality. Like Sean Connery, who became in his forties the first romantic leading man after Yul Brynner to exhibit a bald head, Nicholson receives credit for daring to make his body an object precisely and paradoxically by not being narcissistic about it. However, only *Prizzi's Honor* (1985, John

18. While showing his age and paunch, Nicholson asserts a "boys will be boys" essential nature. With Shirley MacLaine.

Huston) is in the sardonic, absurdist spirit of extreme oedipal trouble that marks so much of Nicholson's seventies work. When Nicholson asserts the "natural," familiar double standards set in. Men, after all, expect to be accepted as they are. What is refreshing about the "role-playing" Nicholson is that he reveals that men *cannot* actually be "as they are," but as the masculinist standard requires them to be. When Nicholson acts otherwise, the man's prerogative to do what he pleases free from standards and requirements imposes itself. Nicholson shifts his persona from one that parodies and challenges white middle-aged masculinity to one that reassures it. Could Shirley MacLaine's character display a flabby tummy and still be credible in a sex scene?

This issue becomes more pointed in *The Witches of Eastwick* (1987, George Miller), another film in which Nicholson exhibits his paunch and plays a comically flabby satyr. Nicholson's "honesty" about his body plays opposite two fortyish actresses, Cher, the health-spa spokeswoman whose debt to modern cosmetic science has been well documented in the media, and Susan Sarandon, whose staying power seems due to a chameleonlike talent by which she can be mousy and housewifely in one film (*Compromising Positions* [1985]) and sultry and exhibitionist in another

19. Flabby, balding, and irresistible? Nicholson as the devil in *The Witches of East-wick.*

(*Bull Durham* [1988]; she moves between both extremes in *Witches*). With *Thelma and Louise* as well as her well-publicized pregnancies by a much younger man, Tim Robbins, her project appears to be an active expansion of the definition of "female star." Meanwhile, Nicholson's candor about the expansion of his waistline and his advancing age calms male fears of growing old (this is precisely what Nicholson has said he wanted to do) but also asserts that men can let themselves go and still attract women while females have to work out and submit to tummy tucks in order to remain sexual subjects into middle age; if Cher and Sarandon put on weight they would be playing supporting roles as Julia Roberts's or Marisa Tomei's mother before they knew it.

The confusion of middle-aged male fantasy with frankness about middle age sinks the *Chinatown* sequel, *The Two Jakes* (1990), a sad failure that shows just how much Nicholson has lost his level of irony and his Brechtian edge. Written by Robert Towne and directed by Nicholson after years of delays, *The Two Jakes* is set eleven years after *Chinatown* in a Los Angeles in the midst of postwar expansion, enmeshing Gittes in a complex web of sex, murder, real estate, and oil. "What's changed in the character," Nicholson said during the production,

is Gittes was originally kind of fast, full of piss and vine-
gar; like America, he's been through the war, so he's a
little less likely to go off, a little more laid-back. He owns
the building he works out of now, belongs to the country
club . . . he's got a fiancée, but he's basically watching the
new morality that we've seen come full circle today develop. Because after the war, divorce is about to rise—he
watches people being immoral all day, and he believes in
divorce. So he doesn't believe marriage is an act of God,
and he thinks he's helping people. (Schruers 60)

Gittes is quite far from the original private-eye archetype in that he
now actually believes in his divorce work. Nicholson and Towne may
feel that they are bringing Gittes out of myth and in line with late-twen-
tieth-century mores. However, in rendering Gittes what producer Robert
Evans called "a straight leading role" and moving him solidly into at
least the middle class, the sequel creates a private eye as far from the
unknowing pretender of the Polanski film as he may be superficially from
the hard-boiled myth. *Chinatown*'s criticism of, and ironic distance
from, the thoughtless racist and sexist assumptions of the private eye
archetype are missing from *The Two Jakes*. In contrast to Polanski's
strategy, this film allows the spectator to experience it unproblematically, through the character, with Nicholson adding *film noir*–like voice-
over narration for Gittes, pervading the movie with Gittes's subjectivity.
The film's portrayal of Gittes is fundamentally schizoid in regard to
the hard-boiled myth. The characterization spreads out in all directions—literally, as the actor plays the role in full Nicholsonian girth,
which confuses things even more; Gittes looks older, tireder, and portlier
than the script indicates. The paunchiness might fit a critical view of the
character. But Nicholson appears to have identified with his protagonist;
in this, the intended second installment of a never-to-be-realized Gittes
trilogy, the detective was meant to be exactly Nicholson's age, forty-
eight, at the sequel's original production date, 1985. Forgotten along
with the private detective archetype is the Brechtian "series of comportments" that systematically diminished the spectator's ability to accept
Chinatown's detective as masterful. Jake becomes what Dort dismis-
sively calls "a given" (101); he is now the white male's "normal" guide
through a baffling, dysfunctional world not of his making. Robert Evans
said, "I think Jack wanted to play this character because it's a straight
part—he prefers straight leading roles. His whole career was always
offbeat" (Schruers 60). This strikes me as a complete misunderstanding
of Nicholson's acting career; Buddusky, Gittes, Torrance, and Breed-

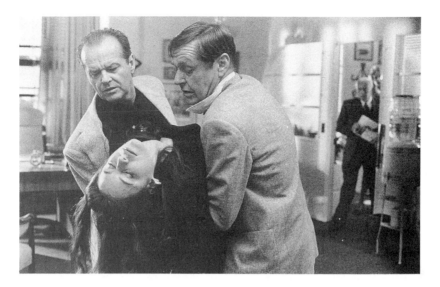

20. The investigator mystified by female hysteria. With Madeleine Stowe and Jeff Morris.

love were *all* "straight parts" until Nicholson bent them (Stephen King even expressed his preference for a "straighter" actor than Nicholson for *The Shining* [Wilson 63]). Yet, from the evidence of *The Two Jakes*, Nicholson finally succumbed to the flattering notion of the straight leading role.

Without critical distance, and with a screenful of middle-aged and elderly male actors, the sexist fantasies of the original genre return with a vengeance. There is on screen scarcely a man under fifty or a woman over thirty. The movie is populated by the comely young receptionists, widows, and fiancées of a forties film like *The Big Sleep*. Nonetheless Nicholson seems out to divest the genre of its glamour and romance in order to emphasize the sordid politics and business deals. Gittes is seduced by the murder victim's widow (Madeleine Stowe), a standard-issue *film noir* hysteric, in a tawdry, joyless scene that seems meant to express the "matrimonial" investigator's cynicism about infidelity but instead summarizes the hard-boiled genre's hatred for female sexuality.

The 1990 Gittes invites conflation with the "real" Nicholson even more than did Breedlove in *Terms of Endearment*. The bevy of young women surrounding the rotund fifty-two-year-old star accords with the press reports of Nicholson's Sunset Strip prowls with Warren Beatty and an actress's accounts in *Playboy* in 1989 of her sexual escapades with the star (Shepherd 171). The frequent gratuitous shots of the actress playing

Gittes's receptionist, the twenty-six-year-old Rebecca Broussard, mother of two children by Nicholson, openly spur such confusion.

Part of the trouble with *The Two Jakes* rests in Nicholson's inability as director to dramatize the intricacies of Towne's ambitious script. The film's deeper problem lies in an uncritical reproduction of the sexism of the original genre. Gittes, grown fat and comfortable, is indeed "less likely to go off." Perhaps the same is true of the actor who plays him.

In the late 1980s Nicholson's exuberant display of impulses that the spectator must suppress also led to his playing villains. *Batman*'s Joker represents both a yielding to mortality and a transcendence of it. Like Jack Torrance he dies with an expression frozen on his face, leading the spectator to suspect that he isn't dead at all—and indeed Nicholson has expressed chagrin that he wasn't asked to revive the Joker in *Batman Returns* (Green 2D). While the threat of Jack's continued reincarnation at the end of *The Shining* promises the horror of endless patriarchy, the apparent interminability of the Joker embodies Kubrick's fear of the optimism of ghost stories as victory over death. The Joker seems the last step in the taming in the 1980s of both Nicholson's acting and his unconventional treatment of masculinity. The Joker is actually object-turned-subject in that the on-screen figure comes to embody the horror-movie machine for eliciting screams from women (Silverman *Acoustic Mirror* 77). Nicholson's "over-the-top" acting is safely enclosed within a literal mask, ruling out any confusion with realism; "there was no top" to go over, Nicholson said (Morgenstern 130). The star's irrepressiblity is not defeated at the end; it is simply held in reserve for the sequel that might yet be made.

Moreover, Nicholson's much publicized deal for a percentage of sales of *Batman* toys and other merchandise, which has reportedly netted him between thirty and sixty million dollars, spells the end of Nicholson's claims to whatever anti-Establishment ideals might be left over from the 1960s (Shepherd 161). *Batman* is the kind of youth-market, comic book blockbuster that Nicholson denounced during the 1980s, swore he would never be involved in, and to which he portrayed his films as alternatives (Wolf 30; Walker 58–59; Rosenbaum 66). "*Star Wars* stinks," he cried in 1983. "Those characters are puppets" (Wolf 30). At the height of the *Batman* merchandising bonanza in 1989, however, Jack Nicholson puppets popped up like Jacks-in-the-box in stores across America. Nicholson's period of antihumanist, antinaturalist experimentation had in the early 1980s brought about a long-threatened collision between an ideological aesthetic that negates the notion of the individual and the institution of stardom that reveres it. *Batman* finally caused Nicholson's cultivated image as a rebellious, visionary artist having his own way with Hollywood to be eclipsed by the portrait of a filthy-rich star in an age of fat percentage deals.

Nicholson has found ways out of the dead ends posed by a persona on the verge of becoming a cliché, as James Stewart's was by the 1960s, and the virtual disappearance of irony from Nicholson's acting style (a result, it would seem, both of his comfortable status atop the Hollywood Establishment and of the refusal of 1980s and 1990s audiences to accept an acting style that undercuts individualism). One alternative is for Nicholson to obliterate the persona and immerse himself in a "serious" role in a prestige film. This strategy worked in *Ironweed* (1987, Hector Babenco) and *Hoffa* (1992, Danny DeVito). *Hoffa* shows that Nicholson is a skillful enough actor to bury his persona under realistic makeup and impersonate a "great man" in a biography. His style reverses the classic-era strategy, exemplified by Stewart's biopics, in which the biographical subject had to adjust to the star persona.

Another, more intriguing solution, one that unleashes irony in a new way, is for Nicholson himself to play a devouring oedipal father figure. He does this for the first time in a scenery-chewing supporting role in *A Few Good Men* (1992, Rob Reiner). In his first military role since *The Last Detail* Nicholson plays Col. Nathan Jessup, a gung-ho rising star in command of the marine base at Guantanamo Bay, Cuba, one of the last places where the Cold War hangs on. Jessup is Noah Cross in camouflage, a self-righteous authoritarian who crows about "saving lives" the way that Cross pontificates about "the future," and whose lines, such as "You can't handle the truth," sound distinctly like Cross's warnings to Gittes.

On screen for 15 minutes of a 135-minute film, Nicholson manages to dominate a lightweight young cast (Tom Cruise, Demi Moore, Kiefer Sutherland), giving a predictable courtroom drama momentary depth and significance underlined by heavy-handed direction that films Nicholson in close-up virtually every moment he is on camera. Nicholson plays the marine in fighting trim, looking years younger than his Jake Gittes from two years before, his head shaved to a slightly spiked bullet cut, his face hard and determined. His Jessup is clearly a true believer in marine discipline, the chain of command, and the polite though unmistakable intimidation of subordinates.

The performance's fascination comes from the fact that this is "Jack Nicholson," whose persona cannot be held in by social strictures, as a character who represents those strictures at their most rigid. Thus the performance strongly etches the character while emphasizing once again a clear space between character and actor. Jessup is in the Nicholson self-destructive mold. Suspected by the lawyer (Cruise) defending two young marines accused of killing a soldier of having given the order himself, Jessup is manipulated on the witness stand into blurting out "what he's longing to say" and incriminating himself. The arrogance, complacency, and pride that goeth before a fall are all here, ready to bring down a man who believes too firmly in his own invulnerability. The intensity that Nicholson brings to *A Few Good Men* suggests that perhaps the actor should look for starring roles that explore the Achilles' heels of powerful men. Perhaps it's time for Nicholson to abandon outlandish villains and impudent little guys and play Charles Foster Kanes about to be toppled from their Xanadus.

The flamboyance and genuine depth of Nicholson's *A Few Good Men* turn notwithstanding, the film itself restricts the impact of Nicholson's malignant militarist in ways that illustrate how much the actor has allowed himself to be compromised by the movie industry of the 1980s and 1990s. *A Few Good Men* is the sort of youth-market narrative that provides a brash young hero a chance to prove his mettle by shooting down the primal father. Jessup is a video-game monster for a video-game audience; any possibility that Kaffee (Cruise) might defeat Jessup only to take his place on the patriarchal ladder is given no hearing. The military setting is even more coyly drawn. In the early scenes the marines of Guantanamo Bay are viewed through the eyes of the hip Kaffee/Cruise. The soldiers look like brainwashed fanatics, their chants of "Unit, Corps, God, Country" sounding nearly like the mantras of a religious cult. By the end the hero's appealing iconoclasm is attributed to lack of discipline and fear of failing to measure up to the high standards of a dead symbolic father who was once U.S. attorney general. By wiping out a bad officer he becomes a good soldier. Even the innocent defendants accept their dishonorable discharges as wise. "We were supposed to fight for people who couldn't fight for themselves"—namely their victim, as if it would have been possible for them to refuse the colonel's order.

A Few Good Men, a visually dull product with the look of television, is a time-capsule item from late 1980s–early 1990s Hollywood. In these movies the young white hero conquers evil and takes his father's place in some benign hierarchy; women and minorities are given lip service but still remain in their assigned slots, and institutions retain a facile morality—moral goodness as a given. Acting up a storm in such a vacuum, Nicholson, to spectators born before, say, 1955, retains some of the aura of sixties protest, a remnant of the counterculture tossed in to enliven late-Reagan-Bush-era conformism. To those born later he is the Joker, an amusing pinball demon with eyes the light up, the embodiment of "evil."

So thoroughly has Nicholson been Cuisinarted by Hollywood's concern not to disturb the status quo that the mild radicalism that produced Nicholson's stardom now appears monstrous. One can even ask what the monster is in *A Few Good Men*—the military man as played by Nicholson, or Nicholson critiquing *one* military man, infusing him with his own individual madness. This is the epitome of mainstream co-optation, a Hollywood conformity that sometimes makes even the studio era (whose conservatism was always blamed on the Production Code) pale in comparison. It is little wonder that a film like *Mr. Smith Goes to Washington*, dismissed in the 1960s as patriotic pabulum, now appears a gem of ambivalence and ideological instability.

Jack Nicholson has enacted in various ways a depressing reversal of the courses traveled by Stewart and, as we will see, Eastwood. His career since 1983 has demonstrated how stars who begin with internal criticism of the dominant order are eventually disciplined and contained by ideology, by the soothing balms of money and success. Nicholson himself, rich and productive, continues to talk in interviews about the power of the actor to shake things up. He appears unconscious of his participation in his own silencing. Like one of the sassy, unaware characters in his films, he doesn't know what's hit him.

PART THREE

□□□

Clint Eastwood:
Male Violence—
Performed, Disavowed,
Unforgiven

□□□

Men with
No Names

□□□

It is the true heroic feeling, which one of our best writers
has expressed in the inimitable phrase, "Nothing can happen to me!" It seems, however, that through this revealing
characteristic of invulnerability we can immediately recognize His Majesty the Ego, the hero of every day-dream
and every story.
           —Freud, *Creative Writers and Day-Dreaming*

Dissolve to . . . a figure on horseback, seeming to emerge out of a distant
horizon, as the opening titles announce the figure and the film: "Clint
Eastwood" . . . "*High Plains Drifter*." As the credits flash, the camera
follows the horseman down from the hills, through a graveyard, into the
seacoast town of Lago. In most of these establishing shots, the camera is
far behind the rider, showing the audience where he's going but also
seeming to tag along. Once he reaches the outskirts of this typical movie-
Western town, the spectator alignment with the stranger has become
quite close. As the man rides through the main street, he seems to put
himself on exhibition in a way untenable to the sort of masculinism that
poses the male as subject of the gaze, not its object.

It is soon apparent that the reactions of the townspeople, who stare at
the horseman from porches, storefronts, and saloon entrances, are as
significant as the character himself. From the point of view of the spectator—an illusory position based on male desire and identification that
create a "subjectivity"—an implied viewer constructed in the ego and in
culturally shared assumptions about gender, race, and class—these
people are also on display. And since the spectator is in the position
of the horseman as he rides past porches and shopwindows, the townspeople are gawking at him or her. But although the spectator is identified with the rider, there is an important difference between them: The

spectator looks at what the stranger passes; the character doesn't. His failure to look indicates, among other things, the townspeople's reaction to him as predictable and beneath interest, and the rider as superior. Only one thing makes him stop and look—the crack of a whip, a gesture that breaks his single-minded riding and will be explained shortly in a subjective flashback.

This opening sequence establishes the spectator position for the rest of the film: he or she is placed as a kind of middle term, aligned with the hero, who knows the town he has come to and why he is there; the narrative will reveal his motives and unfold the action. At the same time, although the citizens are shown at a distance that establishes them as other, the film apparatus—and especially the soundtrack—displays the things that cause their apprehension. As the horse goes by, its hooves and breathing combine to sound like some inexorable machine. When the man gets off his horse, the jingling of his spurs, amplified, sounds like knives slashing at each other; also exaggerated is the sound of his footsteps as he walks up the wooden stairs to the saloon. In the position in which the spectator has been placed, it is he or she who causes the apprehension, so effectively has the spectator been aligned with the stranger.

A male spectator is encouraged to identify with a fantasy projection of himself as a socially constructed male. This projection lures an irresistible narcissism. At times, however, the spectator seems to occupy the position of Mordecai, the dwarf, the only character sympathetic to the stranger. Mordecai is often explicitly a voyeur, burrowing into tight spaces to watch the stranger. He lights his cigars, enjoys his threat to the town, and lives vicariously through him, just as the spectator can. So even dwarfs started small: At the movies they can be six-foot-four, or at least forget their size at the same time that, in another sense, they must remain aware of it.

But in typical Clint Eastwood films of the 1970s, of which *High Plains Drifter* (1973, directed by Eastwood) certainly is one, something else is operating. When the men in the saloon taunt the "flea-bitten range bum," it is the implied spectator, a Mulveyan figure in an illusory position of transcendental power, who is challenged by the stifling proximity of sweaty faces in close-up; the stranger seems unconcerned. When a woman walks by the stranger, daring to initiate the glance at him but framed in an object position, the shot places the spectator right behind Eastwood, who doesn't look; it is the spectator who is interested. The ultralaconic Eastwood figure and the others' "look at the camera" allow for an exaggerated engagement of the spectator as the enunciative source of the film.

The sequence culminates in two events: the stranger, trying to get a shave from a comic barber too nervous to do the job, is surrounded by the thugs from the saloon; the spectators are positioned with the stranger: They, too, are surrounded. The stranger shoots the men with superhuman speed. At the first gunshot the film's constituted spectators are in the stranger's position; they hear the blast and see the smoke and the bullet hole in the target's forehead. In the second and third shots (in both senses of the word), the spectator sees Eastwood's guns in the same position from his or her position: In short, the shots are issuing from the spectator's desire to eliminate these nuisances.

As the thugs' provocation is followed through, so is the woman's. When she brushes up against the stranger in the street, he asks her contemptuously, "If you want to get acquainted, why don't you just say so?" The woman, as the film would have it, pretends to be outraged (her no means yes) and calls him "trash." The stranger, promising to teach the woman "a lesson in manners," as he taught his male antagonists, drags her into a barn and rapes her. Mordecai, who suppresses a smile, looks on as the woman's outrage—in the prototypical male misrecognition of rape—turns to submissive rapture.

In each of these events Eastwood's presence has occasioned a threat and gratified a desire, not in the character but in a spectator whom the highly subjective, centripedal camera style of this and other Eastwood films of the period construct and constitute as male. Any implied female spectator would fall into one of Laura Mulvey's much-criticized *cul-de-sac* alternatives: "masculinized" subjectivity or masochistic identification with the brutalized female. These conclusions follow from the methodology of textual analysis performed by such critics as Raymond Bellour, Stephen Heath, and Thierry Kuntzel. Such analysis isolates the classical film's elements—its "realistic" *mise-en-scène*, editing, and music—and applies semiology and such concepts as Freudian dream theory, the Lacanian mirror stage, and Louis Althusser's theories of ideological subjectivity to show how a spectator is positioned in and constituted by the film apparatus. For instance, Kuntzel's exhaustive analysis of *The Most Dangerous Game* ends as follows: "*The Most Dangerous Game* is uncanny because it constitutes a *mise-en-scène* of my 'love' of the cinema; that is what I go to see (again) with each new film; my own desire—endlessly repeated—for re-presentation" (62). In other words, textual analysis retraces the cinema's evocation of desire, which Kuntzel in this case claims as his own, illustrating what Stephen Heath called "the dialectic of the subject" ("Amata Mo" 50); that is, a spectatorial subjectivity that both constructs and is constructed by the film. Thus while a sequence such as the rape scene just described does not initiate in a male spectator the impulse to rape, it perpetuates misconceptions that continue the culture's tacit tolerance of rape by reaffirming the ideological construction brought to the film by a male in patriarchy.

Textual analysis has been disparaged within film studies because of its ahistorical nature and because of doubts about its ability to account for different audiences for, and multiple responses to, a single film. In his review of Heath's *Questions of Cinema* Noël Carroll charged that such a system of analysis would rule out, for instance, the possibility that spectators of *The Birth of a Nation* could be constructed as anything but racists who cheer the Klansmen as heroes, a reading that would disregard that film's historical reception. My interpretation of the rape scene in *High Plains Drifter* could be similarly questioned: Couldn't there be a spectator who would be appalled by the rape and murders? The answer is that of course there could, but the film clearly was not made for such a spectator. Such a resisting viewer is not the spectator implied by the *mise-en-scène* and the cutting, or even the one drawn to the film by advertising and publicity. On the other hand, given the research on rape by Susan Brownmiller, Anthony Wilden, and others, there is little doubt that attitudes toward rape such as those dramatized in *High Plains Drifter* are pervasive in Western civilization. As a heterosexual male critic I cannot exempt myself under the rubric of "resister" and put malignant attitudes off onto some "other" spectator.

The film's construction of violence, however, does require a disavowal on the part of the spectator who derives pleasure from it: "She deserved it," or, "Those guys asked for it." The absence of character and motivation, combined with the identification techniques the film employs from the beginning, relieves the spectator of moral responsibility for enjoying the rape and murders—even though it's enjoyment the spectator must disavow, as Mordecai does by keeping himself from smiling during the rape. In both events desire is justified by threat and thus displaced onto law: The gunmen are "justly punished" by the gun; the woman, the sexual threat, is "justly punished" by sexual violence. This pattern is similar to the one Tony Bennett and Janet Woollacott find in their study of the James Bond films, noting that in *Never Say Never Again* (1983), "the traditional narrative by which Bond puts attractive women back in their place *sexually* but reserves violence and killing for the villain is reworked to deal violently and finally with those women who cannot be conquered sexually" (41).

Eastwood's films, and none more so than this one, have trouble defining the Bond films' distinction between sexuality and violence, however phallocentric those definitions are. Judith Mayne, in an article on Eastwood's later film *Tightrope*, notes that the film "is . . . unsure of what

21. A symptomatic confusion between sex and violence. With Mariana Hill.

rape is" ("Walking" 69) and unsure of differences between sex and violence. Such uncertainty runs through Eastwood's films of the 1970s and
1980s, which seem fairly obsessed with the topic of rape, as I'll discuss
in the third section of this chapter.

At the same time the disconnection of the rape and murders in this first
scene of *High Plains Drifter* from any sort of moral rationalization reveals those images as pure pornographic projections from the imaginary.
The spectator can trust, because this *is* a Hollywood movie, that a moral
framework—although a singularly masculine and egoistic one—rooted

in language and law will be provided in good time. In the meantime the Eastwood film provides a tentative answer to a question posed by Paul Smith: "What does a man writing his imaginary actually produce? . . . If the structures in which we are caught, in which our egos are constructed, are accurately described by theory and feminist theory, is our imaginary anything but a pornographic defence against the mother's body?" ("Men in Feminism" 37).

The film needs spectators to complete the scene; they supply the desire and passion missing from Eastwood. This is because Eastwood in his persona and his presence is oddly incomplete; the cause of his phenomenal success might lie partly in the fact that he is only a schematic figure whose desires and motivations the spectator willingly fills in.

The Eastwood Westerns of this period thus strip the genre of its moral dimensions, making it serve a egoistic function. This point was not lost on Pauline Kael, who told Eastwood biographer Iain Johnstone in the late 1970s:

> People used to think the Western was such a popular form because of its morality, but really it was because of the melodrama and the action. In a sense Eastwood has removed the hypocrisy from those characters by getting rid of all the morality. . . . The Eastwood character expresses a new emotionlessness about killing that people think is the truth now. It used to be that the man who stood for high principles was also the best shot. Now we no longer believe that in order to be a great shot you need principles at all. And Clint Eastwood is a totally unprincipled killer. (50–51)

The three "spaghetti Westerns" for Sergio Leone that launched Eastwood's film career in the sixties, and his later American-made Westerns in the "Man with No Name" vein, represented new stages in the breakdown of the genre's "high principles," which began in the early fifties with such Westerns as Anthony Mann's. Rather than personify "good" or "justice," Eastwood's heroes represent the ego; they expose the extent to which the moral grandeur and "Americanness" of previous Western heroes had been based upon a glorification of self in which subjectivity translates, probably by definition, as "good."

This is made explicit in Leone's *The Good, the Bad, and the Ugly* (1966) in a prologue in which the title "characters" are introduced. The Eastwood figure, known to audiences as the Man with No Name, is revealed as part of a scam in which he goes from town to town and turns in the outlaw Tuco ("the Ugly," played by Eli Wallach) for the reward money. Later he shoots the rope as Tuco is about to be hanged, and the two split the money once they get out of town. The sequence ends with Eastwood leaving his hapless partner to die in the desert, as the camera and narration freeze his image into a kind of portrait with the ironic caption "the Good." Leone and Eastwood expose "good" as a subject construction built on codes of power and heroism familiar to the audience. They do this by showing just how far they can push the moral boundaries of "hero," while maintaining a viselike spectatorial identification with said "hero." By reducing heroism to ground zero—narcissism—Eastwood recuperates the myth of the subject in an era when ideals seem to have died.

Freud defined narcissism, after Näcke, as "a perversion . . . in which an adult treats his own body with all the caresses that are usually devoted to an outside sexual object" ("The Libido" 416). This extreme self-love leads the libido away from objects and into the ego where it "cannot find its way back to objects" (421). "It is probable," Freud writes, "that this narcissism is the universal and original state of things, from which object-love is later developed, without the narcissism necessarily disappearing on that account" (416). If "objects" include not only love objects but everything on which the subject's integration into civilization depends—family, society, allies—then we have named everything from which the Man with No Name stands apart. Moreover the figure's narcissism and isolation lead to reactionary if not fascist fantasy and nostalgia when Don Siegel gives him a somewhat differentiated identity and moves him to the polarized settings of late-sixties-early-seventies New York (1968, *Coogan's Bluff*) and San Francisco (1971, *Dirty Harry*). To paraphrase the epigraph of *For a Few Dollars More* (1965)—"When life had no value, death, sometimes, had its price"—"When the outside world has no value, the only thing of value to the ego is itself."

Leone told an interviewer: "I looked at [Eastwood] and I didn't see any character, just a physical figure" (Cumbow 154). The character is fabricated out of spare parts that nonetheless add up to a rehabilitated myth. The traditional Western loner is made strange. He wears a Mexican-style poncho and gaucho's flat hat, disrupting the "Americanness" of Hollywood cowboys, and he smokes thin Mexican cigars that Eastwood said "just put you in a sour frame of mind" (Johnstone 40). He is unshaven, although in Westerns this usually signifies a lack of civilized manners unbecoming a hero. For example, in John Ford's *My Darling Clementine*, the first thing the bearded Wyatt Earp does on arriving in town from the range is get a shave. The problematic John Wayne protagonists of *The Searchers* and *The Man Who Shot Liberty Valance* decline in moral stature while losing their daily inclination to shave. The stranger in *High Plains Drifter* has his shave interrupted and goes bristling—in more ways than one—through the rest of the film. The figure in the Leone films rarely goes near a razor.

In these films, in which human flaws are embodied by grotesque figures, the Man with No Name kills or tricks people who manifestly deserve to be killed or tricked. Christopher Frayling calls him "a super-efficient trickster" (78) who leaves at the end of the film when "the various groups he has tricked cannot be exploited anymore" (130). However, his apparently selfish ends coincide with a "moral" structure based on ego, whereby the clearly bloodthirsty elements ("the bad") are destroyed and the merely foolish and garrulous ("the ugly") receive milder punishment. In short, the Man with No Name provides audience pleasure because he profits from turning the greed, stupidity, cowardice, and brutality of others against themselves, although—or perhaps because—he is as selfish and amoral as they are.

Leone and Eastwood put the Man with No Name in front of the camera sparingly and, it seems, with caution. When he is shown in full figure, that figure is heavily cloaked—by the poncho in the Leone films, by a nondescript long coat in the American Westerns. These coverings flatten out and obscure the lean muscularity that is displayed in some of Eastwood's other films. In fact, they blur the body almost entirely; in the Leone films, the presence of the "shroud" is often called attention to, usually in a shot in which one corner of the poncho is dramatically drawn back like a curtain, sometimes in close-up, revealing the six-guns traditional Western heroes openly wear.

The stranger's physical presence is often amorphous and elusive both to the camera and in the world of the fiction. As in the opening of *High Plains Drifter*, Eastwood is often felt to be a presence not so much before the camera but in its place, and not simply as the momentarily out-of-frame character in a point-of-view or shot-reverse shot. His first "appearance" in *The Good, the Bad, and the Ugly* is a good example. Tuco is being captured by three Mexicans. One of them, who about half faces the camera on the far left of a wide-screen shot, gloatingly unfurls the reward poster for Tuco and says, "Hey, amigo, do you know you got a face beautiful enough to be worth two thousand dollars?" At this moment Eastwood's calm, even voice, completely disembodied and seeming to emanate from the screen, says, "Yeah, but you don't look like the one who'll collect it." At this the men draw, toward the right of the screen, as the Man with No Name enters the shot from behind, the back of his head and shoulders taking up the right half of the frame. When he finally faces the camera, his head is bent down to light his cigar, and his face is shadowed by the brim of his hat. The elusiveness does not stop here; in the same film his presence is sometimes indicated merely by a cloud of cigar smoke wafting from around a corner. And all of this in films full of huge close-ups of sweaty, grimacing, blemished faces.

The American films go farther still in stressing the figure's amorphousness. In *High Plains Drifter* the audience learns only at the end of the film that the stranger is an avenging angel, the ghost of a marshal who had been conspired against and put to death by the town of Lago. It is obvious, however, that he has appeared in a different incarnation, a changed body, because no one knows him—not the outlaws who whipped him to death ("Who are you?" one of them stammers again and again) or the dwarf who apparently was the marshal's only friend. Eastwood's personage (though not his persona) is insubstantial enough to be easily changed.

There is, moreover, a recurring violent sight gag that revolves around Eastwood's physical slipperiness. The villain's henchmen think they see the stranger isolated in a room and file in to beat him up or shoot him. Each time the stranger has managed, usually unbeknownst to the audience, either to slip outside and toss in a match or a stick of dynamite (*Fistful of Dollars*, *High Plains Drifter*) or to hide elsewhere in the room and shoot the men after they've used up their ammo firing at his decoy (*For a Few Dollars More*, *Pale Rider*). The device even finds its way into a late Dirty Harry sequel, *The Dead Pool* (1988).

Besides discreet camera placement and narrative legerdemain, Eastwood's movements only suggest rather than delineate character, effacing any individual characteristics and mannerisms. In a tradition in which even the most "masculine" stars, such as Bogart and Wayne, had unique, eccentric voices and ways of carrying themselves, Eastwood is a minimalist. There is nothing distinctive about his walk—unlike James Stewart, whose slightly stooped gait emphasized the ungainliness of his long arms and legs, or Wayne, whose way of hitching up his shoulders and letting them point his body in a given direction called attention to his overall size and strength. Eastwood's gestures are tiny, his movements economical. When Eastwood was younger, his voice was thin and reedy and seldom rose above a whisper; as he aged, the voice deepened, but his use of it remained understated. Some of the later, self-reflexive films, such as *Bronco Billy* and *Honkytonk Man* (1982), in which Eastwood embodies a much more relaxed persona, reveal just how much he had been limiting the range and timbre of his voice.

Similarly Eastwood's face is inaccessible but not inscrutable. As the Leone films alternately hide and reveal the presence of Eastwood's body, the face is also hidden—not just behind the scruffy beard and the cigar with its attendant stream of smoke, but also by Eastwood's and the films' manipulation of these things. Although Eastwood's face is always a mask, except in the films in which he eschews conventional heroism for a more naturalistic demeanor (*The Beguiled*, *Play Misty for Me*, *Honkytonk Man*, *Tightrope*, *Unforgiven*), the mask in the Leone films is paradoxical in its inconsistency. For seven years Eastwood was the pleasant second-lead TV actor on *Rawhide* (1959–1966); he played a role Johnstone likens to the callow Montgomery Clift character in *Red River*. In the Leone Westerns, the first two of which were filmed during Eastwood's summer hiatuses from the TV series, he makes the transition to unprincipled desperado. The Man with No Name's accoutrements compensate for basically soft facial features. The amiability of *Rawhide*'s Rowdy Yates often shows through the surly mask.

Accordingly the Leone films seem interested in the contradiction in traditional Westerns between a hero's politeness and his brutality. Leone and Eastwood learn to capitalize on this incongruity, reserving Eastwood's smile and humor for his most sadistic and ironic moments and playing the young Eastwood's fair-skinned downiness against the invincibility of the character. Later, in the American films, the mask hardens and Eastwood's trademark squint predominates, as does a neutral look that makes the figure seem self-occupied and disinterested. The face, already paradoxical in the Italian Westerns, manages to appear both overdetermined and blank in the American ones.

Robert C. Cumbow—in the sort of film criticism that attributes everything to the director—calls Eastwood "a *tabula rasa* on which Leone would write ineradicable capital letters" (*Once Upon a Time* 154). I would call him instead a *tabula rasa* on which spectators can write their own "letters," but on which nothing is written because nothing actually needs to be. For example, when the French actress Isabelle Huppert performs in a laconic style, she acts out in an ironic way the patriarchal convention of woman as mystery (much as Jack Nicholson ironically "plays" machismo). But when Eastwood employs understatement and cuts his dialogue, as he says, "by the carload, big paragraphs" (Giddins 142), he's not read as inscrutable or mysterious—even though the film may ostensibly posit him that way—because, as Steve Neale theorizes, where woman is seen in patriarchy as mystery, "masculinity, as an ideal at least, is implicitly known" (16).

The values embodied in the indomitable American hero of legend had been largely discredited by the early sixties. The Man with No Name, a more abstract and stylized figure than any hero the American cinema had seen, appeared as a deadpan ironic recuperation of the Western hero. In coldly acknowledging the death of heroism, Eastwood propped up the

22. The frontier lawgiver replayed with "blank irony" in a postmodern age.

spectatorial ego ideal and went through the motions of enforcing justice, without ideals—a postmodern John Wayne.

The macho Eastwood persona could be called—in Fredric Jameson's definition—a pastiche, in which the discredited myth of the late-nineteenth-century frontier lawgiver is replayed in the late-industrial age with "blank irony." Accordingly the pastiche is "a statue with blind eyeballs" ("Postmodernism" 65). The operatic, ironic, amoral, international Westerns with which Eastwood began his star career are products of a postmodern condition whereby "the producers of culture have nowhere to turn but to the past: the imitation of dead styles, speech through all the masks and voices stored up in the imaginary museum of a now global culture" (Jameson "Postmodernism" 65).

In short, Eastwood's persona was based on a realization that the foundations of masculine identity had been lost and needed to be massively reconstructed and reperformed. While Eastwood has never joined the chorus of complaints about acting as "unmanly," he hasn't needed to; his acting is more than "masculine." However, the self-awareness required by Eastwood's minimalism leads to a tension between the behavior of the persona (who is taken as "Clint Eastwood" by the audience) and the way a "real person" behaves.

The feeling persists that for a major star, Eastwood in these films is a schematic and insubstantial figure. He would seem to possess little of the individuality and distinction of a studio-era star. In the "Man with No Name" films that first established him, he doesn't even bear the most basic signifier of identity—a name. (Although the "Man with No Name" might itself come to sound like a name because it does serve to identify the character, the phrase comes from English-language publicity for these movies and is never spoken in the films themselves.)

To leave the Eastwood figure unnamed is to decline to locate him in national identity (although there is no doubt about this, outward defamiliarizing devices notwithstanding), and in specific time and place. If the Eastwood figure doesn't have one of the most basic signifiers that grounds a subject to his or her existence in society—another being gender—then he and the spectator positioned to identify with him elude responsibility to anything but the figure's own distinctly Darwinian survival needs—he has no "good name" to protect. The lack of a name takes the narrative one remove farther from realism, as it relieves the character and the spectator of language and the responsibilities that follow from it. The figure's frequent placement *in* the cinematic apparatus itself—in the place of the camera or of the spectator or both—situates him as a free-floating presence who is never exactly fixed, not confined even to the designation "character"; he is farther from an objective "he" and closer to a preverbal "I."

Yet for all the amorphousness and seeming contradiction of the Man with No Name, what he signifies is unmistakable—the phallus, the salient male imaginary image that requires no name, that simply *is*. With the elaborate paraphernalia of the Man with No Name reduced finally to the male imaginary essence, language is a hindrance to be kept to a minimum. Spectators can forget their symbolic connections and experience the film as Men with No Names. Jacques Aumont writes about spectatorship as "caught up in a kind of 'turnstile' effect (alternating between the Imaginary and the Symbolic) that allows us both to *believe* the image as real and to disengage ourselves from it sufficiently to endow it with meaning" (Saxton 24).

Eastwood's 1960s and 1970s films construct a solipsistic order organized around the phallus, and in the service of an imaginary projection of the self. In his structural study of the Superman comics, Umberto Eco writes that although twentieth-century superheroes differ from the heroes of classical myth because they live in a representation of our everyday world (that is, they are not gods), what keeps such heroes at a pleasurable distance from the viewer or reader is their freedom from chronological time. In Eco's words, such a hero does not "consume himself" (111); he draws no closer to death, and his previous adventures have no consequences in the next. The Leone films operate within a comic book's lack of responsibility for time. In the second film, which takes place some years after the Civil War, the Man With No Name is referred to in dialogue as a young man; however, the next film is set *during* the Civil War, with the character no younger than in the previous movie. Moreover, in each of the Leone films and in Eastwood's American Westerns, other characters do suffer with a vengeance, so to speak, the consequences of previous actions; these are usually brought home to them by the Man with No Name.

The spectator is apt not to be bothered by or even notice these inconsistencies, just as Christopher Frayling is able to write an entire book—an often perceptive one—about Italian Westerns without mentioning that it's not clear in the second Leone film that Eastwood is even playing the same character as in the first! So persuasive is the combination of the amorphous and the monolithic that these uncertainties do not ruin the spectator's pleasure or go against the genre's logic. And if the Italian Westerns defy time, the American ones defy death. The ghostly figures in *High Plains Drifter* and *Pale Rider* are more substantial dead than alive.

The psychoanalytic theory of identification articulated by Christian Metz in *The Imaginary Signifier* has become so commonplace that to apply it to a single mainstream narrative film or group of films may appear naïve. As Metz himself emphasizes, his theory refers not so much to film texts as to spectators. However, because Eastwood films so foreground the spectator's ego as having a stake in the fantasy, while they place that ego in a threateningly real situation, and because all that is tangible about the schematic "stranger" persona is its phallic power, Metz's theory is the best with which to define the original appeal of Eastwood.

Metz sets up the model of the mirror stage and specifies differences between a child's identification with a representation of him- or herself in the primordial mirror and a spectator's identification with images on the screen—that is, the spectator's ego has long since been formed; he or she stays aware of watching a representation because he or she is "wholly outside the mirror, whereas the child is both in it and in front of it" (49). Metz seeks to answer the question, "*With what*, then, does the spectator identify?" (46). He brushes aside, but doesn't exactly eliminate, the usual suspects—a character in the fiction, or an actor; these are "secondary" identifications—and concludes that "the spectator *identifies with himself*, with himself as a pure act of perception (as wakefulness, alertness); as the condition of possibility of the perceived and hence as a kind of transcendental subject, which comes before every *there is*" (49). Metz ties this crucial concept to the cinematic apparatus, at whose center is a perceiving spectator in "identification with the (invisible) seeing agency of the film itself as discourse . . . the agency which *puts forward* the story and shows it to us" (96). Metz's theory, as he acknowledges, is closely akin to Jean-Louis Baudry's concept of an apparatus dependent on the infantile regression described by Freud (this regression is sometimes confused with the imaginary, although to Lacan, the imaginary is not a phase in temporal development to which the subject returns, but part of an ever-present dialectic that functions to coordinate the subject's social identity with his or her desire).

More crucially, although the spectator does identify with him- or herself to some extent in all films, the Man with No Name films take Metz's principle to its most monolithic extreme—as, in a different way, do the Dirty Harry films. Eastwood's low voice, his economical movements and dialogue, his frequent absence from the shot and seeming embeddedness in the apparatus, the dreamlike qualities of his mobility and lack of embodiment—all these make him a figure who performs in our place, whom we release, as Metz would put it, at the same time we receive him (51). He is a figure perceived by the spectator's symbolic but projected from the imaginary.

Eastwood's impassivity contributes to audience engagement. The spectator fills in the desire of a character in a point-of-view shot in which the character doesn't look. In other words, many theorists talk about spectator positioning in terms of an alignment with a character's look in a shot–reverse shot. Ed Branigan notes, for example:

> The importance of character vision for the activity of representation has often been emphasized. In psychoanalytic criticism the dialectic of "looking at" and "being looked at" is a crucial articulation of desire. Eisenstein, Foucault, and Gombrich have emphasized the use of eyelines and pictures of eyes in the modeling of space. Thus we may define narration in the visual arts as a *positioning of the*

viewer with respect to a production of space, and subjectivity as a *production of space attributed to a character*.
(64)

What to do then with a character who doesn't look? The disconnection
of the Eastwood figure from sight is one of the features that make the
stranger omnipotent but also amorphous. He does not need to see in
order to know. In *For a Few Dollars More*, for instance, he knows
somehow that there are three men in back of him and turns and fires three
shots; then, while looking in the opposite direction, he shoots a man who
is trying to get away. In all cases we see what he doesn't, but he acts on
the visual information as if he does see it, thus making mastery for the
spectator complete. The Man and the spectator make a team; the spectator has the sight, the Man is the agent. Eastwood understood this in the
first of the Leone Westerns. When he cut dialogue, "I'd just say, 'Well,
Sergio, in a B western, you'd have to explain. But in an A western, you
just let the audience fill in the holes'" (Biskind 57).

The Man with No Name also does not need sight in order to desire,
because he wants nothing. Frayling points out that even the Leone character's lust for "dollars" is not a desire for money itself, since he never
seems to spend it or get rich from it; it's simply that "dollars are the
prize" (161). As a trickster the stranger functions to keep the dollars out
of the wicked hands of others, such as "the Bad," and/or of greedy hands
such as those of "the Ugly," and not to satisfy a desire that would, after
all, mark him as a mortal, fleshly subject. In *High Plains Drifter*, therefore, the townspeople's looks at an "absent" Eastwood go to a subject
who both is and isn't there. The looks go to him, but they also go through
him—to the spectator. Because these looks are not returned in the usual
way, the film makes explicit the position of the spectator as the one who
directly returns the looks and whose desire animates the film.

In an article entitled "The Look at the Camera," Marc Vernet addresses a similar sort of look. Vernet refers to a shot–reverse-shot pattern
common in horror films, whereby the victim's look makes him or her
(usually her) scream:

> At the beginning of *While the City Sleeps*, the first victim
> of the young killer is seen at the moment of the murder
> from a slight high-angle shot, screaming with terror and
> addressing a frightened look toward the camera. This shot
> is in fact subjective because the axis and position of the
> camera are situated in the place that the killer occupies,
> there where he can already no longer be struck back at.

> The mortifying look is a sort of anti-communication be-
> cause it affirms itself without allowing for a reply and
> adopts an attitude of superb impermeability to all reactions
> of its spectator. The look here is impersonal, unreachable
> . . . it is an unbearable look. It is that look that condemns
> without appeal, that crushes whomever it is addressed to:
> it is the look of murderous folly, a devouring look, the
> look of the Law, the look of Death. (59)

Here finally we have a description of the Eastwood look in these films—opaque, impenetrable. Two elements, however, differentiate it from Vernet's explanation of an "unbearable look." The spectator in horror films is invited to feel contempt, or at best, indifference, for the *victim* simply for making him- or herself so disposable (thus the furor when Hitchcock killed off his presumably-not-negligible "star" halfway through *Psycho*). This invitation is made explicit in the Eastwood films. Also, the stranger is the protagonist and, as we've seen, the ego ideal; the spectator is put in the invincible position of the hero, while being able virtually to program him to do his or her bidding. Thus, "the look of Death" becomes an agent of spectatorial desire. The spectacle of death is acted out upon others as in a dream-wish, with the Eastwood persona inextricable from the desire to rape and murder.

High Plains Drifter shows not only how Eastwood's persona had solidified in the United States by 1973 but how the American realist tradition dictated that the stranger be much more grounded in circumstance, coherence, and cause-and-effect motivation than in the Italian films. For one thing the codes are clear: The stranger is a "range bum." He is dressed simply and shabbily. The Mexican connotations are gone, although the bristly beard and thin cigar from the No Name persona do remain. Missing from this character is any hint of playfulness or mischievousness; he means business—and the audience finds out why. The stranger turns out to be a ghost, back to exact revenge on the venal town that had him killed, and to earn himself a marked grave so that his spirit can stop wandering. By making the *seemingly* otherworldly Man with No Name *concretely* otherworldly, the American films base spectatorial pleasure in an overwhelmingly imaginary image. They justify that pleasure by grounding the action of the film in elemental symbolic principles of law and justice and language (the grave needs lettering, a name).

In short the films become really dangerous. Eastwood's films from the late sixties through at least the mid-seventies confuse individual and community values. In *High Plains Drifter*, the powers of a community must be punished for violating the individual. This represents a further assault on the community values of the traditional Western, one that moved John Wayne to write to Eastwood, protesting "that isn't what the West was all about. That isn't the American people who settled this country" (Biskind 59).

In the Dirty Harry films, the individual purports to protect the community. However, the two series share a contempt for community that goes far beyond the dialectic of individual/community described by such writers on the Western as Will Wright and Robert Warshow. Critics who call *High Plains Drifter* a satire on social hypocrisy and capitalist greed overlook this point. In these films it is *others* who are greedy and vicious. The considerable achievement of the Eastwood persona at this stage is that it keeps a male spectator from recognizing his probable likeness on the screen by tainting such figures with the stigma of weakness. The mirror stage, whereby a basically incoherent existence is rendered coherent by an idealized reflection that the subject embraces, finds its cinematic apotheosis in the fundamental Clint Eastwood persona as articulated in his films, a monolith Eastwood would spend much of his later film career distancing himself from and condescending to.

Authority of One:
The Dirty Harry Films

□□□

Vice President Bush boasted today that the Reagan Ad-
ministration had turned around "the permissive philosophy" of the 1960's and 1970's, helping to change a society
that savored movies like *Easy Rider* into one preferring
Dirty Harry films.
—News story, *New York Times*, 7 Oct. 1988

Unlike those cultural products that mask their apparatus and keep their
ideological agenda invisible, the Dirty Harry films—and particularly the
first one, released in 1971—appear to be conscious demonstrations of a
political strategy. The films were embraced by conservative U.S. politicians, as in the Bush quotation above and Ronald Reagan's use of "Go
ahead, make my day" in a 1985 news conference. Hunter Thompson
claimed that Richard Nixon lifted a policy against showing R-rated films
in the White House theater so that he could see *Dirty Harry*, declaring,
"Eastwood can do no wrong. Let's see the picture" (58). Moreover,
mainstream reviewers, who are usually blind to the politics, and especially the gender politics of films, condemned these Eastwood *policiers*
as reactionary, forcing Eastwood in interviews to deny that he was "a
right-wing fanatic" (Cole 124). In her 1972 *New Yorker* review of *Dirty
Harry*, Pauline Kael concluded that "this action genre has always had a
fascist potential and it has finally surfaced" ("Saint Cop" 388).

Eastwood's four films with Don Siegel between 1968 and 1971—five
if one includes *Play Misty for Me* (1971), which Eastwood directed and
in which Siegel acted in a supporting role—have a defensive, reclama-
tory spirit, as if grabbing back the standards and traditions the white
patriarchy perceived it had lost to feminism, the civil rights movement,
anti-Vietnam protest, sixties youth culture, the so-called sexual revolu-

tion (in particular the short-lived tolerance of homosexuality in the 1970s), the civil-libertarian decisions of the Supreme Court led by Earl Warren, and the "permissive philosophy" in general.

This backlash shows itself in Siegel's 1968 *Coogan's Bluff*, Eastwood's first American film set in the present, in which he plays a deputy sheriff from Arizona sent to New York to extradite a prisoner. There the bureaucracy is seen as keeping criminals from justice because of useless red tape and convoluted legal theories. The locals are greedy and parochial, the town is an open sewer, and especially, women are in need of being put in their place: When Julie (Susan Clark) takes out her purse to pay for her dinner, Coogan says, "You're a girl, aren't you?" "There are rumors to that effect," she answers. "Then sit back and act like one," he says, taking out his wallet.

While rightist impulses can be found in the Dirty Harry cycle (it would be harder not to find them), the films, as the classical Hollywood entertainments that they are, cover their tracks at the same time as they push the spectator's "hot buttons" (to use late-eighties Republican terminology). Are the films' contradictions unconscious admissions of ideological instability or are they part of a conscious and canny strategy of audience address? My approach to these films assumes that they are clever mixtures of traditional and countercultural—or at least anti-authoritarian—codes, manipulated to make a reactionary point that is hard to resist. I am uncomfortable reflecting "the view which once predominated in Marxist writings . . . that works of popular fiction could be regarded as the mere containers of ideology, conveyer belts for the reproduction and transmission of dominant ideology from the 'culture industry' to 'the masses'" (Bennett and Woollacott 2). However, these films do more than "transmit" ideological content to their spectator; they establish a powerful complicity with him or her in which the films take a demagogic role, playing on the "silent majority"'s presumed resentments and desire for cleansing violence.

The contradictions of these films begin *outside* them and redound ironically on the filmmakers. The films use San Francisco as a frightening site of the counterculture, of gays, drugs, lenient law enforcement, and life-styles that are depicted as threatening the working-class position Harry occupies. However, San Francisco is also Clint Eastwood's hometown. He reportedly enjoyed making the Harry films in San Francisco because he felt comfortable there and would even "meet childhood friends and old neighbors while filming" (Johnstone 92).

The first *Dirty Harry* is a polemic, while the sequels take the original's political arguments as little more than a convention of the series. Since the 1971 film does ostensibly make a political argument, it needs to do what Hollywood narratives have always done: make the political personal and hence disavow it. This is a task that the Eastwood persona, in its essential egoism and solipsism, carries off with ease. Because these films pretend to a "realism" eschewed by the No Name films, Eastwood becomes a three-dimensional presence, with motivations and the suggestion of a past. Eastwood's physical presence is far more substantial than in the Westerns. The film's use of him in the *mise-en-scène* partakes of conventional heroic subject placement. He develops a characteristic walk—although it does recall Leone's description of him as "a block of granite"—and he gives his voice some variety, within the still-straitened limits of the character.

Like the Man with No Name, Eastwood's Harry Callahan seems made to order for Laura Mulvey's now-classic characterization of the male protagonist as the force that defines the look and controls the narrative. The films are built around Harry/Eastwood as the symbol of a desire for law and order, as the agent of the spectator's desire, as a show-business performer, of whom a certain "act" is expected, and as part of a subgenre ("Clint Eastwood is Dirty Harry") whose pleasure for the spectator, to return to Umberto Eco's "Superman" thesis, lies in the repetition of the formula.

In an article on Ian Fleming's James Bond novels, Eco breaks down the 007 formula into a sequence of events that he says can be found in each of the novels in his study. Although the topicality of the 1971 *Dirty Harry* made it an unlikely candidate for a series of five films spanning seventeen years, the Harry series transcended historical change by borrowing plots "from today's headlines," by maintaining a consistent subject position, and by re-producing a standard formula each time. Here is a breakdown of the formulaic events that can usually be found in some order in each of the films:

1. The introduction of an ongoing series of crimes by a perpetrator whose identity is not yet revealed. The first crime makes up the opening scene—in the first film in a precredit sequence; in the sequels, just after the credits.

2. Harry arrives at the scene of the crime and begins an investigation.

3. The case is potentially explosive and embarrassing to Harry's superiors; they assign Harry to the case while warning him about his methods, which they call "unconventional" but which the spectator reads as violent and "effective."

4. Before the main plot really gets started, there is a gaudy, violent set piece, such as a bank robbery (*Dirty Harry*), airplane hijacking (*Magnum Force*), liquor store holdup (*The Enforcer*), or coffee shop robbery

23. Spectacle of calm amid the chaos. Eastwood's "opening number" in *Dirty Harry*.

and hostage taking (*Sudden Impact*), which Harry settles in spectacular and bloody fashion. The film's tag line—"Do I feel lucky?" or "Make my day"—often comes from this scene. These scenes serve an identical function to the solo numbers Fred Astaire's MGM musicals, such as *Easter Parade* (1948) and *The Band Wagon* (1953), gave him to perform before the story got under way in earnest. In these cases the genre star performs his signature "routine" outside the narrative, and is presented as a star performer before character and story claim him entirely. Character and performer are hard to separate from each other and from the artifice; however, although Astaire was dancing in front of the camera, Eastwood was not actually killing people, but the set piece makes it more difficult for a spectator to remember this—that is, it effaces its own production. At the same time the killings are not experienced as *deaths*; there is no sense of loss of those killed—they are strictly expendable—and there is no responsibility for their deaths. They are nothing but obstacles to be cleared out of the way, just as the scenes in those Astaire numbers were humdrum places waiting for him to enliven them with song and dance. Thus these scenes actually ground Harry in verisimilitude while introducing and reasserting his extraordinary masculine mastery in a spectacle the spectator both watches from outside and is part of. In other words violence is used as catharsis for the audience. This violence is not connected to real death—except that it desensitizes a spectator to violence and death by connecting an aggressive drive to pleasure in looking.

5. Harry is given a partner who, besides being "green," represents equal opportunity employment at the police department—a Hispanic (*Dirty Harry*), a black (*Magnum Force*), a woman (*The Enforcer*)—occasioning initial jokes at the partner's expense. The partner comes to do well in his or her job and to prove useful to Harry; furthermore the partner overcomes initial skepticism about Harry and comes to admire him, signaling (in the first film especially) that the spectator should, too. The partner either dies by the end of the film (*Magnum Force*, *The Enforcer*) or is injured and quits the force (*Dirty Harry*), in either case leaving Harry alone once again for the climax.

6. Harry eventually identifies the villain but is stymied by laws upholding the rights of the accused and prevented from bringing him to his kind of rough justice.

7. Harry's brash actions infuriate his superiors, who take him off the case. Harry then completes the case and kills the villain independently.

8. The audience, in a sense, knows more than Harry does, in that they are shown the crimes before he knows about them, often being put visually in the position of the murderer. The pattern of the films is always the same: We see the scene of the imminent crime and watch the killer arrive on the scene and commit the murder. What these scenes show, however, is the chaos of a world without Harry; the absence of the hero indicates a kind of voyeuristic (we often see from the killer's point of view through telescopes and gunsights) bloodlust in which the audience is implicated at the same time as it is isolated from it, secure in the knowledge that Harry will put things (including their proper subject alignment) right.

9. In the later films Harry forms an alliance with a social "undesirable"; e.g., a black revolutionary leader in *The Enforcer*, the avenging rape victim in *Sudden Impact*, a sleazy movie director (apparently modeled after Adrian Lyne) in *The Dead Pool*.

10. The film's tag line is repeated at the end, again inviting comparison with the musical genre, in which songs are reprised at the finale. This device gives some symmetry to the narrative and gives Harry the last word.

We can define the political text in this way: that American life is no longer "safe" and "stable" (assuming, as such fantasies do, that it once was) and that there must be reasons, culprits. The films find aberrant, out-of-control villains of a primal, unfathomable evil. While the threat of these killers would seem to call for a strong authoritarian power, the films deny any suggestion of police-state control (an issue the second film, *Magnum Force*, specifically addresses, following criticism of the first) by celebrating the authority of the individual. The films vest vigilante power in an "official hero" (he belongs to the police force) who defies the authority of which he is ostensibly a part. This paradox—an authority figure rebelling against authority—allows the films to avoid actually advocating authoritarian repression, although they condense a wish for it. They pull off this sleight-of-hand by embodying that wish in a fantasy figure who appears to be acting in the "public interest" when he is actually fulfilling the wish-dreams of the ego. In other words Eastwood is "acting" in the solipsistic interest of individual members of a "public" addressed as individual spectators.

Earlier I said that when Eastwood's "stranger" films begin to combine the imaginary self-image with the symbolic order of law and language, they become dangerous. In the Dirty Harry films it would seem that a hostile imaginary image (as in Paul Smith's "pornography against the mother's body") rampages through the world of the symbolic order, rendering language, law, personal connections, responsibilities, and consequences puny and unimportant. There is so much evidence for this that it becomes difficult to accept the assumption, made by most critics, that Harry is out to protect ordinary people, since the films regard ordinary people and their concerns with ridicule and contempt. For example, in *Dirty Harry* Harry talks a suicidal man off a roof by insulting and belittling him, provoking him to lunge at Harry instead of jumping. When Harry goes to a hospital emergency room to check out a report that Scorpio had been there, his conversation with the doctor is repeatedly interrupted by a woman's demands that the doctor tend to her husband's chest pains; these demands appear unreasonable in light of the more pressing requirements of a goal-oriented narrative. In *The Enforcer* DiGiorgio, Harry's sometime partner, already a figure of fun for the "too much linguini" that makes him unable to chase suspects and climb chain-link fences, says that if he's late from work his wife will kill him "because she has a nine-church novena tonight." Even the terrified children on the school bus hijacked by the villain Scorpio scream at the spectator and become nuisances. The "look at the camera" once again threatens and annoys, while in another film the same situation, with different camera placement, would easily move an audience to empathy—an alien emotion in these films. Thus Johnstone writes that the moment when the bus driven by Scorpio runs a Volkswagen off the road "usually got a cheer from Californian audiences familiar with the irritating presence of old VW bangers clogging the road" (86).

With personal problems and crises seen as nuisances, community safety and society's well-being are not what is at stake in these films. The spectators view ordinary humans from such a height that they identify with the height itself and with themselves there, rather than with the ordinary people going about their business on the streets and in apartments. From the spectator's vantage point, the people look like ants and the superhuman-but-real-seeming Harry becomes the fantasy-mirror image. In the first film private lives are objects for titillation as well; Harry peeks through a window at a man bringing a suitcase full of sexy lingerie to his girlfriend. At another point Harry, on a roof with a telescope, watches an orgy apparently about to take place in a nearby apartment and misses seeing the sniper Scorpio, whom he is supposed to have under surveillance, come out onto a neighboring rooftop. The narrative *can* wait for these things; they're not impediments to spectatorial pleasure. Not until *Tightrope* do the Eastwood films deal with the fact that hero, sniper, and spectator have in common voyeurism and the hostile objectification of others.

Harry Callahan was one of many antiauthoritarian male protagonists in sixties-era American films. However, the anti-Establishment hero should be distinguished from his cousin, the antihero, as I describe him in the section on Jack Nicholson. The anti-Establishment hero rebels against and replaces a system that has either lost its authority or represses individual freedom or both. The codes of behavior that allow freedom of action for the male individual are bogged down in excessive diplomacy and protocol (as in *Patton* [1970], whose original ads disingenuously subtitled it "A Salute to a Rebel"), numbed by a desensitized and dehumanized—that is, "emasculated"—society (*A Clockwork Orange* [1971]), or restricted by straitened economic conditions (*Bonnie and Clyde* [1967], an anomalous film in which the subject position is split into two characters, the more dynamic of whom is female).

Unlike an antihero, Harry doesn't question his identity; he knows why he is rebelling. The villain is the evil against which the hero must act. In order to do so, however, he must circumvent the system that stands in his way, prevents him from acting, and allows the villain to continue his terrorism. Harry is the primal man who discards an overly civilized, refined, and intellectualized system because it does not recognize and reward male virtues. In the first film especially, the mayor and the police are willing to capitulate to the murderer's demands for money in order to stop the killing, with disastrous results. They also show misgivings about Harry's methods, which to the spectator are self-evidently sensible, as seen in Harry's "I shoot the bastard" comeback to the mayor in the first film and, in the same film, in Lieutenant Bresler's reaction as Harry straps a stiletto to his leg before going to meet Scorpio—"It's disgusting that a police officer should know how to use a weapon like that."

There is also a strong class connotation in Harry's characterization. Harry is a working-class hero. He tells the doctor tending his wounded leg to risk causing him pain by pulling off rather than cutting off his pants: "These cost twenty-nine fifty; let it hurt," he says, stressing not only the hero's stoicism but also the fact that in 1971 $29.50 is a lot of money on a policeman's salary. He's shown eating only at cheap diners; the cars he drives are always a few years old. His apartment, in the one film (*Magnum Force*) in which we're shown it, is very modest. A sign over a supply table in the precinct in *The Enforcer* reads: IF WE DON'T HAVE IT, YOU DON'T NEED IT.

The austerity in which Harry lives and works allows the films to establish a sort of solidarity with a working-class audience, increasing the feeling that he is put upon, exploited. Harry gets his nickname, as he tells his partner, Chico, in the first film, because he draws "every dirty job that comes along." Chico soon echoes this sentiment, complaining to Lieutenant Bresler that Harry "always gets the shit end of the stick." The films' mounting evidence of Harry's exploitation allows them an ambivalent position with regard to authority, positing Harry both as the ideal source and victim of authority. It also helps the films to straddle the race issue; Harry terrorizes black criminals, but he also forms friendships and alliances with blacks—and this careful negotiation of racial issues remains constant throughout Eastwood's career.

The treatment of African Americans and other minorities in these films is surprisingly complex. The films pursue a careful strategy of pleasing blacks without alienating racist whites, and vice versa. A good example is in *Dirty Harry*; Harry faces a wounded black bank robber (Albert Popwell) on the street, and as the robber reaches for his gun, Harry recites the "I know what you're thinking—'Did he fire six shots or only five'" speech. In a shot–reverse shot, with the black man on the ground and Harry towering above him, the man puts his gun down, but as Harry walks away, the robber cries, "Wait—I gots to know"; Harry points the gun at him, it clicks, and Harry laughs as the robber curses. Cut to the hospital, where Harry's wounded leg is tended to—by an African American doctor who is a friend of his. Thus, while the film dwells on the black criminal, it also shows professional, respectable blacks who know the hero on a personal basis—almost before the first impression can completely sink in.

Another example of the same strategy is in a non-Harry film, Siegel's *Escape from Alcatraz* (1979). Eastwood, as a hardened inmate at Alcatraz, strikes up a friendship with English (Paul Benjamin), a black prisoner who was sent up for life for killing two white men in self-defense. The film is set in the early 1960s, so that the injustice against blacks that the film takes for granted can be consigned to the past. English, presented as the "king" of Alcatraz's African American contingent, sits atop his steps in the prison yard. When English sees Morris (Eastwood), he asks, "The way I figure, there are two reasons why you didn't sit down on my step. Either you're too scared, or you just hate niggers. Which is it, boy? You too scared?" "I just hate niggers," Eastwood answers through his teeth—*as he sits down*. So again the film gets a laugh from a racist line while negating it at the very same moment.

More fundamentally, many of the films position the Eastwood figure partway between white and minority cultures, fully belonging—like the classical Western hero—to neither. His solidarity with minorities underlines the films' antiauthoritarian class conflicts. In *High Plains Drifter* the stranger enters a store in which the shopkeeper is shooing a poor Native American family away from some blankets; when the store owner tells the stranger that he can have whatever he wants as part of the town's agreement with their new "protector," the stranger picks up the blankets and gives them to the family. In *The Outlaw Josey Wales* Josey, a Rebel outcast on the run from the U.S. government just after the Civil War, finds his only friends in an old Indian (Chief Dan George) and a squaw. The members of *Bronco Billy*'s Wild West Show troupe, all of them (including Billy) former prison inmates, make up a veritable who's who of social outcasts—a black petty thief, a prostitute, a Vietnam deserter (the film treats this issue with ambivalence), and a Native American. The troupe performs free at orphanages and old-age homes, and when they need a new circus tent, they appeal to a friend who runs a mental institution, whose denizens sew a new tent out of American flags, which is all they know how to make (conveniently). *Honkytonk Man*, a depression-era tale about a country singer on the road to Nashville, includes a scene in which the protagonist plays with a black band in an all-black nightclub and is accepted there—an obligatory scene in such films, from *The Glenn Miller Story* to *New York, New York* (1977, Martin Scorsese).

All these things suggest that the Eastwood figure is not quite connected to the dominant white culture (a trait he shares with the classic Western hero) and has an affinity for those on the margins of society. This theme is made as clear as the films want to make it in a scene in *The Enforcer*. Harry visits Mustafa (Albert Popwell), the head of a black separatist group, and the two establish a bond of trust. "Callahan," Mustafa tells him, "you're on the wrong side . . . you go out there and put your ass on the line for a bunch of dudes who wouldn't even let you in

24. "I'm doing it for you." Eastwood with Albert Popwell in *The Enforcer*.

the front door anymore than they would me." He answers, "I'm not doin' it for them." "Who then?" "You wouldn't believe me if I told you."

As ambiguous as the last line may seem, what's implicit in it is this: "I'm doing it for you." The Eastwood figure's alignment with those whom society scorns betrays a brand of white-man's-burden paternalism that keeps minorities in their place by setting up the white hero as protector. After *High Plains Drifter* the ceaselessly repeated scene in which Eastwood rescues women from rape serves the same purpose. These films keep a white male subject at the center, with others either adversarial or dependent.

Along these lines the authorities in *Dirty Harry* play the role of the protesting Eastern woman in classical Westerns—for instance the Quaker bride played by Grace Kelly in *High Noon* (1952), who tries to restrain the hero from using violence on his enemies, even if it means protecting the town. (*High Noon* is an appropriate example since *Dirty Harry* ends with Harry throwing away his badge as the Gary Cooper character did at the end of *High Noon*, and *High Plains Drifter* works a full variation on that earlier Western's plot.)

In the "disguised Western" (to borrow Robert B. Ray's term), *Dirty Harry*, Harry's adversary is the killer, but he can overcome him. His real antagonist—and obstacle—is the law. Scorpio, by screaming for a lawyer and demanding his rights when Harry has caught him at last, aligns himself with the system to frustrate Harry's—and the audience's—instinct for violence. The obstacle that keeps Harry from reaching his goal of ridding the city of the villain is the system, which, according to the film, has smothered the sense of right and wrong Harry retains behind a thicket of restrictions. The law, which will not allow the hero to kill the villain and sets the criminal free on legal technicalities, holds back the protagonist from action within the story. It also defers the spectator's pleasure in the violence that is sure to erupt and obstructs the progress of the narrative along its linear and active—that is, violent—way.

Although law is the product of the symbolic order and acts as its arbiter in society, it fails in *Dirty Harry* to perform its function as regulator and facilitator for the phallus. It has been "feminized." To quote Freud in "Femininity," "passivity now has the upper hand" (128). This "feminization" of the powers that be is apparent, on one level, in the female representatives of the Establishment who scold Harry for his methods—a female judge (*Sudden Impact*), a woman chair of a personnel board (*The Enforcer*), a woman journalist (*The Dead Pool*). It is also apparent in the male characters' concern over cosmetic details, suggesting a narcissism that in the Freudian scenario is displaced onto woman: The police chief fusses with the lint on his blue serge uniform, the mayor in the first film talks on a gold-handled telephone receiver and a new mayor in *The Enforcer* constantly primps his blow-dried hair. These peripheral characters are regarded in the same way as the everyday people referred to earlier: Their actions—or more precisely, non-actions—mark them as frivolous and extraneous.

The crowning irony amidst this displaced narcissism is that Harry is a narcissistic figure for the spectator. He is constructed, like the Man with No Name, from colliding signifiers; while the effect of No Name's incongruous coding was to defamiliarize the character, the effect for Harry is to make him appealing to the polarities in 1971. Thus his hair has a retro pompadour in the front and a counterculture shag in the back. When Bresler asks Harry probably the most frequently asked question of the late 1960s, "When are you going to get a haircut?" younger males hear a reassuring echo of recognition; their fathers have already been assured of Harry's authoritarian values.

The institutions and figures of official authority in *Dirty Harry* are perceived as feminine in that they reflect two limitations in particular that Freud attributed to woman—"We can consider women as having very little sense of justice" and "society holds little interest for women" ("Femininity" 133–134). Freud, as analyzed by Luce Irigaray in *Spec-*

ulum of the Other Woman, sees woman, in her preoccupations with home, husband, and son, as the ultimate protector and sustainer of the phallus. However, while the law in the late 1960s was perceived by the political right as severely restricting a male right to authority and action, woman was renouncing her role as "venerator of the phallus." Hollywood film, in which woman had been celebrated as the helpmate, the hero's restoration and salvation, begin angrily to drop women characters from its films, creating interdependent male relationships ("buddy films"—but remember that the film that started this "outlaw couple on the run" genre was *Bonnie and Clyde* [1967]; in the many buddy films that followed, including Eastwood's *Thunderbolt and Lightfoot* [1974, Michael Cimino], the original female character was replaced by a male).

If women could no longer be depicted as supporters and satisfiers of men, then they were of no value as commodities and as representations in dominant films. Women were depicted in films of this period in two ways: One was as perfunctory sex objects, whose function is to demonstrate that the protagonists of the buddy films aren't gay. The other was the displacement of coded female weaknesses onto institutions and male characters. As Harry in *Magnum Force* witheringly says to a young rookie upset over having killed a robber at a shootout, "You better go take care of the women."

In *Dirty Harry* the law, cast in the role of withholding mother, threatens Harry's ruin. The law has been feminized, and it will feminize Harry, too, unless he leaves the nest and breaks out on his own. His superiors order him to capitulate to Scorpio and take him the money he demands "with no tricks," resulting in Harry's humiliation and near death. Authority deprives him of the phallus—his 457 Magnum, "the most powerful handgun in the world." It renders him impotent, unable to kill the villain when he has him presumably dead to rights. To Harry, this law is tangled, enigmatic, incomprehensible, like woman herself in man's eyes—precisely because to man the failure to preserve the phallus *is* incomprehensible, mad. If the effeminate district attorney rejects Harry's evidence against Scorpio as inadmissible under the law, "then the law's crazy," as Harry says, and the male ego withdraws to its own devices.

"Veneration of the phallus," writes Irigaray, "defies the laws of the city, challenges their rulings and penalties. It doesn't give a fig about issues of legitimacy in men's conflicts. All it cares about is keeping the phallic emblem out of the dirt, covering over its dissoluteness, veiling its decay. Preserving it from derision, insignificance, and devaluation" (*Speculum* 117–118). I can't imagine a better characterization of the project of Siegel's *Dirty Harry*; however, Irigaray is describing woman's patriarchal role as keeper of the order. By 1971 the Hollywood cinema,

25. "Then the law's crazy." Harry confronted with incomprehensible, "feminized" institutions. With Harry Guardino and Reni Santoni in *Dirty Harry*.

finding the male without a credible helpmate and supporter, takes upon itself the role of protector of the embattled phallus. At the same time it reveals male contempt for women by attributing everything that is passive to those female "weaknesses" engendered by excessive devotion to men. Since the law will not uphold men's right to dominate, then after Harry has settled his own battle of egos with Scorpio, he throws authority's emblem—his police badge—into the dirt of a polluted river. Once again in Eastwood, the pretenses are dropped. In egoistic Eastwood fashion, man is not meant to preserve the social structure; it is meant to preserve him. By taking support for the phallus into its own devices, Hollywood perpetuates the fantasy that if law, government, and woman abandon phallic authority, the male subject can always maintain it himself, while letting the world feel his bitter resentment.

While this generalized "femininity" threatens to bring down Harry, who represents the "last real man," I disagree with recent work by Paul Smith and Adam Knee that emphasizes what Smith calls an "objectified" Eastwood in narratives that take him through rituals of "masochism" and "transcendence." Smith asserts, but does not demonstrate, the presence in the films of a "hysterical residue, . . . an unresolved or uncontained representation of the body of the male as it exceeds the narrative processes" ("Action" 103). This hysteria, as it turns out, comes not from a loss of control over a masculinity that threatens to exceed its allowed parameters and show its artificiality, but from an "alliance . . . with the hysterical woman protagonist" (104). I've discussed masochism and hysteria at length in the chapter on James Stewart, an actor whose imperfect fit with conventional male roles and capacity for projecting anguish openly overwhelm masculinist definitions. It seems to me that the Dirty Harry films avoid issues of masochism and project hysteria onto the feminized institutions as well as the crazed villain.

Harry's body is indeed often mutilated, but at the hands of feral evil, which the feminized authority structures would allow to run rampant, not from the moral masochist's drive to self-punishment or the martyr's willing submission of self to a cause. Harry/Eastwood, unlike the Stewart protagonists of Capra, Mann, and Hitchcock films, fights and resists a creeping feminization. These movies never suggest that Harry releases femininity in himself, although later Eastwood films will.

In *Dirty Harry*, masochism and male hysteria are displaced onto Scorpio (Andy Robinson), the polymorphous villain, who plays "the bad" *and* "the ugly" to Harry's slightly ironic "good." Scorpio embodies an unrestricted omnisexuality as well as a hysterical reaction to it. He targets (in a long-held point-of-view shot) a bathing-suit-clad young woman, the sort of image that the culture both idealizes and despises (the essence of fetishism), and a stereotypical gay man. His later victims, however, a ten-year-old black child and a fourteen-year-old girl, are not shown to the audience. His leg wound, unlike Harry's, elicits an agonized masochism that the stoic Harry cannot show (it also heals much more slowly than Harry's wounds). A particularly perverse scene, in which Scorpio pays a man to beat him up for reasons unknown to the audience until later, plays on a pleasure in pain that the film associates with the unlimited monstrosity of its villain to the extent of twice placing the camera in Scorpio's position as he is beaten. Given the film's white suburban suspicion of blacks—are they solid citizens or threats?—the fact that the man whom Scorpio pays is black increases the sadomasochism of the scene, stressing the perversity of a white man's submission to a mythic "black beast" (who himself wears glasses and approaches his task with the professionalism and systematic intelligence of a mechanical engineer).

The film carefully contains any perversity displayed by Harry and confines it to the film's first half hour. Harry drives by a porno strip of the sort that Wes Block will frequent in *Tightrope*, snarling, "These loonies—they ought to throw a net over the whole bunch of them."

Moments later Harry is taken for a "peeping Tom" as he voyeuristically looks through the window of a suspect who turns out to be a "wrong number." After Harry criticizes helicopter surveillance men for "talking instead of looking," allowing Scorpio, the rooftop sniper, to get away, he himself watches an orgy in progress while he is supposed to be looking for the sniper. Both of these scenes draw the spectator into the voyeurism, whose implications the films will not explore until *Tightrope*.

The film pays lip service to early 1970s trends whereby authority figures such as cops and military men are posed as antisocial bastards whom the culture still needs to uphold law and order. Even the title is recuperated from the suggestion of a tainted protagonist to the valorization of a hero who must clean out the "dirt" of the culture. The "outlandish" texture of the films deals roughly with contradictions to its masculinism. I am very uncomfortable with theories about how the films' violence and extreme male domination "prompt the idea that all is not as it should be for the male sex" (quoted in Smith "Action" 88). This may be so, but trying to infer insecurity from images of a dominant group's invincibility seems a dangerous mistaking of wishful thinking for critical awareness. Indeed, a man who beats his wife is probably "not as he should be"; his resort to violence may even have something of a "hysterical residue" attached. But ever-more-hyperbolic depiction of his behavior is not likely to invite him to recognize its destructiveness, just as extreme idealizations of male aggressiveness are unlikely to construct anything but more of the same.

Dirty Harry, with its reliance on Western genre conventions, draws numerous parallels between the hero and the savage (Cawelti *Six-Gun* 52–56). Harry and Scorpio are both loners, they both "hate everybody," and they regard modern society and its institutions with contempt. Both are voyeurs who are drawn to and repelled by the women who seem to them to purposely attract their gaze. Harry's point-of-view shots of women differ from Scorpio's in that they aren't shown through a gun sight. Otherwise, they are identical. The original, unused tag line for *Dirty Harry* read: "Dirty Harry and the Homicidal Maniac. Harry's the One with the Badge" (Giddins 134). The fact that the film offers the spectacle of objectification from the point of view of a "loony" and a law enforcer who is ostensibly sane shows the difficulty of distinguishing between "good" and "bad" killing and between the object of a gaze and the target of one.

15

"That Buried World": Eastwood and Sexuality in *The Beguiled* and *Tightrope*

□□□

> CHICO: I was just thinking . . .
> HARRY: About what?
> CHICO: Oh, about why they call you "Dirty Harry"
> —After Harry has been found peeking
> into a window in *Dirty Harry*

> SARAH: You're a man who makes people afraid, and
> that's dangerous.
> STRANGER: Well, it's what people know about them-
> selves inside that makes them afraid.
> —*High Plains Drifter*

A contradiction in the Dirty Harry series is that the "permissiveness" it scorns allows the films themselves to exist. The San Francisco kinkiness that cavorts all around these films may provide a straw man against which they can rail, but it is also part of their attraction. Through these films runs a puritanical streak that by a Freudian slip becomes a prurient one. The same Harry who wishes that someone would throw a net over the denizens of a red-light district also peeks through windows at kinky goings-on. From the dialectic of puritanism and prurience, embodied in the clash in American life between sexual prudery and the commercial culture that uses sex to sell products, comes a dark and unsettled view of sexuality. In Eastwood's films in which it fully emerges, this "dark side" raises questions not often dealt with in Hollywood films.

In *Tightrope* a court psychiatrist tells Wes Block (Eastwood) that "there's a darkness in all of us . . . you, me, the man down the street. Some have it under control. The rest of us try to walk a tightrope be-tween the two." The choice of words is telling, because in the film's context, a number of impulses—heterosexual desire, rape, homosexuality, S/M, murder—all seem included in the category "darkness." As Judith Mayne points out in an article on the film, *Tightrope* is unsure of the difference between male sexuality and male violence, between sex and rape, perhaps because the culture itself is unsure of these distinctions (68–69). Sexuality in Eastwood's films is seldom anything healthy; the films don't know the difference between "dirty" and "normal" sex, between desire and "darkness," and between "love"—as in the "Lookin' for Love" tattoo worn by two prostitutes in *Tightrope*—and manipulative sex or, in the world of prostitution and pornography surveyed in *Tightrope*, commercial sex (a world of which, it could be argued, mainstream film is also a part). The idealized heterosexuality so often endorsed by Hollywood spells trouble in the Eastwood films that hold it out as a possibility. Heterosexual desire leads to disaster in the two films before *Tightrope* that center around sexuality—*The Beguiled* (1971, Siegel) and *Play Misty for Me* (1971, Eastwood). Men and women in these films reach an impasse; they do not know how to coexist.

Sexuality seems something to be feared, as in the many films in which Eastwood characters save women from being raped (for example, *The Outlaw Josey Wales*, *The Gauntlet*, *Bronco Billy*, *Pale Rider*). Heterosexual relationships are to be suffered over and survived, as in the numerous films in which the Eastwood character recounts a ruined love affair in his past, scenes that evoke the sometimes woeful lyrics of country music, a form for which many of the films display great fondness.

As we've seen, masculinity and femininity are defined very narrowly in the Dirty Harry series. Male subjectivity according to these films is best isolated not so much from women individually, but from the idea of woman. Women are "safest" to deal with in these films when they are like men (but still certifiably heterosexual). Officer Moore (Tyne Daly) is a hazard for Harry until she shows that she possesses the requisite "male" attributes—courage, logic, ability with weapons—to measure up to his standards.

Similarly, these films, like the homophobic culture at large, characterize male homosexuality as "feminine," because it poses a similar threat to men's notions of themselves. Male homosexuality is regarded, albeit furtively, as permissible so long as gay men exhibit masculine standards of competence. In *Magnum Force*, for example, when Harry hears rumors that a group of crack-shot young rookies might be gay, he answers, "If everybody could shoot like that, I wouldn't care if the whole damn department was queer." If, as in the Western, masculinity is measured by competence with guns, then Harry's standards for acceptance of women and gay men are clear: Throw off the stigma of your "affliction" by living according to my criteria.

This conditional acceptance goes a few steps further in *Sudden Impact*. By the time of this film, twelve years after *Dirty Harry*, the murderer has become a woman who, like Harry, has given up on institutions of law to guarantee justice. This turns the victims from nameless targets into those who deserve to die, and it aligns Harry with the figure positioned by the formula as the villain. Moreover, the artist, played by Sondra Locke, and the artist's comatose sister are rape victims; in a repeated subjective flashback, the gang rape of the young women is shown as a horrific violation, the fullest expression of the later films' virtual preoccupation with rape.

However, *Sudden Impact* gives masculinity an out. As if the sight of men as rapists were not convincingly brutal by itself, the rape scene is made truly horrible to male subjectivity by the inclusion of a woman, coded as lesbian, who laughs demonically through the rape, encourages it, and is shown in a later flashback to have set it up. Here is a characteristic displacement of Eastwood's films up to this time: The onus for male sexual violence is shifted onto woman, with woman somehow as its instigator. The film separates out the threat and the male dread of woman by condensing them into a figure in which, it is assumed, women would not recognize themselves any more than men would recognize themselves as Scorpio. If men can no longer argue that women indirectly want, invite, and enjoy rape, then this film demonstrates how the impulse to rape can still be located by patriarchy outside the male—women must somehow share the blame. The questions to ask of Eastwood's films are these: If sexuality is threatening, does the threat come from a male fear of castration, or as Karen Horney suggested, from a fear of the vagina itself—and do both fears constitute displacements from the real issue, man's suspicion and fear of his own sexuality, his dread of the consequences of his own desires and impulses?

The film to look at first for these issues is *The Beguiled*. Although the better-known film from the same period that raises the specter of male fear of women is *Play Misty for Me*, I find *The Beguiled* much more interesting and troubled. *Misty* is strictly one-sided in its view of sexuality; it finds literally horrifying the prospect of women as autonomous sexual agents. The film can imagine only two related types of female sexuality. One involves role reversal, with the woman the aggressor and the man forced to submit. The film's ad image displays this reversal: a crazed Evelyn (Jessica Walter), looking remarkably like Andy Robinson as Scorpio in *Dirty Harry*, stands over Eastwood, brandishing a knife while he cowers in fear. The tag line, "The Scream You Hear May Be Your Own," puts a male spectator in the untenable position of having a scream elicited from him in a scenario dominated by a knife-wielding (castrating) woman.

The other alternative to male-determined female sexuality that *Misty* can imagine is hysteria. Evelyn's psychosis stems from her inability to stay within the one-night-stand agreement proposed by the Eastwood character at the beginning, a problem another sort of film might find acceptable and even admirable. Her monstrosity grows from her refusal to be ruled by the heterosexual arrangement whereby the woman waits for the man to initiate things, to "sit back and act like a girl." She is aggressively dependent—an oxymoron that expresses the man's fear of a female sexuality inside which he could lose himself; the Jessica Walter character virtually embodies the myth of the "vagina dentata" described by Horney.

This film's plot—and spirit—seems closely copied by the 1987 Glenn Close–Michael Douglas hit *Fatal Attraction*. While the later film sees autonomous female sexuality as a threat to the family, the favored myth of the late eighties, *Misty*'s hysteric threatens the "swinging single" male heterosexuality celebrated in the late sixties and early seventies as a by-product of the "sexual revolution." In short, each film puts an endangered patriarchal myth of its era on the line in order to restore it finally— Eastwood is reinstated at the end of *Misty* in an "open" relationship with his properly "feminine" girlfriend; *Fatal*'s last shot is a framed portrait of the newly reasserted, holy family.

The Beguiled, on the other hand, anticipates *Tightrope*. Patriarchal films—and Eastwood's are certainly no exceptions—tend to code female sexuality and femininity itself as frightening and dangerous, or to neutralize them by fetishizing them. However, these two films, made thirteen years apart, explore sexual repression and desire; they peer into the darkness, and often they look away, but what they turn up asks more questions about male sexuality than the film themselves seem comfortable with.

The Beguiled, directed by Don Siegel, was the first of three Eastwood films released in 1971, the other two being *Misty* and *Dirty Harry*. It is perhaps Eastwood's least-known film and one of his rare commercial disasters, although Siegel in interviews calls it his own best work. It is perhaps Eastwood's only film not designed as a vehicle for him, but this is not to say that he is miscast. On the contrary, his performance as a mendacious opportunist is the best answer in his early career to those who have called Eastwood "limited" or a "non-actor" (Patterson 92). In fact, the film, which takes place entirely on the grounds of a private girls' school in the South during the Civil War, was so out of character for Eastwood that Universal Studios, according to Johnstone, "appeared to have a corporate breakdown over its release" (74), showing the sort of confusion that can result in the Hollywood system when a star commodity—especially one so narrowly defined as Eastwood—offers a product different from what the marketers know how to sell. "*The Beguiled* wasn't a picture where Clint wins the Civil War single-handedly," Siegel said, "but from their publicity you'd have thought it was" (Johnstone 74). Eastwood attributed the film's failure to the audience's expectations: "It probably would have been a more successful film if I hadn't been in it . . . [Eastwood's fans] didn't like seeing me play a character who gets his leg cut off, gets emasculated. They wanted a character who could control everything around him" (Johnstone 74).

Consider this plot: In the South during the Civil War, a schoolgirl comes across an injured Union corporal named John McBurney (Eastwood); she brings him to the Farnsworth Seminary for Young Ladies, a plantation-turned-boarding-school whose student body has dwindled to six. The matriarch, Miss Martha (Geraldine Page), lets the wounded man convalesce at the school, planning to turn him in to the Confederates as soon as he is well enough to travel. The women, who include a virginal young teacher, Edwina (Elizabeth Hartman), and a black slave, Hallie (Mae Mercer), become attracted to him. McBurney tells the women stories that are contradicted by quick cuts to the actual events. Martha has much to hide as well; subjective flashbacks reveal an incestuous relationship with her brother.

Martha, Edwina, and Carol, a libidinous seventeen-year-old, all fall in love with McBurney. One night, unbeknownst to the others but shown to the audience in an elaborate montage, each waits for him to hobble on his crutches to her room. McBurney goes to Carol's room, where Edwina finds them in bed; furious, she pushes him down a flight of stairs. Martha directs the students to carry the unconscious McBurney to a long table. She decides to cut off his shattered leg—in order to guard against gangrene, she says. The next day McBurney, horrified and wrathful, wreaks havoc in the house. He threatens the women with rape. They respond by preparing a supper in which he will be fed "mushrooms." McBurney, eating the fatal fungi, announces that he is leaving, taking Edwina with him as his wife. As Martha warns Edwina away from the "mushrooms," the poison takes effect. The film ends with the women sewing McBurney a winding sheet and preparing to bury him in the garden as a plaintive period ballad, "Come All Ye Pretty, Fair Maids," sung a cappella by Eastwood, comes onto the soundtrack.

Obviously, this is a far cry from the Eastwood formula; the film's resounding box-office failure assured that he would not veer from it again until his stardom was secure enough to weather such risks. The bizarre story, with its macabre irony, overtones of gothic melodrama, and its spectator distancing, is worthy of Claude Chabrol, a director with a taste for poisonings, for poisonous sexual and family relations, and for absurdist twists on melodramatic situations. The film's irony, underscored by the ballad, which warns young men, "Don't go for a soldier; don't join no army," is that while armies rage against each other on the outside, the real war is between men and women. McBurney is on enemy territory in a dual sense—he's a Yankee on Rebel territory and he's the sole man in a female environment; but in the same dual sense, he is himself the enemy. The film is entirely uncertain about whether he is the one threatened, as in *Play Misty for Me* (whose very title is a woman's order to a man), or whether he is the threat. Who is the beguiler and who "the beguiled"? Similarly the spectator positioning is difficult to pinpoint. The film is not shot in a subjective style so that the spectator experiences the action as the Eastwood protagonist does, as in *Misty* and *Tightrope*; nor does it pose Eastwood as an omnipotent figure who supplies the narrative action, as in the Man with No Name and Dirty Harry films.

However, it is tempting simply to dismiss *The Beguiled* as a misogynist film. As in *Misty* its Eastwood protagonist is forced into a passive role in relation to women. The three main female characters fall into familiar types—Carol, the tart, a type that embodies both a male fantasy and contempt for aggressive female sexuality; Edwina, the virgin, a type that adheres to nineteenth-century patriarchal law at the same time as men despise her for her withholding aloofness; and Martha, the aging woman whose active control over her life must be seen as a cover for some unspeakable secret and whose sexual desires are so threatening to a male audience that they must be rooted in some monstrous motivation—they must, in effect, be taboo; thus, the association here with incest. By 1971 the aging Southern female with a scandalous past was a familiar type from the plays and films of Tennessee Williams. The casting of Geraldine Page, who had starred in film versions of Williams's *Summer and Smoke* (1961) and *Sweet Bird of Youth* (1962), reinforces this connection. The reaction of the three characters to events is true to the types: Carol and Martha, rejected and humiliated, live the adage, "Hell hath no fury like a woman scorned"; Edwina's forgiveness and ecstatic acceptance of McBurney illustrate the cliché of the grateful deflowered virgin whom male sexual attention turns into an insatiable sex partner. The spectator can infer from the ending that McBurney's death and Edwina's commitment to stay at the school as Martha's partner condemn her to

26. Amid the gothic shadows of *The Beguiled*. Is he sexually threatened or a sexual threat?

lifelong "spinsterhood" and saddle her with a repressed secret like Martha's incest; in the last scene Martha is already rehearsing the girls in the official story—that McBurney died because "his heart just gave out on him."

Edwina is a pivotal character because she is an innocent surrounded by guile and lust. First deceived by McBurney, later ignorant of the group's plan to poison him, she is posited as sympathetic because she is a passive victim. The more active characters, Carol and Martha, must be punished for their aggressive desires. McBurney's victimization by Martha, Carol, and even little Amy, all motivated by jealousy, and by the others, who are motivated by hatred of Northerners, seems judged by the film as more final and insidious than Edwina's victimization by the dissembling McBurney.

In contrast to the destructive war that men wage just outside the demilitarized zone that is the Farnsworth School, the women's warfare is stealthy, veiled, and indirect. The poisoning is done under the guise of a reconciliatory supper. Martha in one scene approaches McBurney with a hatchet wrapped in a towel. Carol goes to see him on the pretense of going to her room. McBurney's "masculine" confrontations in the climactic scenes can be read as preferable to the furtive, euphemistic approach of the women with their "feminine wiles." Furthermore, the cinematographer, Bruce Surtees, uses a sepia tone that grows especially intense in the night interiors. It casts a sinister, jaundiced pallor over this female domain, suggesting a sickly dread surrounding female desire, or perhaps this film's version of sexual desire in general.

However, the film leaves unsettled the matter of whether or not McBurney's leg needed to be amputated. McBurney immediately concludes that he's been the target of vindictive, castrating women—and the amputation clearly is a symbolic castration. However, Hallie, the African American slave who has been established as one of the few reliable characters, tries to convince McBurney, "You're wrong to blame her, Mr. Johnny. Your leg was busted bad." In another sort of movie Eastwood's wrath and his move to take matters into his own hands would carry an overriding authority because the character would be acting as the agent of the spectator. Although the film finally seems clumsily to tip the balance toward the male character, enough doubts have been cast on masculinity to undermine its authority, even when represented by Eastwood. We can regard *The Beguiled* after all as a Hollywood film that throws up more contradictions than can be recuperated.

Early on, the film sets up a dialectic between the women's wariness of an enemy soldier in their midst and of a man on their premises and their desire for him. We could say that the disaster that follows is logical given the tenet of feminist film theory that holds that when a woman initiates the gaze and desire, the narrative will punish her in some way. However, in this film the women's desire for McBurney is seen as natural and involuntary. Early in the film, when Martha compliments Edwina on her appearance, she adds, "The corporal seems to be having an effect on all of us." Even the hen starts laying eggs. Hallie tells McBurney, "You must have rooster blood in you"; Hallie tells a cow that won't give much milk, "You're dryin' up like all us other women around here."

The alignment of women with nature is nothing new in patriarchy, and as we've seen, the various women's desires for McBurney are problematic. But the film is ambivalent about the women's desires because it is ambivalent about its male protagonist. In the opening sequence in which Amy is guiding the wounded man, who walks using a long branch as a cane, one of the girls, in close-up, asks Edwina if it's true that "if the Yankees win, they'll rape every one of us." At this moment there is a quick cut to McBurney, panting and lurching past the camera. Thus McBurney is almost immediately associated with the prospect of rape. It's pointed out early that despite the self-other dynamic of the war, the women are afraid of even the men on their own side, and with reason. As Martha leaves the house, ostensibly to tell the passing Southern patrols about her prisoner, she asks a student who wants to go with her, "You want them to see you, girl?" Later, after Martha in a scene laden with danger and threat gets rid of three frightening Southern soldiers who want to stay at the school, one of the younger girls asks Edwina why they should be afraid of their own soldiers. At another point Edwina tells McBurney that she doesn't trust any man and later, he justifies her distrust by deceiving and betraying her. And in a exchange between McBurney and Hallie, in which he tells her that as a black she should want the North to win, she says, "You white folks ain't killin' each other 'cause you care 'bout us niggers. White men are the same everywhere in this world." McBurney replies, "You should say that men are the same everywhere, no matter what color."

The film strongly hints that all men are indeed the same. One of the points argued by Anthony Wilden in his article "In the Penal Colony: The Body as the Discourse of the Other," is that the rapist is the man who actually perpetuates the social order by making women dependent on other men for protection (38–39). McBurney is different from other male outsiders only by the values and desires the women project onto him. Moreover, the Man with No Name's identity is consistent in that it's not specified; later Eastwood characters have simple names; however, McBurney's many names show a fragmented identity. He is variously "John," "Johnny," "Mr. Johnny," "Mr. McB," "the Yank," "Mr. Yank," and "the corporal," the latter also indicating his status as "the body" or "the object." This variety of names shows the extent to which he is defined by each of the women rather than assuming his own salient identity.

Actually, however, he is a sexual predator; if it is true that men are seen in patriarchy as implicitly understood, then this film takes as given man as a manipulative, omnivorous sexual aggressor. While the film makes clear that the women's flashbacks and voice-overs are subjective,

27. Overpowered but lying in wait. With Melody Thomas, Darleen Carr, and Geraldine Page.

McBurney's seem the intrusions of omniscient narration charged with telling the "true" story. As soon as he says, "I have a great respect for land," a loud crackling is heard on the soundtrack and a flashback shows him running wildly through a Southern field, torching stacks of wheat. Thus the narration itself undercuts McBurney, introducing evidence that exposes him as unreliable.

While McBurney doesn't actually become a rapist, the film indicates that he'd be capable of rape. He sees himself as a kind of sultan with his sexual "run of the place," dreaming a soft-core-porn montage in which he cavorts individually with each of the three women. After his amputation he angrily tells Martha and Hallie, "I'm gonna be with any young lady that desires my company," but he then tells Hallie that maybe he'll start with her, a quick elision of the women's desires with his own, not to mention a confusion of sexual impulses with violent, contemptuous ones. But what his postamputatory threats about how he won't leave "till I've had my fill" suggest is that what sexual "conquests" he can't make by charm and cajolery he'll take by force, even though his "missing extremity" renders him less than forceful. There are no men to come to the rescue (as peculiar as a rescue *from* Clint Eastwood, rather than *by* him, would be, especially in an early 1970s film). McBurney simply takes his place among victimizers and scoundrels like Martha's brother. The film refuses to allow that either side in the gender war might be less rapacious than the other. It is thus no wonder that *The Beguiled* has never found an audience.

While the film depicts the women as castrating, jealous, ready to give over everything for a man, it also shows them as more than capable of living without men and as justified in their fear and wariness of them. Conversely, McBurney tries to act out a male fantasy that many Hollywood films would endorse. He is physically and numerically dominated by women, while he manipulates them in spite of his diminished position. Moreover, by his calculation and sexual gluttony, he brings much of what happens to him on himself. Through it all the film seems to vacillate, almost from scene to scene, between sympathy for McBurney and sympathy for the women. This is a film divided against itself, fascinating and maddening in its contradictions, contradictions exacerbated by obligatory last-minute attempts to redeem the Eastwood character, a stab at recuperation of which the film itself doesn't appear convinced.

Readers familiar with Karen Horney's concept of "the dread of woman" might find the preceding analysis naïve and obtuse. A story that shows a man surviving warfare but dying at the hands of women surely sounds like a classic example of the condition described in the first sentence of Horney's article: "Men have never tired of fashioning expressions for the violent force by which man feels himself drawn to the woman, and side by side with his longing, the dread that through her he might die and be undone" (134). The dread of femininity that pervades much of Eastwood's work in the seventies and later seems to be operating here at full mythic force. Moreover Don Siegel is notoriously on record as calling *The Beguiled* "a woman's picture, not a picture for women, but about them. Women are capable of deceit, larceny, murder, anything. Behind that mask of innocence lurks just as much evil as you'll ever find in members of the Mafia. Any young girl, who looks perfectly harmless, is capable of murder" (quoted in P. Cook 144).

Given this statement by the director, the wonder is that *The Beguiled* is not more misogyist. Indeed, it is as if Siegel realized what a dark vision of *man* he had created and looked for a disclaimer. In back of the statement is the assumption that we already know that men are capable, to quote Siegel by way of John Huston in *Chinatown* "of . . . *anything*." Interviewee Siegel sought to heap all the film's "evil" onto the women in one fell displacement, and after the fact: One can hardly imagine him explaining the script in this way to the actresses on the set. The movie that Siegel describes is not exactly the one he made. Unlike *Play Misty for Me*, in which dread of woman transposes the archetypal horror elements of male assailant/female victim, this film allows for the possibility that man covers his dread of woman, his fear of passivity and subordination, with aggression and domination. Arnold M. Cooper writes that " . . . all men have spent a significant formative part of their lives totally in the care of women who wiped their bottoms, fed their mouths and egos, and held their hands whenever there was danger or difficulty. The prevalence of forms of macho behavior can be generally understood as counteracting the inner fear of reversion to this earlier state" (113).

McBurney, reduced to a situation in which women tend his wounds, bathe and feed him, and decide whether or not he goes to prison, spends his conscious moments scheming about how to turn things his way and return to his accustomed dominance. The difference between *The Beguiled* and the works of myth cited by Horney as examples of man as victim and woman as destroyer—Samson and Delilah, Judith and Holofernes, John the Baptist and Salome—is that the film contains the competing myth of the trickster who gets tricked, the lecher who gets caught in the wrong bed and receives his comeuppance. For example, in Chaucer's "The Miller's Tale" the conniving young lover and the foolish cuckolded husband are punished by the narrative, but not the young wife, whose desire for sex sets the plot in motion and is viewed by the narrative as legitimate and unexceptional.

In this film, with its thesis that "all men are the same," questions of male myths and motives come to the surface. Referring to a comic-relief scene in *Tightrope* in which Wes Block's (Eastwood) little daughter asks, "Daddy, what's a hard-on?" Judith Mayne writes: "The film has no answer for the question she asks . . . but what indeed is a hard-on? Is it the desire to kill, *or* the desire for sex, and is it possible to resituate the polarities of violence and sexuality in any but either-or terms?" (68).

Remembering that some of Eastwood's other films are explicit about guns as phallic substitutes, and that the amputated McBurney's answer to his newly diminished state is to find a pistol, Eastwood's films are incapable of imagining meaningful sexual relationships because they are caught up in what Wilden calls a "basic male axiom . . . that sex is an act of violence" (42). The seldom-glimpsed but ever-present dialectic of sex and violence as weapons of power and domination shows its ugly face in *The Beguiled*; once exposed it does not vanish from the mind and cannot be convincingly displaced onto woman.

I need to conjure with the seeming incongruity (in 1971) of Eastwood's presence in this film. The remarks of Iain Johnstone, in which he seems to conclude that Eastwood's appearance in *The Beguiled* was a mistake, a bad career move, tell much about what this film might have been without Eastwood, and how his presence contributes to its ambiguity:

> As McBurney, Eastwood had an unaccustomedly wordy role. At times he was required to be the life and soul of the dinner table and his technique for winning the ladies over, especially Edwina, consisted of a considerable amount of questioning and persuasion. The audience is left with few clues as to how truly calculating McBurney is in his pursuit of the ladies; he could be merely lustful. Eastwood's performance, though suffused with charm, gives little away. When he switches to the gun-toting drunk at the end, there is still nothing in the character to indicate he would be ruthless with his captives. (74)

Johnstone, in a book just a cut above hagiography, criticizes Eastwood for inscrutability and fails to see the irony. In the heroic films, in which Eastwood is less demonstrative than he is here, the motivations are so clear that no delineation on the part of the actor is necessary. However, the audience in *The Beguiled* is still left wondering what McBurney wants as Freud's famous question is turned on man. This is an unpardonable lapse in a male protagonist, and it pervades the film with unwelcome mystery and disorientation, the latter all the more so because no controlling desire directs the proceedings. If McBurney were played by an actor who made the character's appetites and motives more specific, the spectator could participate in McBurney's desires and conquests in ways tending toward voyeurism and scopophilia. (In fact, the film could be something like Nicholson's *The Witches of Eastwick*, which has a similar plot.) A different sort of actor might make McBurney such a despicable lecher as to render the spectator superior to him and the women familiar victim figures. Eastwood, however, gives the film an edge of ambiguity that keeps it queasily ambivalent and distinctly dialectical.

More than *The Beguiled*, *Tightrope* is the film Eastwood's movies to date had been repressing. It opens with a concise reprise of that earlier film's theme. A woman is followed through ominous, deserted streets by a shadowy figure wearing tennis shoes; when a man does lay a hand on her, it is the protective hand of a police officer. The woman and the audience relax—until the camera pans the length of the cop's body to reveal the tennis shoes. Once again a woman's attacker and her would-be savior are the same man.

A match cut to another pair of tennis shoes heightens the confusion between male subject and other. These shoes are worn by the star, another man on another street, with young females. This street is bright and suburban; the girls are the man's daughters. Their toss-football game abruptly ends when they find a stray dog eating out of a trash can. Wes Block (Eastwood) tells the younger girl that they should take the dog to the pound, where "they'll find him a good home." She asks, "What happens if they don't?" Block, caught in a lie, is confronted by the first in a series of unpleasant questions into a furtive, adult world, questions the narrative will spend most of its time fielding. Furthermore, in a penultimate scene at a brewery to which the cops have tracked the serial killer, the tennis shoes that will supposedly identify the murderer have the opposite effect: All the men are wearing tennis shoes; instead of one male suspect, there are, as Block says, "120,000 of them"—the male population of New Orleans, where the film takes place. Anyone constructed as a male subject is capable of violence, the film suggests obliquely: "Men are the same everywhere."

If *The Beguiled* was not ready to confront the male subject as the source of sexual darkness, *Tightrope* finally appears to deliver on that film's promise, to correct its displacements as well as the self/other fantasies of Eastwood's films throughout the seventies. *The Beguiled* displaces much of its sexual trouble onto the secrets of the Geraldine Page character; *Tightrope*, acknowledging the patriarchal arrangement in which woman is the embodiment of sexuality and man is its source, attempts no such shift. In *The Beguiled*, when Martha charges at McBurney, crying, "You beast," he replies, "Yes, but I don't run a school for young girls." In *Tightrope* Wes Block runs a home for young girls and harbors a beastly secret. In *The Beguiled* it is still the women who stay at home and wait for love and romance. In the later film it is Block who is lonely and disillusioned. The women of the Farnsworth School mean to treat the enemy soldier's wounds and then do their patriotic duty by turning him in, but they give in to his calculating charm and their own desires. Block is supposed to be questioning prostitutes as part of his investigation, but he gives in to their conditioned seductiveness and his (implied) sadomasochistic fantasies.

It would be wrong to see the film as just another instance of role reversal, dominant cinema's superficial variation on the active male/passive female paradigm, which it affirms by positing the exception that proves the rule. The film centers around the very issue of the male as desiring subject. But since the star is Eastwood, the subject of desire itself is new because, as we've seen, the essential Man with No Name/Dirty Harry persona is superior to the base desires of ordinary males,

28. As a father of young girls, the Eastwood cop moves into a less-imaginary world in which he has responsibilities and attachments. With Jennifer Beck and Alison Eastwood.

satisfying those of the spectator but not succumbing to them himself. However, in those films in which Eastwood is paired with a female character—the films with Sondra Locke in particular—the male identification figure does not usually vie with another, less magnetic man for the hand of the heroine; instead he fights off rapists and other "undesirables."

The Beguiled is exceptional because it refuses to categorize men in these ways, but *Tightrope* goes further. By using the classic device of the doppelgänger, the film pits a responsible citizen who supports children and lives in the suburbs against a weaker side of the same man, which succumbs to the carefully constructed commercial temptations of the sex shop section of the New Orleans French Quarter. The film then hints at just what the latter might be capable of. The dialectic of the puritanical and the prurient comes to the surface here, with a protagonist who can't explain sex to his children despite, or because of, the fact that he consorts with prostitutes. Here again is an Eastwood film that knows what exploitative or "dirty" sex is but can't arrive at a heterosexual norm. This film deconstructs Eastwood's films' exploitation of cathartic violence by implicating its hero's involvement in—or desire for—the deaths of women and, again like *The Beguiled*, comes close to naming man as the author of most of the things for which men blame and dread women.

In *The Beguiled* I identified several types of women. I won't call the women in *Tightrope* "types," but they do fall into four distinct categories: young daughters (Amanda, played by Eastwood's own daughter Alison, and Penny [Jennifer Beck]); Block's wife, who left him; the prostitutes of the French Quarter; and the feminist, Beryl Thibodeaux (Genevieve Bujold), who runs a rape crisis center. In this film the hero's success or failure depends not on competence, the quality Eric Patterson considers the most important to the Dirty Harry films (99), but on how he relates to each of these categories of women (indeed, Block's preoccupations render him less than competent). Of these four the daughters and Beryl seem to belong together because Block cares about them, they seem to want to help him, and his actions and proclivities indirectly leave them vulnerable. I want to discuss the ex-wife and the prostitutes first, however, because Block's wife's departure drives him to the prostitutes, with whom he acts out fantasies and drives that the film poses as the main problem of the narrative.

Christine Holmlund writes that *Tightrope* contains elements from the thriller, *film noir*, and soft-core pornography: "the movie's point of view shots indicate just how strong patriarchal vision is in this movie. They are overwhelmingly male, and they overwhelmingly position women as sexual objects and little more" ("Sexuality and Power" 38). While the prostitutes are presented in the codes of pornography, the film advances a critique of the position in which women are placed in life and in representation. However, this critique is as ambivalent and underdeveloped as the dark insinuations about masculinity in *The Beguiled*. Holmlund sees a split in the film between good women and bad women, "reminiscent of the Victorian angel/whore split" ("Sexuality" 38). However, the film hints that all women, except those whom it defines as feminists, simply accept and play the roles to which they are assigned by patriarchy—and the film's feminist winds up playing some of these roles too.

The film is unclear about why Block's wife has left him. She is seen briefly in two scenes, and she never speaks. The second time she appears, in the hospital after the attack on Amanda, Block's visit there is interrupted by a phone call, perhaps an endlessly repeated event in their marriage, since ringing phones often cut short Block's time with his daughters. Block tells Thibodeaux that his wife left him "for anyone else," and we see her with her new man in his Mercedes. These details make the wife less threatening to a male audience than is a character such as the wife played by Meryl Streep in *Kramer vs. Kramer*, who leaves her husband and child for a new life on her own, not for another man. *Kramer* finds abhorrent the possibility that a woman could find something better outside of marriage, and creates a double standard by demonstrating that the former husband can do just fine at his role *and* hers. The wife in *Tightrope*, however, doesn't object to marriage—just marriage to *this* man, suggesting that the problem is with him. While the suggestion that Eastwood could be lacking is a radical idea in his films before the 1980s, to male spectators a flesh-and-blood rival is preferable to a suggestion that their institutions are found wanting. Such a lack turns the character, however, and the star persona bound up in it, into a subject in the therapeutic sense. It also moves the spectator into the reliable male role of investigator, implicated in the star/protagonist's fantasies and drives.

In running to prostitutes after the failure of his marriage, especially when the images of these women are familiar from pornography, Block acts out a common scenario. Ethel S. Person, in an article about the male fantasy of the "omni-available woman," writes that men create for themselves in fantasy a woman who is always ready for sex, always ready to please the man. This figure is in effect a representation of the man's adolescent sexuality projected onto woman. "Such women cannot accuse men of being beasts, barbarians or dirty" (78); they represent how "men cope with . . . anxieties about performance and female rejection" (83). Susan Lurie takes a similar tack in "Pornography and the Dread of Woman," in which she says that "pornographers literally attempt to shape female sexuality in the image of male sexual fantasies" (159). Lurie works a reversal on Freud's notion of fetishism as a response to man's realization that the woman has been castrated and that the same could befall him. Lurie writes:

> The terrifying problem, of course, is not that Mother is "castrated," but that she isn't. *Males would be castrated, mutilated if they had no penises* [emphasis in original], and the idea that women possess the whole range of individual powers that the male identifies with his penis and yet have "no penis" is what is so terrible. Eventually men embrace the project their socialization meticulously designs for them: To convince themselves and all the world that women are what men would be if they had no penises—bereft of sexuality, helpless, incapable. (166)

Having experienced rejection, baffled at his failure to please his wife but suspecting that the problem is his, not that of always-culpable woman,

Block flees to women who do not find fault with him and cannot leave him. They are made-to-order products offered by an industry that, like Hollywood film, carefully effaces its production and presents an illusion of reality—in this case, the omni-available woman, seductive and aroused, with no purpose but to provide pleasure. They are fetish objects to whom Block looks for a validation of his virility. He is searching, but again the film doesn't know for what; is it for love, for an understanding of his impulses, or for what happened to the myths of male control like those Eastwood's own films had served to perpetuate?

The film seems unsure of what to make of these women. Are these really "bad" women (as Holmlund suggests)? Is the film buying into (and, of course, selling) the "omni-available" fantasy? Or is it conscious that the women wear masks and practice the learned behavior of "temptresses"? Are they depicted as "bad" women or as performers who have learned to project a persona, as in Hollywood cinema, in order to perpetuate their commodity value in a system of mutual dependence? The mask, the persona, the performance are, after all, items Eastwood films know something about, adept as they often are at displaying the star's expected performance of violence. In *Bronco Billy*, which virtually takes image-construction as its subject matter, Eastwood's children's-carnival cowboy, an ex-convict, ex–shoe salesman from New Jersey, explains that "I'm who I want to be." While the freedom to be the person one wants to be is not an option for all men, it is even less possible for women. If Billy has made himself into who he wants to be, then these prostitutes, perhaps like all women in conventional roles, have been made—or have made themselves—into what men want them to be. *Tightrope* cannot quite bring itself to probe the difference between the omni-available woman as a male turn-on or as a female masquerade, dressing up indifference to men and occupational boredom.

Fleetingly but frequently, the film finds cracks in their poses. *Tightrope* opens with several of the women later identified as prostitutes at a birthday party; this seems an odd way to introduce *femmes fatales*. The scene is shot by only the light of birthday candles, using the Zeiss lens Stanley Kubrick originally commissioned for *Barry Lyndon* (1975), but which by 1984 had become a way of coding warmth and togetherness, as in the scene of the Henry Fonda character's eightieth birthday party in *On Golden Pond* (1981). In a later scene a young woman named Becky, interviewed by Block about one-night stands, asks, "Is there any other kind?" dropping for that instant the seductive pose she had been striking. Her question is significant not only because it shows a poignant hopelessness through the mask, but because it is a question Block himself might ask.

Similarly, when the police are at the home of the first victim, Block listens to an answering machine tape from the young woman's parents, wishing her a happy birthday, indicating that she, like Block, has had a "normal" home life separate from her secret life. This idea is taken further in a puzzling segment, in which Block has sex, viewed by the killer-double, with a woman who doesn't look like the other prostitutes. She wears horn-rimmed glasses and an ordinary flowered blouse and her come-on doesn't seem elaborate and rehearsed like those of the other women. When she turns up dead, the newspapers identify her as "a nurse." Who is this woman? Is she a prostitute? Is she, like Block, a visitor from another sort of world, exploring a dark side of her sexuality (and, since she is female, being punished for her transgression)? The film offers no answers.

I've said earlier that these glimmers of contradiction and sympathy for the prostitutes are only that—glimmers. The film seems finally not to know who these women are (perhaps, as Mayne suggests, "it doesn't know what a woman is" at all). Certainly the women show little reaction to the multiple murders. It doesn't occur to the film that the women might grieve for each other or be afraid. Instead they continue going about their business as sex toys.

Anthony Wilden discusses rape as "a means of communication between men" (39). Using Susan Brownmiller's book *Against Our Will* and citing examples of war atrocities, Wilden writes that woman is a term of exchange, and that a way of claiming another man's property is to violate that man's female relatives. Brownmiller says that in such cases "women are used almost as inanimate objects to prove a point among men" (quoted in Wilden 41). Stephen Heath makes nearly identical points about pornography, calling it "a relation between men, nothing to do with a relation to women except by a process of phallic conversion that sets them as the terms of male exchange" ("Male Feminism" 2).

I've discussed the ways in which the women of pornography and prostitution in *Tightrope* have been remade in the images of male sexual fantasies; the men in this film use women as slates on which to write messages to each other. The pornographers remake women into images that Block, the consumer, wants to re-create for his own pleasure. For example, Block watches Becky wrestle with another young woman in a pool of Vaseline on the stage in a bar; later they have sex—with her in handcuffs, oiled up as she was onstage. In another scene Block questions a tattoo artist who was said to have beaten one of the victims, as the man inscribes a "Lookin' for Love" tattoo on Becky—two men literally writing messages to each other, using women. The women in this film earn no rest from male scrutiny and violation. The men in the forensics lab where this film spends much of its time (unlike the *Dirty Harry* films whose hero would never bother with such picayune processes) delight in proving their competence by combing the victims' bodies for clues. One recites in detail everything one victim ate and drank before she was murdered. Even dead, these women are cheated out of their privacy.

The sneakers-shod double who kills the women Block has sex with wants to get to Block. Women, in time-honored tradition, are his media. Otto Rank theorizes the double in psychology, folklore, and literature as a disastrous wish-fulfillment apparatus that acts out the darkest repressed desires of the subject (76). The double is "that image which has been constructed by one's guardian spirit into a pursuing and torturing conscience" (57). In Eastwood's films in which women figure prominently—especially the six with Sondra Locke—they are usually brought under a kind of gentle domination in which they share the hero's adventures (as in *The Gauntlet* and the two *Every Which Way* movies) and/or become part of his world, due to his protective love and benevolence (as in *Bronco Billy* and *Sudden Impact*). These motifs are opposed by the frequent mentions of failed relationships in the Eastwood character's past. In *Tightrope* the two motifs merge in the character of the wife, who refuses to be part of the hero's life and whose rejection of him is not an old story narrated in passing but the event that propels the plot. Because of this the man's desire to control, which usually displaces his need for love and hence his vulnerability, is rebuffed, and his resultant hurt brings to the surface the aggression and resentment that drives much of man's relation to woman.

Wilden sums up the paradox: "In [men's] depending for their own sense of identity—and above all for their sense of security as 'real men' among other men—on their relationship to their wives or woman friends, they resent them" (49). So in taking to its murderous extreme the aggression Block rehearses with sadomasochistic handcuff sex (blurring once again any distinction between violence and sex), the double acts out both of the functions identified by Rank: He carries out the protagonist's repressed desires, and by exposing those desires in all their horror, acts as his conscience. Thus the violence becomes self-directed and nearly destroys everything close to Block.

Most of those who have written about this film criticize its ending, which falls back on crime genre conventions. Block rescues Beryl Thibodeaux; the murderer turns out to be a former cop whom Block had arrested for rape years earlier, making the double's actions too easy to explain away as acts of revenge. This fancy plotting is contrived to resolve a conundrum that might just resist resolution; I am reminded of Henry James's comment on Ibsen's *Hedda Gabler* as "the picture not of an action but of a condition" (Le Gallienne xxiv), and thus not resolvable dramatically. The classic doppelgänger plot, according to Rank, is resolved by the "slaying of the double, through which the hero seeks to protect himself permanently from the pursuits of his self"; the slaying, however, "is really a suicidal act" (79).

Modern literature on the doppelgänger theme has retained this "double-suicide." For example, in Nabokov's *Lolita* Humbert's absurd and self-destructive tracking down of Quilty results in his own arrest and death. In O'Connor's *Wise Blood* Hazel Motes's "New Jesus" double suffers an equally absurd death when Hazel runs him over with his car. On the other hand, Hollywood has often made of the hero's killing of the double an act of cleansing, a redemption. The death of Lin McClintock's (James Stewart) murderous double, performed in water like a baptism, in Mann's *Bend of the River* is one example. Guy's ridding himself of Bruno in *Strangers on a Train* (to whose ending *Tightrope*'s trainyard conclusion may be alluding) is another.

The difference between the classical double and characters like Block and McClintock is that they are granted a recognition. In the other they recognize the dark instincts they themselves repress. Block finally confronts himself in the mirror, illustrating the Hegelian notion that the need to change is motivated by self-disgust. The film doesn't go nearly far enough, however, in showing how he sheds his violent impulses and his taste for prostitution and pornography. In *Tightrope* the contradictions are just too great to be swept away by a recuperation.

The awkward and unconvincing slaying of the double is not all that critics have found wrong with this film's ending. The character played by Genevieve Bujold, despite her feminism and the fact that she runs a rape crisis center, needs to be rescued by the hero in the finale, even though as Mayne points out, "Beryl Thibodeaux may well be rescued by a man, but the man himself was saved by a dog" ("Walking" 68). The film refuses to allow for any ultimate authorities, be they police, male subjects, fathers, or rape crisis counselors. However, it will not permit the heroine to be competent at the very thing she teaches—how to ward off an attacker. Beryl Thibodeaux is presented as a determined, witty, likable person who doesn't need a man. She is explicitly a feminist ("remarkably free of the 'libber' stereotype one might expect in an Eastwood film" [Mayne "Walking" 70]). However, the role she plays is not so different from that of the conventional "love interest." She is peripheral to the plot, and the spectator finds out very little about her. Her function, as Mayne points out, is to provide Block with his "salvation." What's more, his case is too serious to be solved by "true love," the constitution of which this film doesn't pretend to know. It takes a feminist.

Thibodeaux is coded as a feminist without that label taking on a negative connotation. Furthermore, her instructions to women about rape seem the product of some solid research into the work of real-life rape crisis counselors on the part of the screenwriter (Richard Tuggle). However, outside of her work, which is shown in one scene, she doesn't really appear to practice feminism. When the topic comes up, it is handled gingerly with the vaguest dialogue in the film: About the work she does Thibodeaux says, "We all need it." But what is it that "we all need"—an understanding of why men rape, of why violence is confused in the culture with sex, of what to do to change attitudes, of how women can empower themselves? The film presents a feminist while meeting the question of her project with euphemisms.

Moreover, the film attributes to Thibodeaux the oldest of "feminine" characteristics—intuition. She just knows, as if by magic, Block's problem, his fear of intimacy. She accepts with earth-motherly placidity Block's carousing (which she intuits) and his sadomasochistic sexuality (ditto). In the film's strangest scene, she offers her wrists to Block to be handcuffed. "Nobody can get to you in these?" she asks. "They'll stop just about anybody," he responds. Is her offer a test to see if he will shut out intimacy with her? Is the film suggesting that women—even feminists—might like to be handcuffed and dominated? Does Block refuse because as his partner in a socially sanctioned "dating" relationship (one with whom "you can have a hard-on anytime you want," as the younger daughter innocently puts it), Thibodeaux is in the wrong category for handcuffs? The film posits (uncertainly) a feminist as the Eastwood character's redemption, while also saying (uncertainly) that redemption must come by way of Block's recognition of his condition and his elimination—in the death of the double—of "the darkness inside of him." Thus, as a "Clint Eastwood" film, *Tightrope* switches (uncertainly) from the male subject's monolithic independence to his use of a woman for validation—something a woman who really tries to live out her feminism would probably not consent to.

As it is, however, this is still an extraordinary film to have been produced in Hollywood, let alone as a vehicle that Eastwood's audience was apparently able to accept. Unlike other films up to this time in which he departed from his persona, this one was a box-office success, perhaps a reflection of its titillation value. However, in 1984 it was seen as a not-quite-satisfactory first step. J. Hoberman wrote that if Bujold were to make more films with Eastwood, "she might draw from him something extraordinary" (46), suggesting not only that the function of the character—and of Bujold as actress—is to "draw something" from the star, but that this very ambitious genre film doesn't accomplish all that it might have.

When I saw *Tightrope* on its original release, I felt that it didn't go far enough in implicating the Eastwood protagonist. The film seemed to shield the character/star even while setting out to expose him. While I am more appreciative now of what the film does and fault it less for what it doesn't do, the discretion that I sensed then lies in what the film opts not to show. Not only is it puritanical about sex, fading out like a Production Code–era movie at the suggestion of it, but uniquely for an Eastwood film it is also discreet about the handling of violence. Like the Dirty Harry films, this one revolves around serial killings; however, *Tightrope*'s murders, like its sex scenes, take place off screen. We've seen that the voyeuristic views of murders in the Harry films—often of pretty young women—show the chaos of a world awaiting the hero's intervention and perhaps give the audience a misogynistic, misanthropic pleasure it can easily disavow.

However, a guilty, horrific aura surrounds both the sex and the murders in *Tightrope*, linking them to each other and showing the trepidation that comes into play when the subject becomes (a) suspect. The dialogue of the other Eastwood police films, which is strictly of the "hard-boiled" school of detective writing, is exposed here as a self-protective cover for hidden drives and hurts. Moreover, the star's face is photographed here with emphasis on the mask—as if the face of Clint Eastwood were a shield protecting man from truth about himself. The narcissism that excludes all others doubles back on itself in *Tightrope*. In close-up Block/ Eastwood's look doesn't squint off into the distance at some threatening menace. It winces at the consequences of its own excesses, as in the scene in which Block sees the tie he left with a prostitute at the scene of a murder; it appears as if it would rather look away, as the film itself does with its demure fade-outs.

Ethel S. Person concludes her article on male fantasies by writing that "phallic narcissism, reinforced by the male cultural ego ideal of macho sexuality, tends to obscure . . . underlying dynamics. The fantasies of the omni-available woman . . . are 'windows' on that buried world" (93). That some of Eastwood's late films unearth the dynamics of "that buried world" of male sexuality—with the very same hands that helped keep it buried—provides its own criticism of the dominant order. *Tightrope* presents the contradiction of a star who tries to convince his audience that the qualities on which his successful persona has been based are lies.

Eastwood's films in the early eighties—*Bronco Billy*, *Honkytonk Man*, *Tightrope*—seemed passionate attempts to critique and break out of one of the most monolithic star personas ever devised. After *Tight-rope*, Eastwood filled the rest of the decade with kinder, gentler remakes of *High Plains Drifter* (*Pale Rider*, 1985) and *The Gauntlet* (*Pink Cadillac*, 1989) as well as a Reaganite paean to militarism (*Heartbreak Ridge*, 1986). While some of these mildly represented new departures, there was little in them that continued the deconstruction of his persona. One wondered if *Tightrope* had been a fluke. Then, in the early 1990s, came two mature works with much more to say on the subjects of manhood and lies, *White Hunter, Black Heart* (1990) and *Unforgiven* (1992).

16

Acting and "Manliness":
White Hunter, Black Heart

□□□

A frequently heard complaint from male film actors is that their occupation is "unmanly," an embarrassment to the actor's male identity. Mickey Rourke was quoted as calling acting "very much woman's work" ("Attitudes" 140). William Holden and Robert Redford were said to have worried about emoting on screen. Clark Gable reportedly agonized over having to cry in *Gone With the Wind*, asking over and over, "Would Clark Gable do this?" Director Billy Wilder said that "only actors who are ashamed to act are worth their salt," adding that he liked working with William Holden because "he dies every time he has to act" (Cohan 63).

Such anxiety stems from the constitution of gender in a patriarchal culture. "In everyday and academic discourse," writes Arthur Brittan, "we find that men are commmonly described as aggressive, assertive, independent, competitive, insensitive, and so on. These attributions are based on the idea that there is something about men which transcends their local situation. Men are seen as having natures which determine their behaviour in all situations" (3–4). Masculinity is thus seen as natural and uncomplicated, making the concept of "performance" problematic. Performance is valued when it refers to the proving of one's potential through action, as in the statement "He performed well under pressure." Performance, as it pertains to athletics, cars, military campaigns, and sex, secures a positive meaning for man because it involves the testing and demonstration of his abilities. However, performance is displaced onto femininity when it connotes a playing of parts, a fragmentation of the self into an array of roles, a creation of a self other than one's own, and a dissembling.

Two ways for actors to minimize the "shame" of acting have been to deemphasize performance and to "act natural." These antidotes to a "feminine" pursuit dovetail with the star system, which has specialized in the commodification of coherent star personas designed to represent the star "as he really is." They also suit the requirements of the classical cinema for realism. Thus, three intersecting systems—masculinism, stardom, and classical cinema—work in part on assumptions that masculinity is natural and nonperformative and that it requires the containment of volatility and emotion. It is no accident that most of the masculine icons of the American classical cinema—Clark Gable, Cary Grant, John Wayne, Humphrey Bogart—have been perceived by audiences and critics as being themselves and not really acting on camera. This perception set up a now-familiar distinction between what Naremore refers to as the "image" star, who "behaves" on screen, and the "thespian," who "acts." Naremore writes that heroes in Hollywood films are "usually noble, honest, and relatively inexpressive. . . . [T]he star is often supposed to 'behave' rather than merely pretend" (224).

Warren Beatty describes acting as "trying as hard as you can to be out of control all the while that you also have to be in control of being out of control" (Mailer 226). The idea of control and of maintaining it is of course central to the continuation of patriarchy. It is also a key to Eastwood's appeal. Eastwood plays soft-spoken but deadly fantasy figures by keeping his facial expressions and vocal range, his inflection and volume, tightly under control. The Eastwood persona "control[s] everything around him," as he put it (Johnstone 74). Yet the figure is "out of control," in the sense that he represents imaginary freedom from outside restriction and authority; he cannot be controlled by external forces. Thus Eastwood shows his "control of being out of control" by suppressing and effacing the performance element in his own performances.

The eclipsing of the person by the persona is not unusual for action stars. There is little sense of a "person" behind the "character" with which Eastwood is identified. The comic mileage that *Back to the Future III* (1990) gets from Marty McFly's giving his name as "Clint Eastwood" when he finds himself in the Old West shows how inextricable the Man with No Name persona is from Eastwood the person and actor.

Eastwood's 1980s revisions seem part of an attempt to draw attention to Clint Eastwood, the real person behind the mask—an effort of which his 1992 Academy Awards were the culmination. Much more publicity was given to his work as director and producer, to his two children, Alison and Kyle, with whom he costarred in *Tightrope* and *Honkytonk Man*, respectively, and to his term as mayor of the small resort town of Carmel, California, not to mention the unwanted publicity from Sondra Locke's 1989 "palimony suit." Even his relationship with Locke had been kept in the public mind through the six films that Eastwood and Locke made together.

Eastwood's revisions culminate in a desire to perform that finally gets expressed in *White Hunter, Black Heart* (1990). Eastwood takes on a role far outside his persona, but also takes a risk many more-acclaimed actors might have shunned, playing a thin fictionalization of a magnetic and singular film personality, John Huston. In his foray from action films into an "acting" film, he manages to treat an Eastwood specialty— troubled masculinity—in the form of the rugged adventurer, the "Hemingway male."

The novel *White Hunter, Black Heart* was written in 1953 by Peter Viertel, who was brought in by John Huston to rewrite *The African Queen* after James Agee suffered a heart attack while finishing a first draft of the screenplay. Viertel, who calls himself Verrill in the novel, roamed the Belgian Congo with Huston in 1950 and 1951. The novel depicts the director, named John Wilson, as a cruel, brave, irresponsible, and brilliant personality obsessed with shooting an elephant at the expense of the film he has been hired to make.

By the time Eastwood optioned the novel, whose rights had been in the hands of numerous producers since the mid-1950s, the film that John Wilson is making in Africa couldn't be presented as some vague melodrama, as it is in the novel; it had to be *The African Queen* (called *The African Trader* in the film). When Wilson and Verrill discuss the script, the dialogue they read is instantly recognizable from Huston's film. The costumes were copied from the photographs in Katharine Hepburn's 1987 memoir of the film's production. The actor playing the director in Viertel's novel couldn't play his own conception of "John Wilson," as he might have if the film had been made years earlier. He had to play John Huston.

In a sympathetic review of *White Hunter, Black Heart*, Janet Maslin wrote: "To know that Mr. Eastwood makes his entrance in one scene dressed in white tie, declaring 'Do come in, chaps,' and stroking a small pet monkey, is to wonder what on earth he had in mind" (1C). Eastwood's film struck many as a curiosity on two counts: One, why would Clint Eastwood want to make a film about John Huston, a filmmaker whose audience, films, career, and way of working were very unlike his own? Two, why was Eastwood in effect miscasting himself, taking on a role that required him to conceptualize, internalize, and impersonate a man whose temperament and behavior were apparently so unlike his own?

Eastwood is, after all, a behavioral "persona" actor, whose films, even the revisionist ones, involve the embodiment of archetypes. He makes his strongest impressions by his presence alone. His effects come from the withholding of affect; the audience has to crane forward slightly to catch the nuances in his voice. Part of the fascination of *Tightrope* comes from the effort to read the small changes and realizations breaking through the face of a man whose "stoicism" masks a repressed male subject whose own emotions, gender construction, and sexuality are unknown to him. Eastwood is essentially a mime who relies on only the slightest physical movements. Every twitch, every arm movement or raising of an eyebrow carries dramatic power. He is an external actor with a repertoire of mannerisms, tag lines, and reactions that the audience takes pleasure in reading. "All he has to do is stand there looking scruffy and intense and people love it" (Fayard 47).

In *White Hunter* Eastwood had to play outside himself, expanding an understated acting style to cover a showy extrovert whose lines—most of them taken from the novel—play more like monologues than parts of conversations. One of the elements that always belied the Eastwood supermale was the small, limited voice; the actor reduced the thin voice to a whisper at dramatic moments when the character was at his most threatening. Eastwood's terse, soft-spoken delivery coded the laconic man who needn't say much because his motives and anger are implicitly understood. However, from the actor's point of view this result was a happy accident, stemming from his need to use a light, whispery voice to his best advantage. "Limited" is not a word associated with John Huston's voice, a booming, growling, one-of-a-kind apparatus with soaring range, eccentric timbre, and generous volume. The voice matches a face that Hepburn described as "ridiculous but distinguished" (59), with eyes set back in deep pockets and a wide satchel mouth.

This comparison between Huston and Eastwood is not fair—and perhaps not even pertinent to a discussion of *White Hunter*—yet it is one that audiences and reviewers invariably make. Surely other actors just as singular as Eastwood have played well-known people and not been held to standards of complete replication; for example, George C. Scott as Patton or Barbra Streisand as Fanny Brice. Yet a close analysis of Eastwood's performance reveals how effortlessly Eastwood does enact Huston. Compared to Eastwood as Harry Callahan, who stands perfectly motionless in his scenes and hardly raises an arm, Eastwood/Huston/Wilson bounces at the knees, waves his arms, bobs his head, and gesticulates with his cigarillo (Eastwood's one allusion to the Man with No Name), using it as an "expressive object," in Naremore's term.

Jean-Louis Comolli, in discussing what is signified when an actor plays a fictional character, considers the extra dimension that comes into play when an actual historical personage is portrayed. "If the imaginary person, even in a historical fiction, has no other body than that of the actor playing him, the historical character, filmed, has at least two bodies, that of the imagery and that of the actor who represents him for us. There are at least two bodies in competition, one body too much" (44). In *White Hunter* there are probably two bodies "too much," Eastwood's and Eastwood's trying to be Huston's. The still-fresh memory of John Huston would intrude on the performance of even an unknown actor in this role. It is easy to think of the semiotic "commutation test" proposed by John O. Thompson, in which an actor's performance signs can be assessed by mentally substituting another actor in the role, the other actor in this case being Huston himself, familiar to audiences from his film performances. With Clint Eastwood in the role, distractions abound. One is the voice, which in Huston seemed a bottomless well and with Eastwood always runs up against a whisper-wall beyond which it cannot go. The ever-present whisper gives the impression of something being held back. The other distraction is, of course, the Eastwood persona itself.

Richard Dyer sees three ways in which a star's persona relates to the character he or she is playing; the one that concerns us here is the "problematic fit" between star and character. Dyer defines this as "a clash between two complex sign clusters, the star as image and the character as otherwise constructed" (*Stars* 147). Dyer's example is Marilyn Monroe in *Gentlemen Prefer Blondes* (1953); Lorelei in the Anita Loos original is a scheming, deceitful character while Monroe's persona in the early fifties was founded on her innocence. Dyer writes that such a "disjuncture," as he calls it, "may indeed be glaring . . . a familiar enough idea, miscasting"; or it "may deny the truth of the star's image *vis-à-vis* the character"—the films in which Warren Beatty plays characters who are shy and awkward around women, for example. Dyer adds that this happens "when the film is deliberately having a joke at the expense of the star's image," as when Eastwood as Bronco Billy tells a character, "Never kill a man unless it's absolutely necessary." Dyer theorizes, finally, that a disjuncture between role and star can occur because "the star's image is so powerful that all signs may be read in terms of it," citing Charlton Heston, who "'means' Heston regardless of what the film is trying to do with him" (Dyer *Stars* 148).

The way the archetypal, motionless Eastwood figure interacts with the other characters in a scene is reversed in *White Hunter*. A 1971 *Life* profile stated that "he has developed the art of underplaying to the point that anyone around him who so much as flinches looks hammily histrionic" (Fayard 45). In other words the hero is so immobile that motionlessness becomes equated with strength, making others in a scene into Others, making them look weak and—when the other characters are men—"feminine." A scene in the mayor's office in *Dirty Harry*, in which the mayor announces that he's agreeing to a serial killer's demand for ransom, contrasts Harry/Eastwood's cool with the blustering and fretting of the city officials in the room. This situation is reversed in *White Hunter, Black Heart*. The star/character is the emotive, active focus of attention rather than a still center, and others tend to take the parts of audience surrogates as they gape at and wonder about an unpredictable, shameless exhibitionist.

In the self/other dialectic of the fantasy "persona" films, supporting characters are often coded as other by point-of-view shots and by camera placements that hold the figures at a distance in the recesses of a deep-focus shot or show them intruding menacingly in close-ups. Such supporting characters, usually criminals and cowards or restrictive authority figures, are threatening at worst, ineffectual and restraining at best— nuisances either way. In *White Hunter* it is the Eastwood character who is often recessed in the shot and placed as an object rather than as an identification figure. Although Eastwood in the "persona" films is often shown appearing from a distance as a powerful, awesome figure with whom his enemies will now have to contend, here the distancing marks him as an object of scrutiny. This objectification is especially potent in a film narrated by a young partner, Verrill, who begins as an admirer of the character and ends disillusioned.

Although *White Hunter* seems a new departure in almost every way, it reveals a structure similar to that of many of the "persona" films, especially the Dirty Harry formula. As in those films the Eastwood character is larger than life. He defies authority and balks at obeying orders but has, as Verrill narrates, "the uncanny, almost divine ability to land on his feet." He is the consummate individualist, who has little use for conventional society and is single-minded in the pursuit of his quarry. As regards women Harry is a chivalrous knight, but he shuns their company; femininity is unquestionably seen as weak and inferior overall. Wilson's sexism is uglier; he discards and belittles women and, in a scene in which he insults a woman who has made anti-Semitic remarks, equates "goddamn ugly bitches" with Nazi-scale racial hatred, managing to strike blows for racial tolerance and misogyny at the same time. The Dirty Harry films give Harry a younger partner who represents a minority group, and whose skepticism toward Harry turns to admiration by the film's climax. *White Hunter* gives him Viertel's surrogate as partner and protégé, and as the partner's respect for Harry signals the shift in the film's point of view toward the protagonist, so Verrill's horror at Wilson's selfishness signals a reverse shift.

Thus *White Hunter, Black Heart* traces the fine line between goal orientation and obsession. It also shows the consequences of the sort of lone individualism celebrated in the Dirty Harry and Man with No Name films. *White Hunter* moves Eastwood from fantasy universes, where there are no limits on phallic power, to reality, where freewheeling behavior has consequences, people get hurt, and plans are destroyed. Wilson's misogyny, arrogance, and paternalism all confront him disastrously in the moment when the black native hunter is killed by an elephant during a hunt Wilson was warned not to go on. Eastwood's softening of the novel's ending—Wilson doesn't kill the elephant in the film version—makes the animal world the punisher of man's arrogance instead of its victim and renders the men "perverse little creatures from another planet, without any dignity," as the Viertel character says in dialogue from the novel.

In short *White Hunter, Black Heart* is not just the product of a sudden urge to act but an exploration of the masquerade of masculinity consistent with other Eastwood films that question the values coded in the core persona. It does show a belated drive in Eastwood of the sort described by John Ellis, in which "a certain section of the star firmament . . . seek[s] to reverse [the] tendency toward underacting in order to produce an effect of 'performance'" (108). The result is confusion in coding and reception. The film is "about" John Huston in that it uses him as a taking-off point. Eastwood's impersonation of Huston and the "body-too-much" phenomenon that it creates belie any suggestion that the film might *not* be about Huston. However, the film also focuses on Eastwood's star persona and the aggressive, unflappable, independent masculinity it has always stood for.

The tension between Eastwood's persona as a star and his ambitions as producer, director, and actor, is finally too much for the film to bear. This can be seen in the split critical reception. Reviews that saw the film as being about Huston dripped with disdain; those that regarded it as a self-reflexive and risk-taking Eastwood film bent over backward to be kind. If Eastwood had not impersonated Huston but had "played himself," audiences might have been forced to confront, as they are in *Tightrope*, the stoical, self-sufficient male archetype as he faces the consequences of his behavior. We see the culmination of stardom's double bind in *Unforgiven*. *White Hunter*'s break in the coherence of the Eastwood persona makes the film unreadable for some spectators as a critique of Eastwood-type masculinism. For others, if the role had continued from the star's image, *that* might have mitigated its impact: How bad can elephant killing be if "Clint Eastwood" does it?

In playing a boyish, loose-limbed, theatrical male, Eastwood acknowledges that patriarchal masculinity is not as narrowly defined as the heroic stoicism that connotes acting as "unmanly" would indicate.

Wilson's masculinity is highly performative. As Eastwood plays him Wilson works hard to attract attention, to maintain control by keeping others off guard, to build up his ego by pursuing his goals. Like the male archetype, he not only has restrictive, worrying father figures turned "feminine" to rebel against, but he also a has a young-son figure to teach and coach. He plays the roles of white hunter, white father, seductive lover, "difficult" artist, and tyrant. If the Eastwood performance seems overly external, it might be because the man he's playing is essentially a showman; his performance is a masquerade of a masquerade.

Eastwood's slow movement toward naturalistic acting and three-dimensional characterization that nonetheless reflects on his star persona reaches a new stage in *In the Line of Fire* (1993, Wolfgang Peterson). Eastwood's first non–Warner Bros. film in fourteen years and first non-Malpaso project in twenty-four, this psychological thriller is designed as something new for Eastwood—not only a star vehicle but an actor's showcase. As such the movie, a Secret Service thriller not without its clichés (the partner whose death must be avenged, the romance between a sixtyish man and a thirtyish woman) shows Eastwood's evolution into full humanity, rather than attempting to work variations on or break off from the monolithic "masculinity" of his persona.

The character Frank Horrigan, an aging Secret Service agent haunted by a failure to protect his president on November 22, 1963, is perhaps the least mythic figure Eastwood has ever portrayed; thus he plays him with an ease and completeness that appear to hold nothing back. Eastwood is paired with an antagonist, a determined assassin played by stage-trained actor John Malkovich. Malkovich is hardly the first Method-oriented actor Eastwood has performed with, the first being Eli Wallach in *The Good, the Bad, and the Ugly* twenty-seven years earlier. However, the encounter of the intense, interior acting of Malkovich and the more externalized personality performance of Eastwood leads to fascinating contrasts, another instance in which an offbeat actor well cast, like Bujold in *Tightrope*, leads Eastwood to relax and let loose previously unrevealed vulnerabilities.

Unlike the persona films in which the hero holds himself in while the villain emotes, Malkovich's Mitch Leary is all carefully calibrated control and release, while Eastwood's Horrigan is free to be more expansive, more imperfect and human. Jeff Maguire's screenplay is written with big dramatic moments of the sort that usually would be prepared to show off the talents of, say, Al Pacino or Robert DeNiro. Thus Eastwood is given a scene in which a flu-stricken Horrigan disorientedly mistakes a bursting balloon for gunfire during a presidential rally. The thriller's rush to the climactic moment in which the president's life will be threatened

29. *In the Line of Fire*: In an example of the compleat star performance, Eastwood appears relaxed and himself on screen while embodying a character in the naturalistic manner commonly recognized as "good acting." Copyright © 1993 Castle Rock Entertainment and Columbia Pictures Industries, Inc.

brings with it an emotional catharsis toward which the film has also been building. In what with another actor might have been a hackneyed calm-before-the-storm quiet moment, Horrigan/Eastwood directly deals with his experience in Dallas, John Bailey's cinematography lighting the scene so as to highlight a tear discreetly daring to roll down the cheek of Clint Eastwood.

Therefore, in the retrospect provided by *In the Line of Fire*, the audacity of Eastwood's self-appointed acting assignment in *White Hunter*,

Black Heart appears to have helped him break from the restrictive, masculinist tightness of his persona and move toward the kind of full-bodied, detailed performance that critics (and Academy members) recognize as "good acting."

Finally, *White Hunter, Black Heart* and *Unforgiven* both reach their dramatic resolutions in the protagonists' reactions to the deaths of black men—the native guide, Kivu, who is trampled by the elephant Wilson has stalked, and Will Munny's partner, Ned Logan. Both men are brought along by the white (bounty) hunter Eastwood on ill-advised expeditions, and both die as an indirect result.

Similar to the way Dirty Harry is posed between white and black, Wilson sees himself perched between whites and blacks, using race as a way to intervene in the white power relations of which he fancies himself a rebellious spoiler. Wilson can't get over exoticizing the black African, much as Hollywood always has; he facetiously proposes bringing Kivu to Hollywood with him, to introduce savage nobility into the home of the crass moguls and bean-counting businessmen he hates.

Wilson's sponsoring of the blacks against the vile racism of the whites casts a harsh light on the white-man's-burden themes of earlier Eastwood films. Wilson's fight with the hateful white hotel manager—"We've fought the preliminary for the kikes; let's fight the main event for the niggers"—puts him at a fashionably liberal distance from the racial mythology of the London nightclub act that stages the rape of a blond woman by a gorilla. However, it is revealed that the real threat is not the danger to white women at the hands of the black male monster that such images have long symbolized. At greatest risk are the black men who must assist the freebooting adventurousness of the white man. Wilson finds in the final scenes that, for all his self-styled liberalism, he is part of a racist pattern, a routine of black African life, in which blacks die for white sport: "white hunter, black heart." The paternalism of the white father kills the black man as surely as hostility does.

Paul Smith argues that Wilson's climactic resumption of his duties as director marks his final taking of responsibility as the "auteur-father." Thus, when Wilson moves physically and psychologically from the African tribal world, telling Verrill that the nihilist ending he had conceived for the film "is all wrong," Smith would interpret the line as Wilson's realization that his duty is to entertain the audience (*Clint Eastwood* 260– 262). However, Eastwood as director is evading such a "responsibility" to his fans in the very film we are watching, one that proved as unpopular as a "downbeat" *African Queen* might have. Indeed, in an interview a couple of years after *White Hunter*, Eastwood gave his philosophy of

30. An animated Eastwood/Wilson/Huston with Kivu (Boy Mathias Chuma). The devil-may-care white hunter/artist identifies with the other, confusing Hollywood make-believe with realities he doesn't attempt to understand.

filmmaking as a paraphrase of Wilson's line to Verrill about "letting eighty-five million popcorn-eaters pull you this way and that." Eastwood said, "I never try and romance the audience. You've got to forget that there's somebody out there eating popcorn and Milk Duds" (Biskind 60). Thus, I have difficulty with the notion that the narrative objective of Eastwood's film is to prove wrong Huston's disdain for the popular audience. For years Eastwood was seen as pandering to the baser instincts of that selfsame audience, and his erstwhile abandonment of it has been one of the keys to his newfound *auteur*ist respectability.

Wilson's movement away from the black community whose mourning he causes, and onto the movie set, can be seen as a retreat from reality and into make-believe. He forces himself to mouth the direction "Action"—the very thing he had been seeking as a big-game hunter, replacing ill-fated "action" with Hollywood fantasy. The movie Wilson makes will obscure his recklessness toward a culture he sought to appropriate. In *White Hunter*, Hollywood cinema serves the same function as the mythmaking dime novelist in *Unforgiven*, remaking colonization and murder into "entertainment." Paradoxically the Hollywood director's reality is make-believe, and his capitulation to it constitutes a kind of defeat but also a transforming refuge.

Therefore, *White Hunter, Black Heart* is not about John Huston, who himself often found male obsession and self-destructiveness fertile subject matter for films. It is about the blocked consciousness of man, who must take "action" but must not visibly put on an act. It is also about the repression of the white man, who may extend his benevolence to all, even while enacting white male privilege.

17

"Deserve's Got Nothing to Do with It," or Men with No Names II: *Unforgiven*

□□□

> There was something about [*Dirty Harry*] I felt some
> people missed. One critic said Dirty Harry shot the guy at
> the end with such glee he enjoyed it. There was no glee in
> it at all, there was a sadness in it. Watch the film again,
> and you'll see it.
> —Clint Eastwood, 1985 (Cahill 22)

In recent years, when Eastwood talks in interviews about *Dirty Harry*, it's often in terms of the character's sorrow. Harry is a "guy who's had some sadness in his life," Eastwood told David Frost in a 1993 TV conversation. In Eastwood's films, the dead wife and the lost relationship are such regularly recurring motifs that *Unforgiven*, his thirty-sixth film as a star and sixteenth as director, opens and closes with rhyming long shots of the Eastwood character, in silhouette, at his wife's gravesite. Unlike in *Dirty Harry* and *The Outlaw Josey Wales* on the one hand and *Honkytonk Man* and *Tightrope* on the other, the loss of the wife is neither the pretext for vengeance nor the occasion for country-music-style self-flagellation. (Eastwood's fondness for the rueful suffering of country ballads, which reverberates in the loneliness of many of his protagonists, seems to be an overlooked symptom of male masochism in his films.) Claudia, the wife of Will Munny (Eastwood), was killed three years before the film opens by smallpox, not by marauders, and not, as the scrolled prologue states, "by his hand." Rather she had been Munny's salvation. Munny, a once-notorious gunman, is left a rehabilitated man, saved from "wickedness" by the love and ministrations of a Christian woman.

Unforgiven strangely echoes Jane Tompkins's thesis that the Western novel originated as male rebellion against the Christianity and social reform movements associated with the feminine. Tompkins argues that the

Western is premised upon the rejection of "the female, domestic, 'sentimental' religion of the best-selling women writers [whose work represented] the deepest beliefs of middle-class America" (37–38). To be a real man, the hero casts aside the Bible for the gun, the town for the wilderness, and the "saving of souls" for the proving of physical endurance.

Classical Westerns, Tompkins concludes, exist "in order to provide a justification for violence" (227), couching it in the moral righteousness of those selfsame "middle-class values." Postmodern pastiches of the genre's conventions, such as the Leone Westerns and *High Plains Drifter*, compensate for the loss of values, even those about which the classical Western was ambivalent, by hyperbolizing the model, intensifying the spectator's egoistic investment in the hero's violent response, and replacing righteousness with "blank irony."

Unforgiven was filmed from a script written in 1975 by David Webb Peoples and apparently inspired by Robert Altman's film *McCabe and Mrs. Miller* (1971) and Arthur Kopit's 1968 play *Indians* (filmed by Altman as *Buffalo Bill and the Indians* [1976]). Richard T. Jameson notes that, "filmed in the 1970s, Peoples's screenplay might well have yielded just another hysterical 'revisionist Western' of the day" ("Deserve's" 12). The script, while beautifully written, is typical of early-1970s, Vietnam-inspired "anti-Westerns," with their reprobate Billy the Kids (*Dirty Little Billy*, 1972), corrupted Hollidays and Earps (*Doc*, 1971), and gruesome cavalry massacres of Indians (*Soldier Blue*, *Little Big Man*, both 1970). Thus on first viewing I had difficulty recognizing the film as a "Clint Eastwood" movie. This, however, is exactly the point the film makes about Eastwood's career: he was always twenty years behind the aesthetic curve. In the 1970s he was a pastiche of fifties manhood: the "prosocial" John Wayne (Schatz *Old Hollywood* 245) and the antisocial James Dean in one sleek package. Therefore the Western parody *Bronco Billy* (1980) was Eastwood's *Cat Ballou* (1965); *Tightrope* (1984), a rethinking of the connections between violence and sex, was his *Bonnie and Clyde* (1967); and *Unforgiven*, an elegiac meditation on masculinist Western myths, is his *McCabe and Mrs. Miller*.

It is no wonder that the screenplay was not produced in the seventies and would never have been made if not by Eastwood. Variously called *The Cut Whore Killings* and *The William Munny Killings* (R. Jameson "Deserve's" 12), the script—with its demythifications and characters based on Wyatt Earp, who made men check their guns at the city limits (a myth replayed in the Stewart/Mann *Winchester '73*), and Ned Buntline, the dime novelist who invented Buffalo Bill (and a character in *Indians*)—would have been passé. However, the star—and later the director—who rehabilitated the Western hero by capitalizing on egoism rather than morality, now decapitates the ego from the apparatus and makes a deeply moral film.

Thus, in order to "demythologize [his] own characters" as Frances Fisher remarked (Weinraub 214), he had to return to the anti-Western impulses that made his films of the 1960s and 1970s look like the convulsions of reactionaries. *Dirty Harry* drew crowds the same year that *Mc-Cabe and Mrs. Miller* demystified the Western before art-house-size audiences. Similarly *Unforgiven* dazzled reviewers and won awards, while such action films as *Terminator II* with Schwarzenegger and *Under Siege* with Seagal seemed more relevant to mass-audience tastes in the early 1990s. Ironically Eastwood shared 1992 critics' awards with Robert Altman (for *The Player*). At Eastwood's full-circle Oscar evening, Altman was the first person seen congratulating him on his way to accept the Best Director prize: both of them were lionized by the media in 1992–93—accurately or not—as two of the last American filmmakers making risky, personal projects.

Unforgiven opens by inverting the model detailed by Tompkins. Eleven years before the plot begins, Munny forswears the life of what the first line of *White Hunter, Black Heart* calls "a violent man given to violent action." He is reformed by the very sort of gentle, peace-loving woman whose protests against violence classical Westerns routinely overrule. After the elegiac prologue, the action opens, as in the Dirty Harry films, with a cut to town to depict the chaos that will await the Eastwood figure's intervention. In Big Whiskey, Wyoming, in a dank, bare saloon and brothel, a cowboy slashes the face of a prostitute (Anna Thomson). The law enters in the person of the sheriff, Little Bill Daggett. As played by Gene Hackman, Little Bill is an ambivalent figure, genial and engaging but menacing and patriarchal. He settles the matter with the saloon owner with an exchange of "property": four spring ponies for a prostitute's face. The women, seeking justice, find power in their own pooled secret savings and issue a reward for the lives of the two cowboys.

Before Eastwood even makes his appearance, the waters are muddied. Unlike the impotent legal custodians of the Dirty Harry series and the stooge sheriffs of the Leone- and Eastwood-directed Westerns, Little Bill is a footloose authoritarian whose subjective style of justice demonstrates the danger of leaving law enforcers to their own devices—of letting Dirty Harry run things. The seventies films (except *The Beguiled*) viewed woman as the enemy, and the eighties films walked a *Tightrope* between sympathizing with women and regarding them as cyphers or tempters. *Unforgiven* sides squarely with women as oppressed people trying to eke out some dignity as human beings. The thousand-dollar reward is the women's only means of striking back from a powerless position; the sheriff's violent opposition to the bounty shows that he recognizes it as an affront to his authority. The depiction of the cut whore as a commodity with diminished market value confirms and strengthens *Tightrope*'s tentative portrayal of female sex objects as creations of man. Unlike the various female types in that film, however, Strawberry Alice and her colleagues are the only women we see, and they are presented as angry, wronged women who fight back, not as "prostitutes" or victims. Thus, the schoolmarm/dance-hall girl split of classical Westerns never comes into play.

The treatment of the women, however, has its ambiguities as well. The price is placed on the heads of two cowboys, although only one is guilty. The women's thousand-dollar reward wreaks havoc on Big Whiskey far in excess of the justice the women seek, revealing the cutting as only one arc in a wide circle of violence. The bounty and the crime that cause it invite killers to justify violence ("They had it comin'") and to professionalize it as "just business," a theme well mined by such Mafia films as the Godfather cycle and Huston's *Prizzi's Honor*.

After this muddy stage has been set, Munny/Eastwood aptly enters the film prone in a pigpen. As director Eastwood eschews one type of entrance for his protagonist in favor of another. The revisionist Eastwood has entered his films before in undignified fashion; as Red Stovall in *Honkytonk Man* he is introduced in close-up falling drunk out of a car. While the camera holds on a close-up of Munny, a failing pig farmer, as he tries with his two small children to separate sick hogs from well, a disembodied voice seems to emanate from the vacant left side of the Panavision frame. The camera moves up to reveal on horseback a young bounty hunter who calls himself the Scofield Kid (Jaimz Woolvett).

The introductory scene with Munny and the Scofield Kid furthers *Unforgiven*'s fragmentation of the Eastwood persona among three characters. While Little Bill takes the persona's authoritarian part, the belligerent Kid is endowed with signifiers of the Man with No Name. The Man often entered a scene voice first, the figure later taking up the shot or the camera panning to find him. After the Kid makes his proposition to Munny for a split of the Big Whiskey reward and goes on his way, Eastwood gives Munny a point-of-view shot, again from the pigpen. Munny sees the distant figure of the Kid on the horizon as an icon similar to Josey Wales about to rescue a woman from rape or Harry about to leap onto a hijacked school bus. Munny/Eastwood's tag line, "I ain't like that anymore," is complemented by the view of the heroic horseman—a pose from Eastwood's filmic past—from which Munny/Eastwood turns away

31. Munny and children standing in the doorway, looking at the horseman, from whose position the shot is taken. This reverses the ride through Lago in *High Plains Drifter*.

to attend again to his pigs. The Kid's first line, "You don't look like no rootin', tootin, son-of-a-bitchin' cold-blooded assassin," pinpoints the irritation of an older man who no longer works to keep his "big rep," as the denizens of Presbyterian Church say of McCabe in Altman's Western. All this emphasizes a separation between the older man and the myth through which the Kid, a young oedipal subject looking for a symbolic father to emulate, continues to see Munny.

The early farm sequence includes another striking point-of-view shot that goes more directly to Munny's state of mind. As he gazes out a window, what appears to be an eyeline match shows Munny placing flowers on the grave. When Munny looks he sees his relation to the dead wife who is his lifeline to peace and sobriety. Once he sets out on the bounty hunt, on the quite-real pretext of needing the money, Munny starts on the long road back to murder by means of denial and rationalization, approaching the killing as business and insisting, "I'm just a fella now, like anybody else."

Like all revisionist Westerns, this one confronts the Western as myth. In Peoples's script Little Bill's debunking of the gunfighter English Bob's mythology as the Duke of Death, which Bill parodies as "the duck of death," parallels Munny's own attempts to counter his myth with the terrible reality of the life he renounced. The changeable meaning of the

word *weak* is one key to this difference. The Kid snarls Munny's legend
like the Eastwood of old: "They say you ain't got no weak nerve nor
fear." When Munny uses the word it connotes recovery and religion. "I
used to be *weak*," he stresses to his children when he has difficulty
mounting his horse, "and given to mistreat animals." The difference between "weak" as the "womanish" failure to pass a male test, and "weak"
as the intemperate failure to live according to a middle-class Protestant
standard upheld by women, defines the story's passage from damnation
to piety and back.

As part of its project of separating myth from actuality and symbolic
from actual fathers, the film takes care to divide explicitly the mere flesh
of the penis from the power and force signified by the phallus. The film
wastes no time getting to this issue: The cowboy cuts Delilah the prostitute because, as Strawberry Alice (Frances Fisher) explains, "All she
did when she saw he had a teensy little pecker was give a giggle. She
didn't know no better." The young woman didn't know she was being
paid not only to have sex with a man but to maintain his fragile self-
importance. The cycle of violence is triggered, so to speak, by a woman's failure to respect a man's phallic pride.

The film addresses the persistent relation between the phallus and guns
to which Eastwood's films, with their equation of shootings and rape and
their "My, that's a big one" innuendoes, have contributed in no small
measure. Little Bill corrects for Beauchamp, an Owen Wister–like Eastern writer of Western myths, the story of English Bob's shooting of
"Two-Gun" Corcoran one night in Wichita. Corcoran got his name not
because he wore two guns but because he had a large penis "which he
was stickin' into a French lady Bob liked." As Bill's debunked version
goes, when English Bob approached him, Corcoran pulled a pistol that
exploded in his hand, "a failing common to that model," and Bob shot
the defenseless man. "If Corcoran had had two guns," Little Bill concludes, "instead of just a big dick, he woulda killed ol' Bob." The scene
calls attention to man's eagerness to endow his genitals with the mystified force of weaponry and vice versa, giving ritual significance to the
mechanical need to "cock a pistol" before it's ready to shoot.

This monologue reduces myths of the gun as an extension of man—as
in Harry's reference in *Sudden Impact* to "us: Smith and Wesson and
me"—to mere matters of machines and flesh. Earlier Munny remedies
his inability to hit a can in his yard with shots fired from a pistol by
resorting to a double-barreled rifle, as machinery compensates for man's
lack. The Scofield Kid names himself after "the Scofield model of Smith
and Wesson pistol," emulating the symbolic father by identifying with a

gun. The film's extensive talk of specific models of rifles and pistols, some of which can malfunction in one's hand, redefines the gun as a mechanical commodity, a product of labor and industry. The Western genre represses the mechanical nature of guns. A reminder that firearms are manufactured machines collapses one of the genre's most prized binaries, that between nature and civilization. It demystifies the gun, brushes aside equivalences between guns and the penis/phallus, and ties rifles and six-shooters to the Industrial Revolution and the very modernity from which the Western represents escape.

Just before dismantling phallic mythology, the film shows a scene in which Munny and his partner, Ned Logan (Morgan Freeman), encounter the Kid and find that he's nearsighted. We've seen, with the Man with No Name, the connections between sight, knowledge, and power. In *Unforgiven* inferior sight restricts mythic power to physical limits. The impenetrable gaze of the stranger, the gunman who knows without seeing, is reduced to the myopia of a would-be gunfighter. The look of death attributed to the Man with No Name becomes the "duck of death," the exposure of a mythology whereby man ducks death twice, once in actuality by compensating for his limitations, and again in myth with a construction of power and heightened significance that seeps its way into what we experience as "reality."

Eastwood's Western career takes him from the supernatural Man with No Name to the undead who wreaks vengeance to the unforgiven whose veneer of renunciation gives way to revelations of guilt and terror. Far from having killed people who "had it comin'," Munny is haunted by those he killed. Delirious from fever in Big Whiskey, Munny tells Ned that he sees one of his victims, William Hendershot, "with worms coming out of him." Minutes later, when Little Bill asks his name, he calls himself "William Hendershot," identifying masochistically with his victim.

Comparisons with James Stewart in the fifties apply to much of *Unforgiven*. While the construction of the distant, impenetrable Eastwood persona is nearly the antithesis of the folksy, vulnerable, often androgynous Stewart, *Unforgiven* finds Eastwood crossing over into the hysteria, masochism, and "femininity" that emerge in the Stewart performance style. The Eastwood "persona films" do not dwell on their hero's pain as Stewart's films for Anthony Mann and Alfred Hitchcock do. They tend to regard his frequent suffering as an intolerable affront to his indomitability and not suggestive of the self-punishment and exhibitionism that most theorists of masochism, such as Freud and Theodor Reik, have found to be a condition of it and that the Eastwood films displace onto gender freaks like Scorpio in *Dirty Harry* or mere mortals like Marshal Jim Duncan in *High Plains Drifter*.

Unforgiven, however, is filmed in a style that could be called masochistic and which is associated, as Freud associated masochism, with women. From the opening scene, when the slashing is shown from the point of view of the prostitute whose face is cut, the camera is in the low position of the victim's suffering and pain in a reversal of the point-of-view structure of Eastwood's earlier Westerns. When a body falls from a horse, the camera is there to meet it. When Munny is kicked by Little Bill, the camera cowers with him. Moreover, Munny/Eastwood's delirium peaks in a scene much like the one in *The Naked Spur*, in which the protagonist's demons burst through in hallucinations. His conscious identity as a changed man is shattered by visions of his wife dead and covered with worms like one of his victims—a flashback to the male fear of his own violence toward women that surfaces in *Tightrope*. He dreams, like Wes Block, that he has killed a woman he loves, an act of which he knows he is capable, and that he is damned to face her after death.

The identification with the victimized position of women is taken still farther on Munny's recovery. We saw in Tania Modleski's study of Hitchcock's *Vertigo*, Scottie/James Stewart's slipping from the position of investigator of women to an identification with his own femininity. When Munny awakes from his stupor, he gazes at the face of the woman who had been brutalized, saying, "I must look kinda like you now." Munny identifies with a victimized woman's pain; his victimization, however, cannot compare with his horror as a victimizer, a terror of which—unlike Scottie, who never realizes the true nature of his complicity in the deaths of two women—he is more than conscious. Munny lives the consequences of his terrorism, empathizing with the oppressed position of women in the culture.

Thus the subject position that powerfully lines up self against other in Eastwood's starmaking films is shown as an illusion. Furthermore, the moral indignation that justifies violence in classical Westerns is shown as a construction of men. Exaggerated rumors fly among the bounty hunters about the extent of the cut prostitute's injuries, enabling men to say, "I guess they got it comin'." There is no detestable villain. Again like the Mann-Stewart Westerns, this one has a charming heavy who is difficult to despise. Little Bill, an aspiring 1880s suburbanite, hopes to settle outside of town in a house he is building with his own hands. His ineptitude as a carpenter, along with his sadism, illustrate the inseparability of the frontier lawman from the savagery he is charged with curbing.

Will Munny's domestic conversion, accordingly, proves shallow and

32. "I must look kinda like you now." When Munny looks at the battered woman (Anna Thomson), he sees not himself magnified but the consequences of his sins. (Compare to figure 6, from *The Naked Spur*.)

short-lived. By agreeing to take the journey that is the plot, Munny creates for himself an occasion of sin, a sin to which he eventually convinces himself he must give in. His justification for doing so finally arrives after the contract has been fulfilled and the Kid and Munny wait under a tree much like the one at Claudia's gravesite. A long shot shows one of Strawberry Alice's women bringing the reward money in a ride as foreboding and inevitable as that of the high plains drifter into Lago. The woman reveals that Ned, Munny's partner, was killed by Little Bill and his men, despite the fact that Ned, like the cowboy Davey, is not actually guilty and had left the killing scene because it sickened him. Munny's first response is denial, delivered in his mock-convinced tone of conversion—"Nobody killed Ned." As the woman relates Little Bill's discovery of Munny's identity—"He said you're Mr. William Munny, that you gunned down women and children"—a high-angle shot shows Munny swilling heavily from the liquor bottle he'd sworn never to touch. With this gesture the murderer is back; the drink of "big whiskey" signals not only his reversion to killing but killing itself as addictive behavior, inseparable from alcoholism and equally impossible for the alcoholic to avoid when drinking, just as Munny has tried to avoid his murderous self while inviting its reemergence by embarking on the bounty hunt. The alcoholic's rehabilitation evaporates in a single image.

With this gesture the familiar Eastwood clenched-teeth line delivery returns. The first indication that the bloody climax should not be read as an Eastwood shootout of old comes when the oedipal son figure scorns him, as Verrill, whom the Eastwood character also addresses as "Kid," does in *White Hunter*. Once the symbolic father and actual father meld, and the Kid sees Munny the murderer rather than the legend, he rejects him. Munny has insisted, "I ain't like that anymore," but the Kid now rebukes him—"I'm not like you, Will."

Soon old Eastwood motifs reappear—the slow ride into town, the subjective track to the saloon, and, most startlingly, the surprise emergence of the stranger figure—or his shotgun—from out of an "objective" camera position (a favorite device of Leone's, which he had borrowed from Kurosawa). In the fervid darkness of Jack N. Green's cinematography the Eastwood gunman now appears as the spectral hallucination he perhaps has always been, the elegant phallic six-shooter replaced by a crude shotgun loaded for bear, fires burning in the sockets of Munny/Eastwood's eyes. The camera placements of the saloon massacre scene are madly disorienting. The film adopts subjective viewpoints at the most senseless moments, such as Munny's shooting of the unarmed pimp from the Eastwood character's point of view, and objective viewpoints at others, as when Munny points his gun seemingly at random—at "everything that walks or crawls."

Unlike in a "make my day" Eastwood killfest, the characters in this scene pose no threat visually. Gone are the sweaty wide-screen close-ups of smirking thugs; these are deputies, depicted as working stiffs, always Eastwood's chief constituency. As we have seen, Eastwood's earlier films make spectacle of killing, with each aim precisely delineated, each crashing body followed lovingly to the ground. Here men become corpses illogically, distantly, as on a battleground, in a slaughterhouse.

Two grace notes summarize the scene. Beauchamp, the mythmaker, sees a new mythology to celebrate and auditions before Munny the theory that "you always shoot the best shot first," when we know that the first victim wasn't even armed. When the dime-novel writer regards Munny/Eastwood with awe, he makes clear who the male spectator is: one who draws strength from transforming the violence of madmen into feats of mettle and courage. "A man's gotta do what a man's gotta do": a sentiment Jeffrey Dahmer and John Wayne Gacy (unfortunate name, his) would surely endorse. *Unforgiven* places the Clint Eastwood avenging gunman in their company. The moral imperative of the Western hero to avenge his wrongs in spectacular fashion is reduced to the "irresistible impulse" of a psychopath (to quote *Anatomy of a Murder*'s legalese).

Furthermore, Munny's growled answer to Little Bill's dying plaint that he doesn't deserve to die this way provides the film with its essence line: "Deserve's got nothing to do with it." This line represents every principled Western provocation, every righteous high-noon gunfight stripped of its justification, including those of the spectators who pay to watch crashing bodies. The Leone, Siegel, and Eastwood films always knew "deserve's got nothing to do with it" and this is why they centered violence so intensely in the ego, knowing that no moral code could truly contain such brutality. Unlike William Munny, Eastwood attains redemption and he does it by spurning his dead symbolic fathers—"Sergio and Don"—to whom he nonetheless dedicates the film. By making a film that admits that his Westerns got "rid of all the morality" in order to dwell on the "melodrama and action," Eastwood acknowledges in his professed "last statement in the genre" his eventual agreement with Pauline Kael, his severest critic in the 1970s.

The most puzzling thing about *Unforgiven* is the casting of Morgan Freeman as Ned Logan, a role that clearly was not written for a black actor. Paul Smith sees the casting as evidence of Eastwood's New Right belief in a society suddenly turned "color-blind," a position that argues that the white race's responsibility for centuries of bigotry suddenly vanishes by willing into existence a kind of instant equality, defined as the denial of racial difference (*Clint Eastwood* 282). Eastwood said of Ned's race that "it's just hipper not to mention it" (Weinraub 216). By not mentioning it, however, the film speaks to the moment of its making, turning the "color-blind" argument against itself by inviting the audience to find racial motivations in actions that seem to deny them. The Scofield Kid's angry reaction to Ned's discovery of his myopia appears tinged by resentment that a black man is getting the better of him. Little Bill's whipping of Ned, moreover, adds to the sheriff's sadism the actions of a slavemaster.

If Eastwood's intention was to deny the importance of race, the effect is the opposite—to show the impossibility of such efforts. The depiction of a black man with a Native American wife revises history; in fact, thousands of African Americans went west in the years following the emancipation. At the same time Ned's race makes Munny's climactic shooting spree more ambiguous. The film could be said to manipulate its audience into wanting to see a prejudice-free white hero avenge the death of a black "partner." On the other hand, the climax, like *White Hunter*'s, seems to show the white protagonist climbing back into delusion on the back of a dead black man. By justifying the bounty hunt to Ned, Will leads him into harm's way as surely as Wilson toys with the life of Kivu. The long-held shot of Ned's wife watching the two of them leave appears to register this understanding. Indeed, Mario Van Peebles's Western

Posse (1993) makes note of the kinship between black cowboys and Native Americans who have in common a well-founded suspicion of whites. If *Unforgiven* is about the violent white male hero's ultimate responsibility for the deaths of others who appear to "deserve" their fates, then the film decodes Dirty Harry's condescending "I'm doing it for you" ethic as a spectacle of murder, masquerading as rescue.

Does this film in general hedge its bets, allowing the conservative reading that Andrew Britton maintains all commercial films must offer ("Stars and Genre" 201)? My guess is that confusion over the film's performance of the expected Eastwood catharsis mutes its critical impact with some spectators. In fact, one reviewer celebrated the film as a "classic tale about coming back, about vitality and virility when youth and optimism are spent. It's about accepting diminished powers and personal demons and still finding the strength to say enough is enough and to act" (Gerstel 4C). The lines "You just shot an unarmed man," "Well, he shoulda armed himself" drew laughter in the theater each time I saw the film. Perhaps, coming from Eastwood, rambling insanity still sounds to some ears like gallows-humor justice.

If *Unforgiven* is not enough to break the blood lust of what Eastwood himself calls his "hard-core fans" (Thomson "Cop" 66), it may just be enough to break critics of the monolithic verities of textual analysis. *Unforgiven* acts out in a deconstructive way what Tompkins calls

> the entire purpose of the pattern . . . to get the audience to the point where it can't wait till the hero lets loose with his six-shooters. . . . Vengeance, by the time it arrives, feels biologically necessary. It's as if the hero had been dying of thirst, and suddenly he's given the chance to take a drink of water. . . . This is the moment of moral ecstasy. The hero is *so right* (that is, so wronged) that he can kill with impunity. (228–229; emphasis in original)

Thus, earlier Eastwood-directed films and those by Leone and Siegel cater to spectatorial desire. *Unforgiven* confronts it, a confrontation that may not necessarily be taken as such when it comes from "Clint Eastwood." I said earlier that while there are those who would be appalled by the rape and murders that open *High Plains Drifter*, those are not the spectators for whom the film was made. Nineteen years later, Eastwood made a film for the resisting viewers of his earlier movies. And they responded, carrying Eastwood into the realm of "serious artist," where his films might be discussed not only for their spectator positioning or as parts of "a cultural production" but, also, for better or worse, as *auteur* texts, despite periodic premature announcements of the death of *auteur-ism* in film studies. The silhouetted William Munny who vanishes in the last shot of *Unforgiven* may be Eastwood the spectatorial agent, withdrawing from male desire. He may be back in future films, or Eastwood's past films may continue to satisfy what his new films do not. It is certain that male violence in films has already outlasted Eastwood's interest in it.

Nevertheless, since the much-honored *Unforgiven* removed the patina of disrepute, it is clear that "Clint Eastwood" will not "mean" the same again. Nor, perhaps, will masculinity. The mask is off and the face underneath is a woman's—scarred, covered with worms—the victim of male insecurity masquerading as power and strength. The face is also a man's, his eyes opened by the recognition of centuries of oppression caused by white male privilege. Can the dialectic of these faces synthesize, resulting in a new kind of gender identity? Will this bisexual "star image" be as persuasive as that of the vengeful, whip-wielding "Stranger"? Or will it be consigned to irrelevance in a gallery of slicker violent males, who by their transcendent indomitability continue to construct and be constructed by their counterparts off screen? Will it be displaced, like Stewart's gender idiosyncrasy, by a portrait more endearing to the status quo, or be tamed, like Nicholson's modernism, by money, fame, and ego? It will be difficult after all to recuperate Eastwood. His career, with all of its missteps, has illustrated a twelve-step withdrawal program from masculinism. The fact that no one in the mid-1970s would have believed that Eastwood could be written about in this way may offer some hope.

The following year that hope appeared to be both fulfilled and somewhat leavened. *Unforgiven*, like *Tightrope*, shouldered the burden of the star's violent, fearsome quality, and *White Hunter* turned its back on Eastwood's stardom almost entirely. *In the Line of Fire*, on the other hand, embraces the actor as the familiar, comfortable star presence that he is. Produced at Castle Rock, where Tom Cruise and Jack Nicholson were showcased in *A Few Good Men*, the movie is a much grander production than the spartan Malpaso films and one in which Eastwood's only responsibilities are to perform and to be Clint Eastwood (which, as we know, are not the same).

As stated earlier the movie treats Eastwood as a star *actor*, providing him with flavorful dialogue that manages to point up nearly every aspect of Eastwood's public image. His male chauvinism gets trotted out early when, upon meeting the Secret Service agent Lily (Rene Russo), he remarks, "Secretaries keep getting prettier and prettier," and one cannot be sure whether the character knew she was an agent and was making a sexist joke or was taken by surprise. The main elements of his mystique are spotlighted: "A good glare can be just as effective as a gun" is a reminder that the key to Eastwood's power has been his firing of looks, not bullets. The line, "You're looking at a living legend, the only active Secret Service agent who has lost a president" takes a self-reflexive line and gives it a masochistic twist.

And that is this film's strategy. Like so many of the later Malpaso films, *In the Line of Fire* delivers the heroic Eastwood, but requires him to overcome obstacles of his own making, and brings in pieces of Eastwood's off-screen personality; one senses that he took this rare role outside of his own shop because he got to play the piano in several scenes. The film tweaks the white male hegemony Eastwood formerly symbolized, neutralizes it by making it appear the stuff of "dinosaurs," and yet rehabilitates it by Horrigan's triumph. Unlike the sometimes ragged Malpaso movies, this one is ultimately too canny and slick for its own good. When Horrigan tells Lily that the few female Secret Service agents are window dressing, tokens that allow the president "to appeal to his feminist supporters," one must be aware that the film is doing the same thing, putting a capable woman out front for its "feminist" spectators, while also supplying the aging star with a much-younger love interest.

Something more disturbing seemed to be happening amid the reception to *In the Line of Fire* (which was designed as a commercial thriller to follow the "personal" *Unforgiven*, and which did become a bigger hit than Eastwood's Oscar winner). In reviews and articles Eastwood was clearly being set apart, no longer an emblem of masculinity but a self-contained institution. Bernard Weinraub wrote in the *New York Times* that the success of *In The Line of Fire* proves "once and for all that Hollywood has few stars like Clint" ("Hits, Misses, and Also-Rans of Summer" 2:17). For an Eastwood protagonist to suggest giving up his career for a woman would have seemed a radical notion five years earlier. In *In the Line of Fire* it causes hardly a ripple, probably because at sixty-three, Eastwood is around retirement age anyway. The love interest is won over to Eastwood by the harmless vulnerability of a crusty old sweetheart, a sure sign, amid all the others (such as the Oscars) that Eastwood may be on the Jimmy Stewart road, en route to becoming a "beloved" figure, the viciousness of his early films and the power of his revisionist movies receding behind a mist of posterity, respectability, and age.

In the selfsame movie summer of 1993 Arnold Schwarzenegger was roasted for making a film, *Last Action Hero*, which attempted to pull off a similar stunt. David Ansen's review in *Newsweek* called it "the first deconstructionist action movie. Admittedly, Columbia Pictures is not selling it as a postmodernist opus ('Quel plaisir! You haven't lived until you've seen Arnold decode his own text!'—Jacques Derrida, 'Sneak Previews')" (64). As surprising as it may be to find references to Derrida and deconstruction in the popular media, the review—as well as the film—can be taken as confirmation that Schwarzenegger is beginning to follow a now-familiar pattern. Machismo cannot hold for long and eventually must call attention to its own considerable artifice. Like Eastwood until 1992 he has paid a heavy price at the box office, the difference being that Eastwood freed himself early from mega-million-dollar budgets like that reported for *Last Action Hero* in order to allow some leeway from the demands of his core audience.

Moreover, demands for conventional masculinism continue to be insistent. In interviews for postmortem on the film's failure published in *Premiere* Schwarzenegger referred to preview cards that said things like, "I don't want to see Arnold dragged down to where he's helpless like that. He's standing there talking about the father's death, and the rain—it's very upsetting." The star said, "Somehow I bring a luggage with me that certain things—although they work very good on paper—it doesn't work with me [*sic*]. What the people want to see at that point is, 'Stop having the kid suggest to [him] what to do next: Arnold should kick in gear and get aggressive'" (Griffin 57).

Therefore, as we head into an ever more intertextual and self-reflexive multimedia age, the dialectics between masculinism and feminism; myths about masculinity and economic and social pressures on the genders to become less monolithic; signs of gender equality (such as a working-couple first family), and signs of gender barbarism (such as the increasing number of rape cases involving teenage sports heroes and parents with "boys will be boys" attitudes) can only grow more complex. Hollywood film, with its need to balance commercial pressures and artistic impulses, will continue to reproduce the cultural contradictions that threaten increasingly to confront and overtake us all.

□□□

Filmographies

□□□

The following is a list of the films to date of James Stewart, Jack Nicholson, and Clint Eastwood. These listings include the films' year of release, directors, and production and releasing companies (when available). Also noted are any New York Film Critics or Academy Award honors that the actor won for a certain film.

JAMES STEWART (1908–   )

Murder Man (1935, Tim Whelan, MGM)
Rose Marie (1936, W. S. Van Dyke, MGM)
Next Time We Love (1936, Edwin H. Griffith, Universal)
Wife vs. Secretary (1936, Clarence Brown, MGM)
Small Town Girl (1936, William Wellman, MGM)
Speed (1936, Edwin L. Marin, MGM)
The Gorgeous Hussy (1936, Clarence Brown, MGM)
Born to Dance (1936, Roy Del Ruth, MGM)
After the Thin Man (1936, W. S. Van Dyke, MGM)
Seventh Heaven (1937, Henry King, 20th Century–Fox)
The Last Gangster (1937, Edward Lustig, MGM)
Navy Blue and Gold (1937, Sam Wood, MGM)
Of Human Hearts (1937, Clarence Brown, MGM)
Vivacious Lady (1938, George Stevens, RKO)
Shopworn Angel (1938, H. C. Potter, MGM)
You Can't Take It With You (1938, Frank Capra, Columbia)
Made for Each Other (1939, John Cromwell, Selznick-UA)
The Ice Follies of 1939 (1939, Reinhold Schunzel, MGM)
It's a Wonderful World (1939, W. S. Van Dyke, MGM)
Mr. Smith Goes to Washington (1939, Frank Capra, Columbia)
   (New York Film Critics Award [NYFCA], Academy Award nomination)
Destry Rides Again (1939, George Marshall, Universal)
The Shop Around the Corner (1940, Ernst Lubitsch, MGM)
The Mortal Storm (1940, Sidney Franklin, MGM)
No Time for Comedy (1940, William Keighley, Warner Bros.)
The Philadelphia Story (1940, George Cukor, MGM) (Academy Award)
Come Live with Me (1941, Clarence Brown, MGM)
Pot o' Gold (1941, George Marshall, United Artists)

Ziegfield Girl (1941, Robert Z. Leonard, MGM)

It's a Wonderful Life (1946, Frank Capra, Liberty Films) (Academy Award nomination)

Magic Town (1947, William Wellman, RKO)

Call Northside 777 (1948, Henry Hathaway, 20th Century-Fox)

On Our Merry Way (1948, King Vidor and Leslie Fenton, United Artists)

Rope (1948, Alfred Hitchcock, Transatlantic-Warner Bros.)

You Gotta Stay Happy (1948, H. C. Potter, Universal)

The Stratton Story (1949, Sam Wood, MGM)

Malaya (1949, Richard Thorpe, MGM)

Broken Arrow (1950, Delmer Daves, 20th Century-Fox)

Winchester '73 (1950, Anthony Mann, Universal-International [U-I]) (made after *Broken Arrow*, but released earlier)

The Jackpot (1950, Walter Lang, 20th Century-Fox)

Harvey (1950, Henry Koster, U-I) (Academy Award nomination)

No Highway in the Sky (1951, Henry Koster, 20th Century-Fox)

The Greatest Show on Earth (1952, C. B. DeMille, Paramount) (Stewart performs entire role wearing clown makeup)

Bend of the River (1952, Anthony Mann, U-I)

Carbine Williams (1952, Richard Thorpe, MGM)

The Naked Spur (1953, Anthony Mann, MGM)

Thunder Bay (1953, Anthony Mann, U-I)

The Glenn Miller Story (1954, Anthony Mann, U-I)

Rear Window (1954, Alfred Hitchcock, Paramount)

The Far Country (1955, Anthony Mann, U-I) (made between *Glenn Miller* and *Rear Window* but released third)

Strategic Air Command (1955, Anthony Mann, Paramount)

The Man from Laramie (1955, Anthony Mann, Columbia)

The Man Who Knew Too Much (1956, Alfred Hitchcock, Paramount)

The Spirit of St. Louis (1957, Billy Wilder, Warner Bros.)

Night Passage (1957, James Neilson, U-I) (marked a falling-out between Anthony Mann and Stewart; Mann considered this a poor script and left the production)

Vertigo (1958, Alfred Hitchcock, Paramount)

Bell, Book, and Candle (1958, Richard Quine, Columbia)

Anatomy of a Murder (1959, Otto Preminger, Columbia) (NYFCA; Academy Award nomination)

The FBI Story (1959, Mervyn Le Roy, Warner Bros.)

The Mountain Road (1960, Daniel Mann, Warner Bros.)

Two Rode Together (1961, John Ford, Columbia)

The Man Who Shot Liberty Valance (1962, John Ford, Paramount)

Mr. Hobbs Takes a Vacation (1962, Henry Koster, 20th Century-Fox)

How the West Was Won (1963, Henry Hathaway, John Ford, George Marshall, MGM)

Take Her, She's Mine (1963, Henry Koster, 20th Century-Fox)

Cheyenne Autumn (1964, John Ford, Warner Bros.)

Dear Brigitte (1965, Henry Koster, 20th Century-Fox)

Shenandoah (1965, Andrew V. McLaglen, Universal)
Flight of the Phoenix (1965, Robert Aldrich, 20th Century–Fox)
The Rare Breed (1966, Andrew V. McLaglen, Universal)
Firecreek (1968, Vincent McEveety, Warner Bros.)
Bandolero (1968, Andrew V. McLaglen, 20th Century–Fox)
The Cheyenne Social Club (1970, Gene Kelly, National General)
Fool's Parade (1971, Andrew V. McLaglen, Columbia)
The Shootist (1976, Don Siegel, Paramount)
Airport '77 (1977, Jerry Jameson, Universal)
The Big Sleep (1978, Michael Winner, ITC)
The Magic of Lassie (1981, Don Chaffey, Lassie Prods.)

JACK NICHOLSON (1937–　　)

Cry Baby Killer (1958, Jus Addis, Allied Artists)
Little Shop of Horrors (1960, Roger Corman)
Too Soon to Love (1960, Richard Rush)
Studs Lonigan (1960, Irving Lerner, United Artists)
The Wild Ride (1960, Harvey Berman, Roger Corman)
The Broken Land (1962, Roger Corman, 20th Century–Fox)
The Raven (1963, Roger Corman, American-International [AIP])
The Terror (1963, Roger Corman, Grand National)
Thunder Island (1963, Jack Leewood; scr. by Nicholson and Don Devlin)
Ensign Pulver (1964, Joshua Logan, Warner Bros.)
Back Door to Hell (1964, Monte Hellman)
Flight to Fury (1965, Monte Hellman, scr. by Nicholson)
The Shooting (1966, Monte Hellman, scr. by Nicholson and Hellman)
Ride in the Whirlwind (1966, Monte Hellman, co-prod. and scr. by Nicholson)
Hell's Angels on Wheels (1967, Richard Rush, AIP)
Rebel Rousers (1967, Martin B. Cohen, AIP)
The St. Valentine's Day Massacre (1967, Roger Corman, AIP)
The Trip (1967, Roger Corman, AIP, scr. by Nicholson)
Psych-Out (1968, Richard Rush, AIP)
Head (1968, Bob Rafelson, Columbia, prod. and scr. by Rafelson and Nicholson) (a
　vehicle for the Monkees)
Easy Rider (1969, Dennis Hopper, BBS-Columbia) (NYFCA for Supp. Actor; Acad-
　emy Award nomination)
On a Clear Day You Can See Forever (1970, Vincente Minnelli, Paramount)
Five Easy Pieces (1970, Bob Rafelson, BBS-Columbia) (Academy Award nomination)
Carnal Knowledge (1971, Mike Nichols, Avco-Embassy)
Drive, He Said (1971, Jack Nicholson, BBS-Columbia); directed only
A Safe Place (1972, Henry Jaglom, BBS-Columbia)
The King of Marvin Gardens (1972, Bob Rafelson, BBS-Columbia)
The Last Detail (1973, Hal Ashby, Columbia) (Academy Award nomination)
Chinatown (1974, Roman Polanski, Paramount) (NYFCA as 1974 Best Actor for
　Chinatown and *Last Detail*; Academy Award nomination)

The Passenger (1975, Michelangelo Antonioni, MGM)
Tommy (1975, Ken Russell, Stigwood-Columbia)
The Fortune (1975, Mike Nichols, Columbia)
One Flew Over the Cuckoo's Nest (1975, Milos Forman, Fantasy-UA) (NYFCA; Academy Award)
The Missouri Breaks (1976, Arthur Penn, Winkler–Chartoff–UA)
The Last Tycoon (1976, Elia Kazan, Paramount)
Goin' South (1978, Jack Nicholson, Paramount)
The Shining (1980, Stanley Kubrick, Warner Bros.)
The Postman Always Rings Twice (1981, Bob Rafelson, Lorimar-Paramount)
Reds (1981, Warren Beatty, Paramount) (Academy Award nomination as Supp. Actor)
The Border (1982, Tony Richardson, Universal)
Terms of Endearment (1983, James L. Brooks, Paramount) (NYFCA, Academy Award for Best Supporting Actor)
Prizzi's Honor (1985, John Huston, ABC–20th Century–Fox) (NYFCA; Academy Award nomination)
Heartburn (1986, Mike Nichols, Paramount)
The Witches of Eastwick (1987, George Miller, Guber-Peters–Warner Bros.)
Broadcast News (1987, James L. Brooks, 20th Century–Fox)
Ironweed (1987, Hector Babenco, Tri-Star) (NYFCA for *Ironweed*, *Witches*, and *News*; Academy Award nomination for *Ironweed*)
Batman (1989, Tim Burton, Guber-Peters–Warner Bros.)
The Two Jakes (1990, Jack Nicholson, Paramount)
Man Trouble (1992, Bob Rafelson, 20th Century–Fox)
A Few Good Men (1992, Rob Reiner, Castle Rock–Columbia) (Academy Award nomination for Supp. Actor)
Hoffa (1992, Danny DeVito, 20th Century–Fox)

CLINT EASTWOOD (1930–   )

Revenge of the Creature (1955, Jack Arnold, U-I)
Francis in the Navy (1955, Arthur Lubin, U-I)
Lady Godiva (1955, Arthur Lubin, U-I)
Tarantula (1955, Jack Arnold, U-I)
Never Say Goodbye (1956, Jerry Hopper, U-I)
The First Traveling Saleslady (1956, Arthur Lubin, RKO)
Star in the Dust (1956, Charles Hass, U-I)
Escapade in Japan (1957, Arthur Lubin, RKO)
Lafayette Escadrille (1958, William Wellman, Warner Bros.)
Ambush at Cimarron Pass (1958, Herbert Mendelson, 20th Century–Fox)
Rawhide series, CBS Television, 1959–1966
Fistful of Dollars (1964, Sergio Leone; U.S. release 1967)
For a Few Dollars More (1965, Sergio Leone; U.S. release 1967)
The Good, the Bad, and the Ugly (1966, Sergio Leone; U.S. release 1968)
The Witches (1966, Italian omnibus film prod. by Dino DeLaurentiis; Eastwood segment dir. by Vittorio De Sica)

Hang 'Em High (1968, Ted Post, United Artists)
Coogan's Bluff (1968, Don Siegel, Universal)
Where Eagles Dare (1969, Brian G. Hutton, MGM)
Paint Your Wagon (1969, Joshua Logan, Paramount)
Kelly's Heroes (1970, Brian G. Hutton, MGM)
Two Mules for Sister Sara (1970, Don Siegel, Malpaso-Universal)
The Beguiled (1971, Don Siegel, Malpaso-Universal)
Play Misty for Me (1971, Clint Eastwood, Malpaso-Universal)
Dirty Harry (1971, Don Siegel, Malpaso–Warner Bros.)
Joe Kidd (1972, John Sturges, Universal)
High Plains Drifter (1973, Clint Eastwood, Malpaso-Universal)
Breezy (1973, Clint Eastwood, Malpaso-Universal); directed only
Magnum Force (1973, Ted Post, Malpaso–Warner Bros.)
Thunderbolt and Lightfoot (1974, Michael Cimino, United Artists)
The Eiger Sanction (1975, Clint Eastwood, Malpaso-Universal)
The Outlaw Josey Wales (1976, Clint Eastwood, Malpaso–Warner Bros.)
The Enforcer (1976, James Fargo, Malpaso–Warner Bros.)
The Gauntlet (1977, Clint Eastwood, Malpaso–Warner Bros.)
Every Which Way but Loose (1978, James Fargo, Malpaso–Warner Bros.)
Escape from Alcatraz (1979, Don Siegel, Paramount)
Bronco Billy (1980, Clint Eastwood, Malpaso–Warner Bros.)
Any Which Way You Can (1980, Buddy Van Horn, Malpaso–Warner Bros.)
Firefox (1982, Clint Eastwood, Malpaso–Warner Bros.)
Honkytonk Man (1982, Clint Eastwood, Malpaso–Warner Bros.)
Sudden Impact (1983, Clint Eastwood, Malpaso–Warner Bros.)
Tightrope (1984, Richard Tuggle, Malpaso–Warner Bros.)
City Heat (1984, Richard Benjamin, Malpaso–Warner Bros.)
Pale Rider (1985, Clint Eastwood, Malpaso–Warner Bros.)
Heartbreak Ridge (1986, Clint Eastwood, Malpaso–Warner Bros.)
The Dead Pool (1988, Buddy Van Horn, Malpaso–Warner Bros.)
Bird (1988, Clint Eastwood, Malpaso–Warner Bros.); directed only
Pink Cadillac (1989, Buddy Van Horn, Malpaso–Warner Bros.)
White Hunter, Black Heart (1990, Clint Eastwood, Malpaso–Warner Bros.)
The Rookie (1990, Clint Eastwood, Malpaso–Warner Bros.)
Unforgiven (1992, Clint Eastwood, Malpaso–Warner Bros.) (Academy Awards as
    director, producer; Academy Award nomination for Best Actor)
In the Line of Fire (1993, Wolfgang Petersen, Castle Rock–Columbia)
A Perfect World (1993, Clint Eastwood, Malpaso–Warner Bros.)

Works Cited

□□□

"Accolade for *Unforgiven*." *Moving Pictures International* 11 March 1993: 2.

Affron, Charles. *Star Acting: Gish, Garbo, Davis*. New York: E. P. Dutton, 1977.

Allen, Jeanne. "Looking Through *Rear Window*: Hitchcock's Traps and Lures of Heterosexual Romance." In *Female Spectators: Looking at Film and Television*. Edited by E. Deidre Pribram. London and New York: Verso, 1988: 31–44.

Althusser, Louis. "Ideology and Ideological State Apparatuses (Notes Toward an Investigation)." In *Video Culture*. Edited by John G. Hanhardt. New York: Peregrine Smith, 1986: 56–95.

Ansen, David. "Bang, Bang, Kiss, Kiss: Summer Movies Suddenly Get Serious." *Newsweek* 28 June 1993:64–65.

"Attitudes: A Thump on the head to . . . " *New Woman* November 1991: 140.

Barthes, Roland. *The Pleasure of the Text*. Translated by Richard Miller. New York: Noonday, 1975.

———. *S/Z: An Essay*. Translated by Richard Miller. New York: Hill & Wang, 1974.

Basinger, Jeanine. *Anthony Mann*. Boston: Twayne, 1979.

———. *The 'It's a Wonderful Life' Book*. New York: Knopf, 1977.

Baudrillard, Jean. *Simulations*. Translated by Paul Foss, Paul Patton, and Philip Beitchman. New York: Semiotext(e), 1983.

Baudry, Jean-Louis. "Ideological Effects of the Basic Cinematographic Apparatus." In *Movies and Methods, Vol. II*. Edited by Bill Nichols. Berkeley: University of California Press, 1985. 531–542.

Bazin, André, Jacques Doniol-Valcroze, Pierre Kast, Roger Leenhardt, Jacques Rivette, Eric Rohmer. "Six Characters in Search of Auteurs: a Discussion about the French Cinema." 1957. Translated by Liz Heron. In *Cahiers du Cinéma: the 1950s*. Edited by Jim Hillier. Cambridge, Mass.: Harvard University Press, 1985. 31–46.

Belton, John. "James Stewart: Homegrown." In *Close-ups*. Edited by Danny Peary. New York: Workman, 1978. 537–542.

Bennett, Tony, and Janet Woollacott. *Bond and Beyond: The Political Career of a Popular Hero*. London and New York: Methuen, 1987.

Bingham, Dennis. " . . . And Now, Crawling into the Spotlight." *Columbus Monthly* August 1979: 20–22.

————. Review of *The Shining*. *Columbus Monthly* August 1980: 119–122.

Biskind, Peter. "Any Which Way He Can." *Premiere* April 1993: 52–60.

Bordwell, David, Janet Staiger, and Kristin Thompson. *The Classical Hollywood Cinema: Film Style and Mode of Production to 1960*. New York: Columbia University Press, 1985.

Bordwell, David, and Kristen Thompson. *Film Art: An Introduction, 4th Edition*. New York: McGraw-Hill, 1993.

Branigan, Edward. *Point of View in the Cinema*. Berlin: Mouton, 1984.

Brecht, Bertolt. *On Theatre*. Edited and translated by John Willett. New York: Hill & Wang, 1964.

Brittan, Arthur. *Masculinity and Power*. London: Basil Blackwell, 1989.

Britton, Andrew. *Cary Grant: Comedy and Male Desire*. Newcastle upon Tyne: Tyneside Cinema, 1983.

————. "Stars and Genre." In *Stardom: Industry of Desire*. Edited by Christine Gledhill. London and New York: Routledge, 1991. 198–206.

Browne, Nick. "The Politics of Narrative Form: Frank Capra's *Mr. Smith Goes to Washington*." *Wide Angle* 3.3 (1979): 4–11.

Brownmiller, Susan. *Against Our Will: Men, Women, and Rape*. New York: Simon & Schuster, 1975.

Budd, Michael. "Genre, Director, and Stars in John Ford's Westerns: Fonda, Wayne, Stewart, and Widmark." *Wide Angle* 2.4 (1978): 52–61.

Burnett, Ron. "Hollywood Corner: the *Tightrope* of Male Fantasy." *Framework* 26–27 (1985): 76–85.

Butler, Judith. *Gender Trouble: Feminism and the Subversion of Identity*. New York and London: Routledge, 1990.

Cagin, Seth, and Philip Dray. *Sex, Drugs, and Violence: Hollywood Films in the Seventies*. New York: Harper & Row, 1984.

Cahill, Tim. "Clint Eastwood." *Rolling Stone* 451. 4 July 1985: 19–23.

Canby, Vincent. "James Stewart's Talent: More Than Aw-Shucks." *New York Times* 22 April 1990: Section 2: 13 + .

Capra, Frank. *The Name Above the Title*. New York: Macmillan, 1971.

Carroll, Noël. "Address to the Heathen." *October* 23 (Winter 1982): 89–163.

————. *The Philosophy of Horror*. New York and London: Routledge, 1990.

Cawelti, John G. "*Chinatown* and Generic Transformation." In *Film Theory and Criticism, 2nd Ed*. Edited by Gerald Mast and Marshall Cohen. New York and Oxford: Oxford University Press, 1979. 559–579.

————. *The Six-Gun Mystique, 2nd edition*. Bowling Green, Ohio: Bowling Green Popular Press, 1984.

Chethik, Neil. "Eastwood's Lines, in Face and Scripts, Deepen." *Detroit Free Press* 28 March 1993: 3J.

Chodorow, Nancy. *Feminism and Psychoanalytic Theory*. New Haven: Yale University Press, 1989.

Clarke, Jane, and Diana Simmonds. *Move Over Misconceptions: Doris Day Reappraised*. BFI Dossier No. 4. London: British Film Institute, 1980.

Cohan, Steven. "Masquerading as the American Male in the Fifties: *Picnic*, William Holden and the Spectacle of Masculinity in Hollywood Film." *Camera Obscura* 25–26 (January–May 1991): 43–74.

Cohan, Steven, and Ina Rae Hark, editors. *Screening the Male: Exploring Masculinities in Hollywood Cinema*. London and New York: Routledge, 1993.

Cole, Larry. "Clint's Not Cute When He's Angry." *Village Voice* 24 May 1976: 124–125.

Comolli, Jean-Louis. "Historical Fiction: A Body Too Much." *Screen* 19.2 (Summer 1978): 41–51.

Cook, David A. "American Horror: *The Shining*." *Literature/Film Quarterly* 12.1 (Fall 1984): 2–4.

———. *A History of Narrative Film, 2nd Ed*. New York: Norton, 1990.

Cook, Pam, editor. *The Cinema Book*. New York: Pantheon, 1985.

Cooper, Arnold M. "What Men Fear: the Facade of Castration Anxiety." *The Psychology of Men*. Edited by Gerald I. Fogel, Frederick M. Lane, Robert S. Leibert. New York: Basic Books, 1986. 113–130.

Corliss, Richard. "A Few Good Women." *Time* 5 April 1993: 58–59.

Cumbow, Robert C. "Jack Nicholson: Badge of Alienation." In Peary. 420–424.

———. *Once Upon a Time: the Films of Sergio Leone*. Metuchen, N.J.: Scarecrow Press, 1987.

Custen, George F. *Bio/Pics: How Hollywood Constructed Public History*. New Brunswick: Rutgers University Press, 1992.

de Cordova, Richard. "Genre and Performance: an Overview." In *Film Genre Reader*. Edited by Barry Keith Grant. Austin: University of Texas Press, 1986. 129–139.

———. *Picture Personalities: The Emergence of the Star System in America*. Urbana: University of Illinois Press, 1990.

deLauretis, Teresa. *Alice Doesn't: Feminism, Semiotics, Cinema*. Bloomington: Indiana University Press, 1984.

———. *Technologies of Gender*. Bloomington: Indiana University Press, 1987.

Doane, Mary Ann. *The Desire to Desire: The Woman's Film of the 1940s*. Bloomington: Indiana University Press, 1987.

———. "Film and the Masquerade: Theorising the Female Spectator." *Screen* 23.3–4 (1982): 74–88.

Dort, Bernard. "Crossing the Desert: Brecht in France in the Eighties." Translated by Colin Visser. In *Reinterpreting Brecht*. Edited by Pia Kleber and Colin Visser. Cambridge: Cambridge University Press, 1990. 90–103.

Dowd, Maureen. "Bush Boasts of Turn-around from *Easy Rider* Society." *New York Times* 7 October 1988, national edition: B7.

Dunagan, Clyde Kelly. "A Methodology of Film Acting Analysis and an Application to the Performance of Clint Eastwood." Dissertation. Northwestern University, 1985.

Dyer, Richard. *Heavenly Bodies: Film Stars and Society*. New York: St. Martin's Press, 1986.

———. *Stars*. London: British Film Institute, 1979.

Eco, Umberto. "The Myth of Superman." *The Role of the Reader*. Bloomington: Indiana University Press, 1979. 107–124.

Ellis, John. *Visible Fictions*. London: Routledge & Kegan Paul, 1982.

Erickson, Steve. "The Myth That Jack Built." *Esquire* September 1990: 165–174.

Esslin, Martin. *Brecht: A Choice of Evils*. London: Eyre & Spottiswoode, 1959.

———. *The Theater of the Absurd*. New York: Doubleday Anchor, 1961.

"An Evening with Clint Eastwood." The actor interviewed by David Frost. PBS. WFYI Indianapolis. 26 February 1993.

Eyles, Allen. *James Stewart*. New York: Stein & Day, 1984.

Falsetto, Mario. "The Mad and the Beautiful: A Look at Two Performances in the Films of Stanley Kubrick." In *Making Visible the Invisible: An Anthology of Original Essays on Film Acting*. Edited by Carole Zucker. Metuchen, N.J.: Scarecrow Press, 1990. 325–364.

Fayard, Judy. "Who Wants to Watch 32,250 Seconds of Clint Eastwood? Just About Everybody." *Life* 26 July 1971: 44 + .

Fischer, Lucy. *Shot/Countershot*. Princeton, N.J.: Princeton University Press, 1989.

Foucault, Michel. *The History of Sexuality*. Translated by Robert Hurley. New York: Pantheon, 1978.

———. *Madness and Civilization*. 1965. Translated by Richard Howard. New York: Vintage, 1988.

Frayling, Christopher. *Spaghetti Westerns*. London: Routledge & Kegan Paul, 1981.

Freud, Sigmund. "Creative Writers and Day-Dreaming." In *The Standard Edition of the Complete Psychological Works of Sigmund Freud Vol. 9*. Translated by James Strachey. London: Hogarth Press, 1963.

———. *Dora: An Analysis of a Case of Hysteria*. Edited by Philip Rieff. New York: Collier, 1963.

———. "The Economic Problem of Masochism." *Standard Edition Vol. 19*.

———. "Femininity." *New Introductory Lectures on Psychoanalysis*. Translated by James Strachey. London: Hogarth Press, 1965.

———. *The Interpretation of Dreams*. Edited and translated by James Strachey. New York: Avon, 1965.

———. *Introductory Lectures on Psychoanalysis*. Edited and translated by James Strachey. New York: W. W. Norton, 1966.

———. *Jokes and Their Relation to the Unconscious*. Edited and translated by James Strachey. New York: W. W. Norton, 1960.

———. "The Libido Theory and Narcissism." *Standard Edition Vol. 16*.

———. "Some Psychical Consequences of the Distinction between the Sexes." *Standard Edition Vol. 19*.

———. *Studies on Hysteria. Standard Edition Vol. 2*.

———. *Three Essays on the Theory of Sexuality. Standard Edition Vol. 7*.

———. "The Uncanny." *Studies in Parapsychology*. Edited by Philip Rieff. New York: Collier, 1963: 19–60.

Friedberg, Anne. "A Denial of Difference: Theories of Cinematic Identification." In *Psychoanalysis and Cinema*. Edited by E. Ann Kaplan. New York and London: Routledge, 1990. 36–45.

Gaines, Jane. "White Privilege and Looking Relations: Race and Gender in Feminist

Film Theory." In *Issues in Feminist Film Criticism*. Edited by Patricia Erens. Bloomington: Indiana University Press, 1990. 197–215.

Gallagher, Tag. *John Ford*. Berkeley: University of California Press, 1985.

Gates, David. "White Male Paranoia." *Newsweek* 29 March 1993: 48–54.

Gerstel, Judy. "Eastwood Redefines the Western Hero." *Detroit Free Press* 7 August 1992: 1C +.

Giddins, Gary. "Clint Eastwood Shoots Us the Bird." *Esquire* October 1988: 133–144.

Green, Ian. "Malefunction: A Contribution to the Debate on Masculinity in the Cinema." *Screen* 25.4–5 (1984): 36–48.

Green, Tom. "Nicholson in Command." *USA Today* 23 December 1992: 1D +.

Griffin, Nancy. "How They Built the Bomb: Inside the Last Seven Weeks of *Last Action Hero*." *Premiere* September 1993. 54 +.

Hansen, Miriam. "Pleasure, Ambivalence, Identification: Valentino and Female Spectatorship." *Cinema Journal* 25.4 (Summer 1986): 6–28.

Hark, Ina Rae. "Revalidating Patriarchy: Why Hitchcock Remade *The Man Who Knew Too Much*." In *Hitchcock's Rereleased Films*. Edited by Walter Raubicheck and Walter Srebnick. Detroit: Wayne State University Press, 1991. 209–220.

Harmetz, Aljean. "Kubrick Films *The Shining* in Secrecy in English Studio." *New York Times* 6 November 1978, late edition: 72.

Harris, Thomas. "The Building of Popular Images: Grace Kelly and Marilyn Monroe." In Gledhill. 40–44.

Haskell, Molly. *From Reverence to Rape: The Treatment of Women in the Movies*. New York: Penguin, 1974.

———. "Gould vs. Redford vs. Nicholson: The Absurdist as Box-Office Draw." In *The National Society of Film Critics on the Movie Star*. Edited by Elizabeth Weis. New York: Viking, 1981. 45–57.

———. "The Great Hollywood Con: Machismo Doesn't Live Here Anymore." *The Village Voice* 18 September 1978: 74 +.

Heath, Stephen. "Amata Mo." *Screen* 17.4 (Winter 1976–1977): 49–66.

———. "Difference." In *The Sexual Subject: A 'Screen' Reader in Sexuality*. Edited by John Caughie, Annette Kuhn, and Mandy Merck. London and New York: Routledge, 1992. 47–106.

———. "Male Feminism." *Men in Feminism*. Edited by Alice Jardine and Paul Smith. New York: Methuen, 1987. 1–40.

———. *Questions of Cinema*. Bloomington: Indiana University Press, 1981.

Hendrickson, Paul. "It's Been a Wonderful Life." *Life* July 1991: 66–77.

Hepburn, Katharine. *The Making of The African Queen or How I Went to Africa with Bogart, Bacall and Huston and Almost Lost My Mind*. New York: Alfred A. Knopf, 1987.

Hoberman, J. "Double Indemnity." *Village Voice* 28 August 1984: 46.

Holmlund, Chris. "Masculinity as Multiple Masquerade: The 'Mature' Stallone and the Stallone Clone." In Cohan and Hark. 213–229.

———. "Sexuality and Power in Male Doppelgänger Cinema: the Case of Clint Eastwood's *Tightrope*." *Cinema Journal* 26.1 (Fall 1986): 31–41.

Horney, Karen. "The Dread of Woman." *Feminine Psychology*. New York: W. W. Norton, 1967: 133–146.

Horton, Robert. "Mann & Stewart." *Film Comment* 26.2 (March–April 1990): 40–54.

"The Innocent Goes Abroad." *Life* 5 September 1955: 50–52.

Irigaray, Luce. *Speculum of the Other Woman*. Translated by Gillian C. Gill. Ithaca, N.Y.: Cornell University Press, 1985.

———. *This Sex Which Is Not One*. Translated by Gillian C. Gill. Ithaca, N.Y.: Cornell University Press, 1985.

"James Stewart: A Wonderful Life." Narrated by Johnny Carson. Written by John L. Miller. Produced by Joan Kramer and David Heeley. Directed by David Heeley. *Great Performances*. PBS. WOSU Columbus, Ohio. 13 March 1987.

"James Stewart—Highest Paid Actor." *Look* 26 July 1955: 94–102.

Jameson, Fredric. "Postmodernism, or the Cultural Logic of Late Capitalism." *New Left Review* 146 (1984): 53–92.

Jameson, Richard T. " 'Deserve's Got Nothin' To Do With It': *Unforgiven*." *Film Comment* 28.5 (September–October 1992): 12–14.

———. "Kubrick's Shining." *Film Comment* 16.4 (July–August 1980): 28–32.

Jeffords, Susan. "The Big Switch: Hollywood Masculinity in the Nineties." In *Film Theory Goes to the Movies*. Edited by Jim Collins, Hilary Radner, Ava Preacher Collins. New York and London: Routledge, 1993. 196–208.

———. *The Remasculinization of America: Gender and the Vietnam War*. Bloomington: Indiana University Press, 1989.

Johnston, Claire. "Women's Cinema as Counter-Cinema." *Sexual Strategems: The World of Women in Film*. Edited by Patricia Erens. New York: Horizon, 1979.

Johnstone, Iain. *The Man with No Name: The Biography of Clint Eastwood*. New York: Morrow Quill, 1981.

Kael, Pauline. "Saint Cop" (15 January 1972). In *Deeper into Movies*. Boston: Little, Brown, 1972. 385–388.

———. "Chance/Fate" (6 April 1981). In *Taking It All In*. New York: Holt, Rinehart & Winston, 1984. 178–182.

Kaplan, E. Ann. *Women and Film: Both Sides of the Camera*. New York: Methuen, 1983.

———. *Women in Film Noir*. London: BFI, 1978.

Kaplan, James. "King Leer: Nicholson Talks about *A Few Good Men*, *Hoffa*, and the Knack of Being Jack." *Entertainment Weekly* 8 January 1993: 12–19.

Kapsis, Robert E. *Hitchcock: The Making of a Reputation*. Chicago: University of Chicago Press, 1992.

Keane, Marian. "A Closer Look of Scopophilia: Mulvey, Hitchcock, and *Vertigo*." In *A Hitchcock Reader*. Edited by Marshall Deutelbaum and Leland Poague. Ames, Iowa: Iowa State University Press, 1986. 231–248.

King, Barry. "Stardom as an Occupation." In *The Hollywood Film Industry*. Edited by Paul Kerr. New York and London: Routledge and Kegan Paul, 1986. 154–184.

Kirby, Lynne. "Male Hysteria and Early Cinema." *Camera Obscura* 17 (May 1988): 112–131.

Kitses, Jim. *Horizons West—Anthony Mann, Budd Boetticher, Sam Peckinpah: Studies of Authorship Within the Western*. Bloomington: Indiana University Press, 1970.

Knee, Adam. "The Dialectic of Female Power and Male Hysteria in *Play Misty for Me*." In Cohan and Hark. 87–102.

Kolker, Robert Phillip. *A Cinema of Loneliness, 2nd Edition*. New York and Oxford: Oxford University Press, 1988.

Kroll, Jack. "Stanley Kubrick's Horror Show." *Newsweek* 26 May 1980: 96–99.

Kuntzel, Thierry. "The Film-Work 2." *Camera Obscura* 5 (Spring 1980): 7–72.

Lacan, Jacques. *Écrits: A Selection*. Translated by Alan Sheridan. New York: W. W. Norton, 1977.

Lang, Robert. "Looking for the 'Great Whatzit': *Kiss Me Deadly* and Film Noir." *Cinema Journal* 27.3 (Spring 1988): 32–44.

Le Gallienne, Eva. Introduction to *Six Plays by Henrik Ibsen*. Edited and translated by Eva Le Gallienne. New York: Modern Library, 1957.

Lellis, George. *Bertolt Brecht, Cahiers du Cinéma, and Contemporary Film Theory*. Ann Arbor: University Microfilms International Press, 1982.

Lurie, Susan. "Pornography and the Dread of Woman." In *Take Back the Night*. Edited by Laura Lederer. New York: Morrow, 1980. 159–173.

Lyotard, Jean-François. *The Postmodern Condition: A Report on Knowledge*. Translated by Geoff Bennington and Brian Massumi. Minneapolis: University of Minnesota Press, 1984.

Mailer, Norman. "The Warren Report." *Esquire* November 1991: 174+.

Maland, Charles J. *Chaplin and American Culture: The Evolution of a Star Image*. Princeton: Princeton University Press, 1989.

Maslin, Janet. "Eastwood Follows the Trail of the Elusive, Essential Huston." *New York Times* 21 September 1990: 1C.

Mayne, Judith. "The Female Audience and the Feminist Critic." In *Women and Film*. Edited by Janet Todd. New York: Holmes and Meier, 1988. 22–40.

———. "Feminist Film Theory and Criticism." *Signs* 11.1 (Fall 1985): 81–100.

———. "Marlene Dietrich, *The Blue Angel*, and Female Performance." *Seduction and Theory*. Edited by Dianne Hunter. Urbana: University of Illinois Press, 1989. 28–46.

———. "Walking the *Tightrope* of Feminism and Male Desire." Jardine and Smith. 62–70.

McBride, Joseph. *Frank Capra: The Catastrophe of Success*. New York: Simon & Schuster, 1992.

McCann, Graham. *Rebel Males: Clift, Brando, and Dean*. New Brunswick, N.J.: Rutgers University Press, 1993.

McCormick, Richard W. "Politics and the Psyche: Feminism, Psychoanalysis, and Film Theory." *Signs* 17.4 (Summer 1992): 173–187.

McGhee, Richard D. "John Wayne: Man with a Thousand Faces." *Literature/Film Quarterly* 16.1 (1988): 10–21.

McGilligan, Patrick. "Corey-ography." *Film Comment* 25.6 (November–December 1989): 38–43.

Mellen, Joan. *Big Bad Wolves: Masculinity in the American Film.* New York: Pantheon, 1977.

Metz, Christian. *The Imaginary Signifier: Psychoanalysis and the Cinema.* Translated by Celia Britton, Annwyl Williams, Ben Brewster, Alfred Guzzetti. Bloomington: Indiana University Press, 1982.

Millner, Cork. "Ah . . . Waal . . . It's Jimmy Stewart." *Saturday Evening Post* May–June 1988: 60 + .

Mitchell, Juliet. *Psychoanalysis and Feminism: Freud, Reich, Laing and Women.* New York: Vintage, 1975.

Modleski, Tania. *Feminism without Women: Culture and Criticism in a "Post-Feminist" Age.* New York and London: Routledge, 1991.

———. "The Terror of Pleasure." In *Studies in Entertainment.* Edited by Tania Modleski. Bloomington: Indiana University Press, 1986. 155–166.

———. *The Women Who Knew Too Much: Hitchcock and Feminist Theory.* London and New York: Methuen, 1988.

Moi, Toril. *Sexual/Textual Politics: Feminist Literary Theory.* London: Methuen, 1985.

Molyneaux, Gerard. *James Stewart: a Bio-Bibliography.* New York: Greenwood, 1992.

Monaco, James, and the Editors of *Baseline. The Encyclopedia of Film.* New York: Perigee, 1991.

Morgenstern, Joseph. "Remember It, Jack. It's Chinatown." *GQ* January 1990: 128 + .

Mulvey, Laura. "Afterthoughts . . . Inspired by *Duel in the Sun.*" *Framework* 15/16/17 (1981): 12–15.

———. "Visual Pleasure and Narrative Cinema." Nichols, *Movies and Methods, Vol. 2.* 303–315.

Murphy, Kathleen. "Lasso the Moon." *Film Comment* 26.2 (March–April 1990): 35–39.

Naremore, James. *Acting in the Cinema.* Berkeley: University of California Press, 1988.

Neale, Steve. "Masculinity as Spectacle: Reflections on Men and Mainstream Cinema." *Screen* 24.4 (1983): 2–16.

"The New Movies." *Newsweek* 7 December 1970: 62–74.

Oscar's Greatest Moments: 1971–91. Academy of Motion Picture Arts and Sciences. Produced and directed by Jeff Margolis. Written by Stephen Poulliot and Hal Kantor. Hosted by Karl Malden. RCA/Columbia Pictures Home Video. 1992.

Patterson, Eric. "Every Which Way but Lucid: the Critique of Authority in Clint Eastwood's Police Movies." *Journal of Popular Film and Television* 10.3 (1982): 92–104.

Perlez, Jane. "Clint Eastwood Directs Himself Portraying a Director." *New York Times* 16 September 1990: 2:1 + .

Person, Ethel S. "The Omni-Available Woman and Lesbian Sex: Two Fantasy Themes and Their Relationship to the Male Developmental Experience." In Fogel, Lane, Liebert. 71–94.

Plaza, Fuensanta. *Clint Eastwood/Malpaso*. Carmel Valley, Cal.: Ex Libris, 1991.

Rafferty, Terrence. "Slow Burn." *The New Yorker* 8 March 1993: 98–99.

Rank, Otto. *The Double*. Edited and translated by Harry Tucker, Jr. Chapel Hill: University of North Carolina Press, 1971.

Ray, Robert B. *A Certain Tendency in the Hollywood Cinema, 1930–80*. Princeton, N.J.: Princeton University Press, 1985.

Riviere, Joan. "Womanliness as a Masquerade." 1929. In *Formations of Fantasy*. Edited by Victor Burgin, James Donald, and Cora Kaplan. New York and London: Methuen, 1986. 35–44.

Robbins, Jhan. *Everybody's Man: A Biography of James Stewart*. New York: G. P. Putnam's Sons, 1985.

Rodowick, D. N. "The Difficulty of Difference." *Wide Angle* 5.1 (1981): 8–15.

Rosenbaum, Ron. "Acting: The Creative Mind of Jack Nicholson." *New York Times Magazine* 13 July 1986: 12 + .

Russo, Vito. *The Celluloid Closet: Homosexuality in the Movies*. Revised Edition. New York: Harper & Row, 1987.

Sarris, Andrew. *The American Cinema: Directors and Directions, 1929–68*. New York: E. P. Dutton, 1968.

———. "Oscar Wiles XI." *Village Voice* 5 April 1973: 71 + .

Saxton, Christine. "The Collective Voice as Cultural Voice." *Cinema Journal* 26.1 (Fall 1986): 19–30.

Schatz, Thomas. *The Genius of the System: Hollywood Filmmaking in the Studio Era*. New York: Pantheon, 1988.

———. *Old Hollywood/New Hollywood: Ritual, Art, and Industry*. Ann Arbor: University Microfilms International Research Press, 1983.

Schickel, Richard. "Elephant Man." *Time* 24 September 1990: 84.

Schruers, Fred. "The Two Jacks." *Premiere* September 1990: 58–68.

Schwenger, Peter. *Phallic Critiques*. London: Routledge & Kegan Paul, 1984.

Segal, Lynne. *Slow Motion: Changing Masculinities, Changing Men*. New Brunswick, N.J.: Rutgers University Press, 1990.

Seidler, Victor J. "Reason, Desire, and Male Sexuality." *The Cultural Construction of Masculinity*. Edited by Pat Caplan. London: Tavistock, 1987: 82–112.

Shepherd, Donald. *Jack Nicholson*. New York: St. Martin's Press, 1991.

Silverman, Kaja. "Male Subjectivity and the Celestial Suture: *It's a Wonderful Life*." *Framework* 15/16/17 (1981): 16–22.

———. *Male Subjectivity at the Margins*. New York and London: Routledge, 1992.

———. *The Subject of Semiotics*. New York and Oxford: Oxford University Press, 1983.

Sklar, Robert. *City Boys: Cagney, Bogart, Garfield*. Princeton, N.J.: Princeton University Press, 1992.

Smith, Paul. "Action Movie Hysteria, or Eastwood Bound." *Differences* 1.3 (Fall 1989): 88–107.

———. *Clint Eastwood: A Cultural Production*. Minneapolis: University of Minnesota Press, 1993.

——. "Men in Feminism: Men and Feminist Theory." In Jardine and Smith. 33–40.

Spoto, Donald. *Camerado: Hollywood and the American Man*. New York: New American Library, 1978.

"The Star with the Killer Smile." *Time* 12 August 1974: 44–50.

Stewart, Garrett. "*The Long Goodbye* from *Chinatown*." *Film Quarterly* 28.2 (Winter 1974–75): 25–32.

Studlar, Gaylyn. "Masochism and the Perverse Pleasures of the Cinema." Nichols, *Movies and Methods, Vol 2*. 602–621.

——. "Valentino, 'Optic Intoxication,' and Dance Madness." In Cohan and Hark. 23–45.

Tasker, Yvonne. "Dumb Movies for Dumb People: Masculinity, the Body, and the Voice in Contemporary Action Cinema." In Cohan and Hark. 230–244.

Thomson, David. *A Biographical Dictionary of Film*. New York: William Morrow, 1981.

——. "Cop on a Hot *Tightrope*." *Film Comment* 20.5 (September–October 1984): 64–73.

Thompson, Hunter S. *Fear and Loathing on the Campaign Trail, 1972*. San Francisco, Straight Arrow, 1973.

Thompson, John O. "Screen Acting and the Commutation Test." 1978. In Gledhill. 183–197.

Thompson, Richard, and Tim Hunter. "Clint Eastwood, Auteur." *Film Comment* 14.1 (January–February 1978): 24–32.

Titterington, P. L. "Kubrick and *The Shining*." *Sight and Sound* 50.2 (1981): 117–121.

Tompkins, Jane. *West of Everything: The Inner Life of Westerns*. New York and Oxford: Oxford University Press, 1992.

Truffaut, François. *Hitchcock*. New York: Simon & Schuster, 1967.

"The Universal Appeal." *Life* 15 June 1953: 103–109.

Vernet, Marc. "The Look at the Camera." Translated by Dana Polan. *Cinema Journal* 28.2 (Winter 1989): 48–63.

Viertel, Peter. *White Hunter, Black Heart*. 1953. New York: Dell Laurel, 1987.

Vinocur, John. "Clint Eastwood, Seriously." *New York Times Magazine* 24 February 1985: 16+.

Walker, Beverly. "'The Bird Is on His Own': Jack Nicholson Interviewed." *Film Comment* 21.3 (May–June 1985): 53–61.

Warshow, Robert. "Movie Chronicle: The Westerner." 1954. In *Focus on the Western*. Edited by Jack Nachbar. Englewood Cliffs, N.J.: Prentice-Hall, 1974: 45–56.

Weinraub, Bernard. "Even Cowboys Get Their Due." *GQ* March 1993: 213+.

——. "Hits, Misses and Also-Rans of Summer." *New York Times*, 5 September 1993: 2:16–17.

Wexman, Virginia Wright. "Absurdist Performance in Hollywood: Boy 'Gets' Girl in Mamet's *House of Games*." Paper presented at the Society for Cinema Studies Conference. Iowa City, Iowa. April 14, 1989.

——. "The Film Critic as Consumer: Film Study in the University, *Vertigo*, and the Film Canon." *Film Quarterly* 39.2 (Spring 1986): 32–41.

————. *Roman Polanski*. London: G. K. Hall, 1985.

Wilden, Anthony. "In the Penal Colony: the Body as the Discourse of the Other." *Semiotica* 54.1–2 (1985): 33–86.

Wiley, Mason, and Damien Bova. *Inside Oscar*. New York: Ballantine, 1986.

Willemen, Paul. "Anthony Mann: Looking at the Male." *Framework* 15/16/17 (1981): 16.

Williams, Linda. *Hard Core: Power, Pleasure, and the "Frenzy of the Visible."* Berkeley: University of California Press, 1989.

————. "Feminist Film Theory: *Mildred Pierce* and the Second World War." Pribram 12–30.

Wilson, William. "Riding the Crest of the Horror Wave." *New York Times Magazine* 11 May 1980: 42 + .

Winchester '73. Laser Disc. Interview with James Stewart. Conducted by Paul Lindenschmid. Universal City: MCA Home Video, 1987. Audio track two.

Witteman, Paul A. "Go Ahead, Make My Career." *Time* 5 April 1993: 54–56.

Wolf, Jamie. "It's All Right, Jack." *American Film* January–February 1984: 36 + .

Wolfe, Charles. "*Mr. Smith Goes to Washington*: Democratic Forums and Representational Forms." In *Close Viewings*. Edited by Peter Lehman. Tallahassee: Florida State University Press, 1990. 300–332.

————. "The Return of Jimmy Stewart: The Publicity Photograph as Text." In Gledhill. 92–106.

Wood, Robin. "The American Nightmare: Horror in the 70s." In *Hollywood from Vietnam to Reagan*. New York: Columbia University Press, 1987. 70–94.

————. "Cat and Dog: Lewis Teague's Stephen King Movies." *CineAction!* Fall 1985: 39–45.

————. *Hitchcock's Films Revisited*. New York: Columbia University Press, 1989.

————. "The Men Who Knew Too Much (and the Women Who Knew Much Better)." In Raubicheck and Srebnick. 194–208.

Wright, Elizabeth. *Psychoanalytic Criticism*. London: Methuen, 1984.

Wright, Will. *Sixguns and Society: A Structural Study of the Western*. Berkeley: University of California Press, 1975.

Index